The Absent Father
in Modern Drama

American University Studies

Series III
Comparative Literature
Vol. 54

PETER LANG
New York • Washington, D.C./Baltimore • San Francisco
Bern • Frankfurt am Main • Berlin • Vienna • Paris

Paul Rosefeldt

The Absent Father
in Modern Drama

PETER LANG
New York • Washington, D.C./Baltimore • San Francisco
Bern • Frankfurt am Main • Berlin • Vienna • Paris

Library of Congress Cataloging-in-Publication Data

Rosefeldt, Paul.
The absent father in modern drama / Paul Rosefeldt.
    p.   cm. — (American university studies. Series III, Comparative
literature; vol. 54)
    Includes bibliographical references and index.
    1. Drama—History and criticism. 2. Fathers in literature. 3. Fathers
and sons in literature. 4. Fathers and daughters in literature.
5. Psychology in literature. 6. Myth in literature. I. Title. II. Series.
PN1821.R67   809.2′93520431—dc20   94-28595
ISBN 0-8204-2629-6
ISSN 0724-1445

Die Deutsche Bibliothek-CIP-Einheitsaufnahme

Rosefeldt, Paul:
The absent father in modern drama / Paul Rosefeldt. - New York;
Washington, D.C./Baltimore; San Francisco; Bern; Frankfurt am Main;
Berlin; Vienna; Paris: Lang.
    (American university studies: Ser. 3, Comparative literature; Vol. 54)
    ISBN 0-8204-2629-6
NE: American university studies / 03

The paper in this book meets the guidelines for permanence and durability of
the Committee on Production Guidelines for Book Longevity of the
Council on Library Resources.

© 1995 Peter Lang Publishing, Inc., New York

Printed in the United States of America.

ACKNOWLEDGMENTS

I would like to thank Dr. William Demastes for his careful and patient guidance in helping me shape my ideas; my wife Peggy, without whose assistance this project would never have been completed; and my mother, the late Mrs. Josephine Rosefeldt, whose prayers and encouragement sustained me through many years of arduous study.

CONTENTS

CHAPTER 1

INTRODUCTION

One major thread in the analysis of modern drama holds that modern drama is a reaction to a sense of profound loss, brought about by the death of God, the transcendental father. Robert Brustein notes that "modern drama aches with nostalgia, loneliness and regret" (11). Reeling from the death of God, the modern theatre of revolt "fails to build its church and records the failure in a growing mood of despair" (12). For Brustein, the modern dramatists hate "reality and labor ceaselessly to change it but are pulled back into setting up the continuous tension between illusion and reality" (15). Like Brustein, Tom Driver also sees modern drama as a reaction to loss. He claims that modern drama begins in a romantic quest for "something unsearchable that must nevertheless be searched" (xiii) and leads to a modern query which asks "whether the quest has meaning and whether all search for meaning is futile" (xiv).

Maurice Valency, Martin Esslin, and George Wellwarth also focus on loss in their assessments of major movements in modern drama. Valency traces modern drama back to the symbolists for whom "the idea of God was inextricably bound up with the idea of nature, the loss of faith in one was necessarily attended by the loss of faith in the other" (vi). According to Valency, the modern dramatists are reacting to a world that has been lost or shattered. He states: "From Eliot to Beckett the artisans of our age speak to us in elegiacal tones as the dazed survivors of a seismic upheaval . . . In the 1880's there was an urgent need to rediscover God, and this time God proved to be more than ordinarily elusive" (viii). Looking at a later stage of modern drama, Martin Esslin also focuses on modern drama's reaction to loss: He explains how earlier in the twentieth century, "the certitudes and unshakable assumptions of former ages" had been "discredited as cheap and somewhat childish illusions," but "the decline of religious faith was masked until the end of the Second World War by the substitute religions of faith in progress, nationalism and various totalitarian fallacies. All this ended with the War" (23). George Wellwarth seems to sum up the school of critical opinion that sees modern drama as a mourning ritual enacted at the wake of a dead god. Wellwarth describes modern drama as "an extended meditation on existential rootlessness . . . a critical analysis of man in the void . . . into which man was cast by the death of religion" (1).

For the modern dramatist, the world must adjust to the breakdown of a God-centered universe that was ordered and hierarchical. In modern drama, even the search for meaning has become a futile quest. God, nature, and the very world itself seems to vanish, and all that is left is unaccommodated man living in a scrapyard of meaningless memorabilia. The reality which was once grounded in a teleological absolute has broken down into a series of fragmented illusions. The modern drama, however, still encompasses the romantic quest for a lost Eden at the same time as it reaches toward an uncertain future grasping for a nebulous missing savior figure, some mysterious and paradoxical being slouching toward Bethlehem.

Since the absence of God as the ground of Being has become a central concern in modern drama, one avenue worth exploring is the use of the absent father in modern drama, for the father image symbolizes creation and the origin of meaning and in patriarchal cultures is subsumed into the Transcendental Father or God, the Father, a figure whose absence seems to penetrate the various strands of modern drama. One way to address and understand how modern drama plays out profound loss for that which once was or, at least, was thought to be, is to explore the workings of the absent father in modern plays. However, in order to better understand the concept of the absent father, the father who is central to the dramatic action but never appears on the stage, one needs to define the nature of the absent character and its unique construction in dramatic literature.

Drama depends upon mimesis, the imitation or direct presentation of an action. A dramatic character is most often presented to the audience through an actor. The dramatic action historically takes place in the conventional present. Since Aristotle, mimesis in drama has been given a privileged position. Over the years, critics who favored mimesis have tried to assure its effectiveness by proposing the contraction of dramatic action and espousing the unities of place, time, and action. One consequence of this contraction, however, has been the increased use of diegesis or narrated discourse. The focus on absence in modern drama brings diegesis to the foreground and emphasizes the dramaturgy of that which is not presented, but which is always represented or mediated through the discourse of an Other.

Critics, however, emphasize the fact that drama focuses on a present action in which events are presented, not narrated to an audience. Peter Szondi, for example, defines drama as "always primary; its internal time is always the present. . . . In the Drama, time unfolds as an absolute linear sequence in the present" (9). Szondi, however, finds that modern drama focuses on internal conflicts that emphasize the welling up of past actions, thus rendering drama more like an epic. For Szondi, modern drama is a drama of reflection in which "the (spoken or unspoken) 'three years later' presupposes an epic I" (9). In discussing Ibsen's drama, for example, Szondi considers the present to be merely "an occasion for conjuring up the past" (16). In examining *John Gabriel Borkman* (1896), Szondi finds that "the past itself, the repeatedly mentioned 'long years' and the 'wasted life,' is the subject of the play, a subject that does not lend itself to the dramatic present" (16). Szondi sums up his position: "Only something temporal can be made present in the sense of dramatic actualization, not time itself. Time can only be reported about in drama" (16). Debating the validity of Szondi's theory is beyond the purview of this study, but Szondi does show how the structure of modern drama depends heavily on recapturing that which is lost. Drama, however, not only takes place in the present, but it also demands a presence that can be seen and heard. Moreover, drama demands an embodied presence. More than poetry or fiction which depend on an imaginative response, drama is an attempt to bring into physical presence that which is absent. As David Cole states in *The Theatrical Event*, "When theatre fails there has been a refusal of presence" (x). Also, according to Herbert Blau, dramatic performance gives "visible body to what is not there" (84).

In a discourse which emphasizes presenting that which is present, there is a need to understand the workings of that which is not present or absent. This understanding can be achieved by analyzing the twofold nature of dramatic discourse. Formalist critics divide dramatic action into two modes: fabula (story) and sjuzet (plot). According to Elaine Aston and George Savona, "Story is the basic narrative outline; plot, the means by which narrative events are structured, organized and presented" (21). In other words, the story may include actions that have taken place before the beginning of the play or during the time between scenes. For example, in *Oedipus Tyrannus*, the story covers all the events from Oedipus' birth to his banishment. Story events are related in the plot through various strands of discourse. Several characters narrate the murder of Laius. However, Laius is never seen or presented to the audience. As a character, he exists in the gaps or margins of the dramatic present; he is part of the story, the overall narrative, but not a part of the plot, the sequence of presented actions. Like all characters who exist in story but not in plot, or in discourse but not in presentation, Laius is an absent character.

Essentially, the absent character is a character who never appears in the plot and, therefore, is never on stage, for his appearance would automatically give him unmediated presence. The absent character may exist in past time prior to the action of the play, in present time but spatially removed from the presented action, or in the ellipses between presented actions. The character's actions and physical characteristics may be recounted in the discourse of other characters, or they may be represented by iconic markers such as photographs or metonymic signs such as the boots that a character wears or the gun that the character owns. The absent character neither speaks directly nor is embodied on stage. Essentially, the character's actions are always filtered through someone else's point of view. Although all characters in a drama are subject to the interpretation of other characters, the absent character is different because such a character cannot explain his or her actions nor can the absent character contradict the representation that others construct. The absent character, thus, becomes a syphon and a magnet, an Other that becomes reflected and refracted throughout the dramatic environment. By its very nature, the absent character maintains a liminal space between absence and presence and is both outside (not in the plot) and inside (in the story) of the drama. Often when focal to the play, such a character can take on symbolic significance.

In an art form which calls for an embodied presence, the absent character never appears but exists only within the discourse of others or through signs or impersonations. The character is always being represented, always one step removed from presence. For example, Captain Alving, the dead father in Henrik Ibsen's *Ghosts* (1881), would be considered an absent character because he is reconstructed in various dimensions of the text but never appears in the play. In J. M. Synge's *Playboy of the Western World* (1907), Christy Mahon's father is considered dead throughout most of the play and his absence is central to the play. However, at the end of Synge's drama, the father appears and affirms his presence and thus cannot be considered an absent character. The absent character cannot speak for himself or herself but only through others or through representations.

Also, the absent character cannot be presented, even in the domain of memory. For example, the character cannot appear in a flashback. In Wendy Wasserstein's *Uncommon Women and Others* (1979), a group of women from a prestigious women's college has a reunion. One member of the group is conspicuously absent; however, when the play flashes back in time, this character is present in an embodied form and speaks for herself. On the other hand, in Jason Miller's *That Championship Season* (1972), another reunion play, one basketball player is missing from the reunion of the championship team. However, he never appears in a flashback but exists only in what the other characters say about him. Thus, the absent character never affirms his or her presence.

Although the absent character cannot be present in the plot, the character must be represented or alluded to in the discourse and, thus, is part of the story. For example, In Ibsen's *A Doll House* (1879), Nora's father never appears; however, he is mentioned by Nora and her husband, Torvald, and the father's forged signature is significant both to the plot and the thematic structure of the play. He is an absent character. However, Nora's mother is absent even from the discourse, for she is never mentioned. Certainly, her absence has ideological implications in a play about wounded motherhood. A Marxist or feminist critic might explore this gap in the text. However, such characters are beyond the purview of this study. They are not just absent, but missing. Absence implies residual presence and has repercussions the playwright wants elevated to audience consciousness.

Thus, the absent character is a liminal figure, halfway between being missing and present, life and death, past and present, the "what was" and "the never will be," a presence that is always being deferred. The absent character may be dead like the father in August Strindberg's *The Pelican* (1907) or alive like the father in Strindberg's *Miss Julie* (1888), a supernatural being like God the Father in Peter Shaffer's *Equus* (1973) and John Pielmeier's *Agnes of God* (1982) or an animal like the runaway dog in William Inge's *Come Back, Little Sheba* (1950). The character may be imaginary like the child in Edward Albee's *Who's Afraid of Virginia Woolf?* (1962) or the skeletal remains of a once-live child as those found in Sam Shepard's *Buried Child* (1979). Or even a mysterious being like Mr. Godot in *Waiting for Godot* (1954).

Most absent characters are not only liminal figures but are also figures moving toward presence, especially in modern drama which takes place in a wasteland devoid of any spiritual presence. Whether as a vengeful force that has been sinned against or as a wished-for savior that holds out the promise of redemption, the absent character is forever being recreated through a series of simulations: metonymic substitutions, iconic representations, psychological displacements, or uncanny doubles. In Ibsen's *Hedda Gabler* (1890) and Marsha Norman's *'night, Mother* (1983), a father's gun is associated with the father and becomes a metonymic representation of the father or a metonymic substitution for him. In both plays, the absent father's phallic weapon is not only a crucial plot device, but a clear representation of the father and his world. The heroines in both plays return to the father through the enactment of a beautiful death. In a world out of their control, both daughters seek salvation through a return to the absent father. Other metonymic substitutions are Julie's father's boots in *Miss Julie* and the manuscript as child in *Hedda Gabler*.

The absent character may also be revealed through iconic representations or pictures such as the ever-present picture of Tom Wingfield's absent father in Tennessee Williams' *The Glass Menagerie* (1945). Or the character may be reconstituted through doubles. Doubling takes place in Eugene O'Neill's *Strange Interlude* (1928) when Nina Leeds has sexual relationships with soldiers who represent her dead lover, Gordon Shaw. She also marries a man who idolizes Gordon, has a son by Gordon's friend, and mistakes this son for Gordon. The absent character may also appear as a supplementary voice from beyond death as he does through the use of secret letters in Arthur Miller's *All My Sons* (1947) and in Strindberg's *The Pelican*.

Although there are many types of absent characters, the one most suitable to understanding modern drama as a reaction to the death of God is the character of the absent father, a figure which generates an enormous amount of symbolic significance. The father is indeed a seminal figure in the drama of absence since fatherhood is closely connected with absence. First, the father who can never be absolutely verified is an absent figure in the process of conception. The mother displays the physical presence of motherhood, but fatherhood needs to be authenticated. Sigmund Freud notes: "Maternity is proved by evidence of the senses while paternity is a hypothesis, based on an influence and a presence" (*Moses and Monotheism* 114). James Joyce calls paternity a "legal fiction" (2: 107–8). According to Peter Wilson "the 'invention' of the father is of necessity founded not on the biological facts of paternity but on the relation of a male to a female and on her offspring." The term "father" denotes "a cultural relationship" (65).

The father is not only absent from conception but is also absent from the gestation process. Even in the initial dyadic relationship, the father is absent, a third party who enters the relationship from the outside. Also, the father is usually absent from the family and is outside of the family, hunting or working. Alex Pirani claims that it is the "father's business to be absent: away hunting, earning a living, functioning in the wider world." He is free from "body ties" and "detached from maternal concerns" (113).

Also, the father is a construct of culture not of nature. According to Andre Bleikasten, "originally father power is derived or delegated power, and only social consensus makes it into a rightful one. . . . Paternal authority . . . is the more firmly settled as time has erased its contingent and hypothetical origin and hallowed its prerogatives as an 'indisputable' right" (118). In other words, paternal authority as well as patriarchy itself is based on an ideology that has privileged the absent and uncertain position of the father. According to Paul Ricoeur, the father figures' "privileged status is no doubt due to its extremely rich symbolic power, in particular its potential for 'transcendence'. . . the father is an unreality set apart, who, from the start is a being of language. Because he is the name giver, he is the name problem" (542). In other words, the father is felt strongly in his absence. He is a disembodied figure behind the scenes, a paternal metaphor.

To understand the nature of this paternal metaphor, it is necessary to examine three psychological theories of the father: the theories of Sigmund Freud, Jacques Lacan and Carl Jung. All these theorists view the figure of the father as an absence, a powerful figure that stands behind patriarchal culture. Sigmund Freud theorizes that at the origin of civilization, the father of the primal horde possessed all the women until his sons killed him and devoured him. Freud clearly notes: "The violent primal father had doubtless been the feared and envied model of all the brothers . . . devouring him, they accomplished their identification with him" (*Totem* 142). In order to alleviate their guilt, they reestablished the father in the totem animal, and "the totem meal would thus be a repetition and commemoration of this memorable and criminal deed" (*Totem* 142).

Realizing that they would destroy themselves in incessant rivalry over the women, the brothers instituted "the law against incest, by which they all alike renounced the women whom they desired and who had been their chief motive for dispatching the father" (*Totem* 144). According to Jan Cook, Freud shows how the murder of the father brings the father to life: "Rather than dissolving his power, death magnifies and perpetuates it. His death in nature produces his life in culture as symbol (a totem god), as source of the law and as the subject of a seemingly unresolvable ambivalence, oscillating between hatred and veneration, identification with the father and rejection of him" (143). In other words, the sacrificed father becomes the absent father standing behind culture and the law, a father that not only promotes identification but establishes an ambivalent relationship between himself and his progeny.

According to Jacques Lacan, the paternal metaphor is seen in the Symbolic Father, a manifestation of Freud's Dead Father. Through the bestowing of his name on the child, this father inscribes the child into the symbolic system of language and determines the child's subjectivity. Lacan holds that "the symbolic father is to be conceived as 'transcendent'" as an irreducible given of the signifier. The symbolic father . . . can only be imperfectly incarnate in the real father" (qtd. in Wilden 271).

In other words, the symbolic father remains absent although his presence is felt. Juliet Mitchell explains the machinations of Lacan's symbolic father: "For whether or not the actual father is there does not affect the perpetuation of the patriarchal culture within the psychology of the individual; absent or present 'the father' always has his place. His actual absence may cause confusion . . . but the only difference it makes is within the terms of the patriarchal assumption of his presence. In our own culture, he is just as present in his absence" (232). Mitchell explains how the absent father is always a given, an assumption that bolsters patriarchal culture and even in its absence exerts a presence.

The Symbolic Father also is the absent father behind patriarchy and the establishment of the Law. Bleikasten notes that "what matters most in the last resort is not the living father but the dead father, not the real father so much as the symbolic father or what Jacques Lacan calls the 'name-of-the-father,' the symbolic function which since the dawn of historical time, has identified his person with the figure of the Law" (114–120). In Lacanian terms, the Symbolic Father is absent in his presence, a figure representing the Law of the Father, the establisher of language and culture, and the initiator of the individual to the chain of desire. Charles Scott notes the Symbolic Father's relationship to desire: "The hidden presence of the Symbolic Father, a hiddenness that is revealed in the presence of rupture and lack, means that desire will not be satisfied by anything. . . . The Law of the Father is articulated always in a chain of signifiers that has no completion . . . the desire for the other is like, perhaps, the other-as-desire for which there is no fulfillment" (125). Thus, the Symbolic Father is an absent presence, the figure behind the Law and the lack or absence that unleashes a chain of desire that can never be satisfied. This quality of the absent father to open up the force of desire allows him to be a propelling force in dramatic action.

Like Lacanians, Jungian analysts also see the father as an absent figure behind the structure of culture. For Carl Jung, the father archetype "determines our relation to man, the law and the state, to reason and the Spirit and the dynamism of nature . . . the father . . . represents authority, hence also the law and the state. He . . . is the creative wind-breath . . . the spirit pneuma, the atman" (*Civilization in Transition* 35). According to Barbara Greenfield, the Jungian father archetype stands outside the world of presence. He is "a mental spiritual principal that is 'above' and 'beyond' the material world . . . a sort of divine perfection . . . beyond the reach of mortals still tied to the physical world" (204). For Jungians, the archetypal Father is the source of creation through the Logos or the Word, not the body, and is the source of order and consciousness. He is an invisible, disembodied presence hovering behind the material world. Feminist critic Patricia Yeager notes that "most critical and philosophical discourse about the father evades the body altogether; it is obsessed with a father who is bodiless . . . who stands for Law, for the Idea, for the Symbolic" (8). The absent father thus becomes a focal character in his absence. Because his presence is never embodied on the stage, he becomes an influential outside force who determines the trajectory of other characters who are absorbed with recreating his presence.

This imposing figure of the absent father has, furthermore, been investigated in the theory of narrative. Robert Con Davis notes "(1) that the question of the father in fiction . . . is essentially one of father absence; (2) that each manifestation of the father in a text is a refinding of an absent father; (3) and that the father's origin is to be found in the trace of his absence" ("Discourse" 3). For some narrative theorists, "a fictional father is not simply a character in a narrative who happens to be a father, but the paradigm of desirable masculinity itself, not simply what stories are about but the motive for telling them in the first place" (Cook 154). In other words, the father and his loss initiates narrative action. According to Roland Barthes, "Every narrative (every unveiling of the truth) is a staging of the absent, hidden or hypostatized father" (10). Following in the same line of thinking as Barthes, Regis Durand reiterates that "not only is fiction haunted by the return of the vanished father, but it wagers its very status and existence as fiction on the question of the symbolic father" (49).

Using Lacanian theory, Davis points out that all narratives are Oedipal in nature and claims that "the father is a 'no' that initiates narrative development by enfranchising one line of continuity over other possibilities, the son's desire is a 'yes' that leaves behind maternal demands, gets bound to the father's law, and proceeds in a narrative advance that plays out the father's meaning in time" ("Discourse" 13). Although Davis' formula is much too global to be applied to all narrative, and is applicable only to male quest narratives, certainly as the forementioned critics point out, father absence does promote one particular line of narrative and so too can be applied to one type of drama which emphasizes the absent father. One way of seeing how these dramas of the absent father come about is to examine the correlation between psychological theories of the absent father and the ritual theories of drama.

Early modern theorists of the origin of drama, known as the Cambridge Ritualists, based much of their theories on the findings of Sir James Frazer in *The Golden Bough*. They believed that drama arose out of a year drama or fertility ritual which was played out in the image of a dying and rising god. These theorists conjecture that the process of sacrificing an old king and replacing him with a new king promoted the death and rebirth of the god as well as the crops which died in winter and were reborn in spring. Though these theories have been largely discredited as anthropological and historical accounts of the origin and nature of drama, they do have validity for myth criticism. Northrop Frye notes that although such theories may not have historical validity they are based on archetypal or mythical principles, and "it does not matter two pins to the literary critic whether such a ritual had any historical existence or not" (*Anatomy* 109). The death of the old king or the dying of the god is another form of the sacrifice of the father. With the death of the god or father figure, the world is thrown into mourning or blight and the cycle moves toward bringing the absent father into presence.

Another theory of the origins of tragedy closely linked to the Cambridge Ritualists is that of William Ridgeway. In *The Dramas and Dramatic Dances of Non-European Races*, Ridgeway argues that tragic drama did not arise directly out of the cult to the dying and rising god Dionysus but "that it sprang out of the indigenous worship of the dead" (1). Ridgeway's tomb theory or hero cult theory links tragedy to rituals for the dead performed before the tombs of heroes. Susan Cole builds on Ridgeway's theory by linking tragedy to rituals of mourning in various primitive cultures. Cole points out that "mourning ritual, like tragedy, is a performance of ambivalence on behalf of an absent presence" (1). In tragedy, Cole sees "the beloved deceased, usually a father or father figure" and a "mourner-inheritor, usually a son or son surrogate," in a relationship "characterized by ambivalence" (2).

Cole points the way toward the elaboration of her premise: "Since ambivalence, absent parents, and a journey as a rite of passage may be found in other dramatic genres, why could this theory of tragedy not as well be a theory of all theatrical entertainment" (5). Certainly, one would have to stretch the paradigm to make it fit all dramatic literature, but the elements pointed out by Cole are certainly a part of many modern dramas which focus on the absent father. Whereas Cole is interested specifically in a dead father, this study focuses on the father's absence in a variety of ways. Cole links mourning to tragedy by pointing out figures of ghosts and other uncanny presences that are visible reembodiments of the dead father. This study will focus on the total absence of the father who is never reembodied. Yet Cole's theory ties in well with the modern psychological theories of the absent father. Freud's powerful figure of the Dead Father as sacrificial victim, Lacan's symbolic father behind the artifice of patriarchal cultural, and Jung's archetypal father as spiritual force and divine speaker of the Word or Logos, all point toward a powerful absent father in a transcendental form. Thus, by correlating these psychological theories of the absent father with Cambridge Ritualists' theories of the dying and rising god who oscillates between absence and presence, and by supporting them with Cole's argument for the linking of tragic drama to the mourning ritual of a father or father figure, one can see a dramatic pattern emerging. This pattern shows how the loss of paternal and divine origins has propelled much of modern drama into a mourning ritual for the lost presence of the father.

Thus, the dramas of the absent father pull together the mythic structure of drama and its ritual base along with psychological theories of the absent father to show how one phase of modern drama is haunted by the presence of the absent father. In this type of drama, the absent father not only controls the dynamics of the plot but also influences the trajectory of the other characters. Through multiple reconstructions of the absent father in the discourse of the other characters, he is projected onto all aspects of the dramatic milieu. Also through various referents and surrogates, the main structure of the dramatic action focuses on trying to represent him or bring him into presence.

In the plays of the absent father a distinct pattern emerges. The father is absent from the family. He has died or has abandoned his children or is away from home at a crucial point in the drama. He is a mysterious figure, connected to the family, yet outside of the family, a representative of the values of his culture, yet a transgressor of those values. His absence shows the diminishing or displacement of fatherhood itself. The name of the father which inscribes the family in a line of descent is often unspoken or displaced. The mother/wife is either missing (not mentioned at all) or ineffectual. She is often a version of the "crazy" mother or the Terrible Mother who ignores, persecutes or betrays her children.

In the absence of the father, his children are failures, alienated from themselves and the world that surrounds them, and henceforth will be described as lost children. They live in a wasteland, a world of mourning and melancholia, filled with sterile objects, an illusory world that is often crumbling around them. Yearning with father hunger, these lost children, both male and female, begin a quest for the father who is usually represented in a highly idealized form. In some cases, the child may become the father, follow in his path, or recreate a part of his life. Lacking the presence of the father and the spiritual ground of Being, the lost child feels compelled to escape the nightmare world of the wasteland and to return to the paradise world of the father, a world which exists in a mythical past, a childhood illusion or a utopian fantasy. However, the world of the father is connected closely with the death and dying, and the search for the father is often a self-destructive one. Harmonious union with the father is not possible, for the father which exists at the point of origin is forever absent in these dramas.

Thus, the absent father is a propelling force in the plays in this study. He presents the origin of the drama, initiates the quest, spawns imitators or doubles who trace his path, and becomes the ultimate goal of the quest. He not only creates the lack but propels the forward action of the drama. His absence at the origin sets off the process of unfolding or deferring that pushes the action forward at the same time as it reveals a continual lack or absence. The need to double the father or retrace his path directs the forward action of the drama toward the ever-compelling need to fill in the gaps. In modern drama, moreover, his absence creates an inconsolable feeling of loss, an eternal mourning for the lost father.

This study does not propose a comprehensive theory of modern drama. The plays analyzed represent a particular configuration and comprise a large enough sample to isolate a significant pattern primarily found in recent modern drama. Although the pattern of the absent father can be found in various strands of European drama, in order to limit the scope of the study and avoid language barriers, the sample plays are drawn primarily from Anglo-American dramas. In order to emphasize diversity, the study includes playwrights who have become part of the canon, like Tennessee Williams and Arthur Miller, as well as more recent playwrights, like Beth Henley and Marsha Norman, who are still on the margins of the canon.

The study also makes no claim to trace the historical progression of the topos of the absent father but moves back and forth discovering him in a variety of time schemes. Plays from the early modern period are linked to more recent dramas. *Hedda Gabler* (1890) is compared to *'night, Mother* (1983) and *The Three Sisters* (1901) is linked to *Crimes of the Heart* (1981) in order to show how the pattern of the absent father spans the scope of modern drama. Although a variety of critical methodologies has been used to analyze the pattern of the absent father, this study does not try to focus on modern drama through one critical school or one particular critic, nor does it take any particular political stance. The study will not attempt to induce global abstractions about the nature of drama but will focus on close comparative readings of individual dramas. My intention is to point out a significant pattern and a unique and important character configuration in modern drama and to show without being reductive how both develop a consistent inner structure within a series of dramas.

Chapter 2 will review Greek and Elizabethan prototypes of the absent father in Sophocles' *Oedipus Tyrannus*, Aeschylus' *Libation Bearers*, and William Shakespeare's *Hamlet*.

Chapter 3 will cover the pattern of the absent father, the weakening of the position of the father in general, and the ambivalence of the father in early modern drama, covering Henrik Ibsen's *A Doll House* (1879), and *Ghosts* (1881), and August Strindberg's *Miss Julie* (1888), and *The Pelican* (1907).

Chapter 4 will show how the absent father plays a part in the American myth of the pioneer hero who escapes civilization to find adventure and riches in a mythical frontier. The pattern of the absent father and the quest of the lost son will be traced through Tennessee Williams' *The Glass Menagerie* (1945) and Arthur Miller's *Death of a Salesman* (1949).

Chapter 5 will continue to explore the romantic image of the father in more recent American dramas, like Sam Shepard's *True West* (1981), and David Rabe's *The Basic Training of Pavlo Hummel* (1969).

Chapter 6 will concentrate on the daughter's more limited quest to follow the path of the absent father. The quest will be examined in Marsha Norman's *'night, Mother* (1983), which will be compared to *Hedda Gabler* (1890) in order to show how the lost daughter becomes enamored of an escape to the father through a romantic death.

Chapter 7 will focus on the daughter's ties to the absent patriarch in *Crimes of the Heart* (1981). *Crimes of the Heart* will also be compared to Anton Chekhov's *The Three Sisters* (1901) to illustrate how the absent father imposes a lifestyle that is impossible for his daughter to live out.

Chapter 8 will investigate the nature of the absent father as a transcendental presence as well as the search to reestablish the aura of the father in a modern wasteland. In John Pielmeier's *Agnes of God* (1982) and Peter Shaffer's *Equus* (1973), the lost child seeks reunion with a divine presence through a mystical experience only to have the divine mystery destroyed.

Chapter 9 will examine *Amadeus* (1980), a play in which a lost son tries to appease a Transcendental Father but becomes obsessed with his revolt against the Father.

Chapter 10 will deal with the social and political ramifications of the absent father as a representative of the class struggle in John Osborne's *Look Back in Anger* (1957).

Chapter 11 will show how racial oppression is projected onto the figure of the ailing father in Athol Fugard's *Master Harold . . . and the boys* (1983).

Chapter 12 will examine Caryl Churchill's *Top Girls* (1982), a play which depicts the absent father as representative of the patriarchal system and its ability to ensnare women who are seeking independence.

CHAPTER 2

AVENGING THE FATHER:
Sophocles' *Oedipus Tyrannus*
Aeschylus' *The Libation Bearers*
Shakespeare's *Hamlet*

The concept of the absent father appears in drama long before the modern period. In fact, part of its dynamics can be seen as far back as the Greeks. In examining Sophocles' *Oedipus Tyrannus*, Aeschylus' *The Libation Bearers*, one can see the emerging pattern of the absent father and discover its workings in the dynamics of drama. Although William Shakespeare's *Hamlet* does not fit the criteria for a drama of the absent father, the play does have a close enough affinity to these dramas and such a prominent standing in the canon of Western drama that it, too, is worth examining as a classical text that has some resemblance to the dramas of the absent father.

The dead and absent father is the crucial figure in all three plays. He is a royal and a military hero, murdered in a less than glorious manner. His murder has been left unavenged and unmourned. In his absence, his children are lost and confused. The son returns home, but he, too, becomes alienated in his homeland and is cast into a state of profound mourning. The kingdom in which he dwells is turning into a wasteland as the father's absence cries out for a return of the father. In order to restore the absent father, whose status is ambiguous, to a state of presence, the son becomes a double of the father (as both son and king), and follows a command from the father which is given through a divine or spiritual figure who serves as an absent father god. He then reenacts the path of the father or mimics the murder of the father through reciprocal revenge—a path which inevitably leads to self-destruction. Thus, in all three dramas the tragic action and its consequences, as well as the dynamics of the characters and their environment, are all driven by the figure of the absent father.

Oedipus Tyrannus has long been cited as a seminal drama in Western literature. In his *Poetics*, Aristotle holds the play up as the model of an ideal tragedy, and Sigmund Freud sees the play as a paradigmatic model for the process of psychoanalysis. Interestingly, both Aristotle and Freud see tragic action in terms of family conflicts. Aristotle believes that the most powerful conflicts in drama are staged between family members. For Freud, the center of all human conflicts begins in the dynamics of childhood as the young child resolves his loves and hates toward his mother and father. For Freud, *Oedipus Tyrannus* mirrors the son's unconscious wish to kill the father and marry the mother. Yet if we go beyond the Oedipus complex, what emerges in the drama is the tragedy of the absent father, a tragedy which puts into question the very nature of fatherhood.

In *Oedipus Tyrannus*, the action of the drama is driven by the search for the absent father. King Laius, the father of the city, has been murdered. However, there has been no investigation into his murder and no mention of retrieving his body and conducting a proper funeral. Thus, the king has not been properly mourned, and the matter of his death has been left unresolved and unavenged. The king as father of the people is doubly absent. He is absent not only in his death but also in his murder which has deprived him of his rightful presence as king and father.

Oedipus is a lost son who has been abandoned by his real father and lied to by his adopted father. However, living in the state of illusion, Oedipus believes that he is both fortunate and wise. Like many a modern lost son, Oedipus is deceived by the physical trappings that surround him. He does not realize who he is nor can he recognize those around him. His riches and royalty are a sham.

In the absence of the father, the world itself has turned into a wasteland. *Oedipus Tyrannus* opens on a ritual of mourning. The people of Thebes are mourning the victims of the plague. In essence, however, they are mourning the loss of the absent father, for the plague is only a reflection of his unavenged and unmourned death. The plague, which is creating the wasteland, centers on the absence of the father in two aspects. First, the concept of fertility in *Oedipus Tyrannus* is linked to the father's seed. Both the seeds in mother earth and the seeds injected into maternal animals and human mothers are not coming to fruition. The father or life-giver who can produce no fruits is thus an absent father. Second, Oedipus is reminded that the plague is destroying "the house of Cadmus" (3). The city is traced back to the original patriarch and the whole patriarchal line, which is now in jeopardy of being destroyed. If the plague is not stopped, the absent patriarch Cadmus and his descendent, the ruling father, Oedipus, will both be relegated to absence.

In his search to uncover the crime against the father and to restore the absent father, Oedipus discovers that he has been propelled through a series of surrogate fathers who have served to reinforce the concept of father absence. As a child Oedipus is abandoned by his father, Laius, who becomes an absent father and is taken by Laius' shepherd, who has a fatherly compassion for Oedipus and wants to save the child from suffering. He, however, must give the child away to a Corinthian shepherd and thus becomes another absent father. The Corinthian shepherd in turn gives Oedipus to King Polybus. Thus, through a series of substitute fathers, Oedipus is thrice removed from the real father.

From here, Oedipus moves further into a maze of absent fathers and a distorted search for the father. Through a chain of substitute fathers, Oedipus goes from Laius, an absent father who abandoned his child and renounced his heir, to Polybus, an absent father who has no children and can produce no heirs. Oedipus claims Polybus as father, but Polybus is only a surrogate or stand-in for the father. Later, Oedipus abandons Polybus, rendering himself permanently absent from his surrogate father, only to put himself on a path of flight in which he confronts his real father. However, Laius too is an absent father to Oedipus because Laius does not bear the sign of the father, thus Oedipus kills a man on the road, unable to recognize that man as his father. At every point Oedipus turns, fatherhood is absent, both as signifier and signified. Polybus signifies fatherhood, but his fatherhood is an empty signifier without a true signified. He is no more than a supplement in a series of supplements. Laius, on the other hand, is the signified, the true father, yet he bears no signifier to Oedipus, who cannot recognize him as the father. Thus, in *Oedipus Tyrannus*, the sign for father is always deconstructing itself and rendering the father absent.

In the continuing absence of the father, the son finds himself bringing the father into presence by doubling or reenacting the father. Oedipus first reenacts the father as king. The play opens with Oedipus as father of the people calling upon the name of the ancient father, Cadmus. According to Pietro Pucci, the Name of the Father "opens the play as a teleological point of origin which reaches Oedipus and through him continues to provide care for the Theban children" (Pucci 5-6). Pucci claims that Oedipus' royal paternity "is grounded on mythological stories that begin with Cadmus and continue without break on to Oedipus, designing a teleological line of good and caring masters and kings" (8).

Oedipus also doubles Laius by becoming Laius' avenger. An avenger must do what the deceased or injured cannot do. He is compelled to act in the place of or to double the avenged. Thus, Oedipus doubles Laius in seeking to punish Laius' murderer. As husband of Laius' wife, Oedipus also doubles Laius as husband. For Oedipus, the doubling of the father leads to disastrous consequences. By taking on the role of king and father, he has become the source of the plague that is destroying his people. As avenger of Laius' murder, he can only destroy himself. In displacing Laius as husband, he breaks sacred taboo and occupies the place reserved only for the father in relationship to the mother, thus the absence of the father leads him to the ultimate doubling as he becomes his own father leaving fatherhood in a state of suspended absence.

Along with the predominant absence of the father, *Oedipus Tyrannus* reflects a strong ambivalence towards the father. Laius is the giver of life yet he tries to kill his son. Polybus cares for Oedipus but lies to Oedipus about his true identity, thus leading Oedipus in the path of harm. David McDonald points out the shepherd's double roles as "substitute fathers, as those who once saved him [Oedipus] and now come to destroy him" (157). Even Oedipus as father of the people is both their caretaker and the cause of their destruction. Pucci calls this "paternal violence an absence in the sense of the absence of his [the father's] teleological presence for the son" (6). In other words, the father is not a stable caretaker and source of origin.

The issue of father absence in *Oedipus Tyrannus* goes beyond the realm of surrogate human fathers and father doubles but leads toward the absence of the transcendental father. When Oedipus finds out that he is not Polybus' son, he first sees himself as a possible son of a slave but soon his slave origins are converted into divine paternity connecting the absent father and the absent god. Oedipus becomes a child of fortune and the chorus points out Pan, Apollo, Hermes and Dionysus as absent fathers. The most conspicuous absent god, however, is Apollo. According to McDonald, Apollo's absence "renders the 'force' of that absence more powerful. When the god cannot be seen, when it exists as not being there . . . then absence is all the more efficient and it shapes what is there by what is not there" ("Absence" 153). McDonald considers the supplicant priest in the prologue as a "surrogate of the absent god" and Teiresias and Creon as "agents for the concealed presence" of Apollo; "both serve to bring the source of light, the word of God to Oedipus" ("Absence" 154). Apollo knows the truth, and can reveal the guilty one, but the absent Father Apollo cannot be made to speak, he can only be heard through his ministers. As Pucci has discovered, "the Father is absent . . . the voice of Apollo is always one of his prophets." However, in the absence of the paternal voice of the god, no one can verify the words of his substitutes.

Following the path of the absent father has left Oedipus bereft of sight, kingdom and family. In the end, he wants to be banished and absent from his "father's city" (32). Even though he is not banished, he is rendered a pollution and hidden from public view. He has lost his position as father king, lost his wife/mother and lost his role as father, as Oedipus deems Creon "the only father left" (33) to Oedipus' daughters.

Oedipus Tyrannus is a search for the father that leads back to the son as a fratricide, whereas *The Libation Bearers* is a search for the father that leads to the son's act of matricide. In both cases the absent father leads to the curse upon the son. Oedipus' choices are not as conscious as Orestes' choices, but in both dramas the absent Apollo is standing in the wings ready to uphold the Law of the Father. *The Libation Bearers* is the middle play of Aeschylus' *Oresteia* trilogy. It stands alone as a separate play. In it, like in *Oedipus Tyrannus*, the father is absent, murdered. The crime against Father Agamemnon, like that against Father Laius, has gone unavenged. In both plays, the god Apollo calls for vengeance but never appears to verify his word. Although Aeschylus brings ghosts and divine apparitions into *The Eumenides*, the third play of the *Oresteia* and uses the ghost of the father in his earlier drama *The Persians*, no ghosts appear in *The Libation Bearers*, and the Furies are only seen by Orestes, not the audience. *The Libation Bearers* is earthbound, a play of solemn mourning for the absent father.

Agamemnon is an absent father. Like Laius, Agamemnon is not only dead but has been displaced as the rightful king by a usurper. Thus, he is also absent as the father king. Furthermore, he has suffered a loss of status and dignity for he has died in an ignominious butchering in his bath. Agamemnon is a hero warrior deprived of his honor and name, buried beneath "one sad mound" (116). Not only was Agamemnon deprived of a hero's death but he was also left unmourned. According to Andre Green, Agamemnon is "twice dead" or doubly absent, "once by murder and a second time by the failure to perform the rites that should have accompanied his burial" (80). Thus, according to Green, Orestes must "restore the name of the father to gain a sense of identity" (80). The dead father, embedded in a chain of absent fathers leading back to Atreus, is beckoning to be made present in his absence. Green concludes about Orestes' mission: "In order to set down a past that he knows only through the marked but not signified place of his father's grave" and "in order to clear the way for the Trojan epic that will be the glory of his life and which remains inaccessible, unavailable to him, he must restore life to Agamemnon" (80). In other words he must bring the absent father into presence.

The drama opens before the tomb of the absent father. The son has returned and the daughter comes to the tomb in a procession of mourning, but behind the procession is the presence of the absent father. Clytemnestra has had a dream which has been sent by Agamemnon. The dream, like the voice of Apollo in *Oedipus Tyrannus*, is the cry of the dead father for vengeance. Frightened by this dream, Clytemnestra hopes to appease her wrong by ordering a funeral ritual. However, her mourning is feigned, and the chorus calls it a "pious blasphemy" (105). Clearly, the unmourned king cannot be appeased by a mere show of mourning. In both *Oedipus Tyrannus* and *The Libation Bearers*, the death of an absent father, unmourned and unavenged, not only initiates the dramatic action but becomes the main impetus for it.

Both Electra and Orestes are the lost children of an absent father. Orestes labels himself "an exile newly returned to his land" (103). Electra lives "like a slave" (108). There is a clear connection between the children of Agamemnon and Oedipus. Oedipus is also an exile, a dishonored child who has returned to his fatherland. Both Oedipus and the Atreid children have lost their rightful places as part of the royal family which has descended from the father. Orestes calls himself and his sister "Orphans and exiles both" (113) cut off from father and fatherland. They have also felt a deeper sense of absence, for they are the last of the patriarchal line which is threatened with extinction, the permanent absence of the father. The house of Atreus, like the house of Cadmus, is on the brink of extinction and the Name of the Father is in jeopardy of being annihilated.

Also, the lost children are living in a wasteland at Argos. The chorus notes that Agamemnon's death has left the world "bruised for a loss whose blow / Leaves life no laughter pain nor rest" (104). In the corrupt world of Clytemnestra and her adulterous lover Aegisthus, "reverence for royal power has resigned," and "fear has his hour. Success is now man's god, man's more than god" (105). The wealth of Agamemnon has been squandered. The world of heroes is reduced to one of idle luxury. Electra complains to her dead father "Where is one single good, not rendered vain" (115).

In the midst of this woe, there is the cry for an avenger to bring back the absent father, for every avenger is the double of the avenged. It is the absent father that summons the son. Electra implores the dead father: "Father, let some good chance bring Orestes here . . . let your avenger, Father, appear" (108–9). Orestes as the representation of the father does appear first in his lock of hair (inherited from the father), then in his presence as son and double of the father. The voice of the father has summoned him through Clytemnestra's dream of a viper that suckled at her bosom. Orestes realizes "the dream commands it: I am her destined murderer" (123). In a Freudian interpretation, Green sees the snake as "the father (Agamemnon) returning from the world of the dead by means of his son" (52).

In his attempt to resurrect the father, Orestes not only doubles the father but invokes Agamemnon to manifest himself. Orestes pleads, "Father, your own son calls you; stand at my side," and Electra follows with "I echo him" (120). Orestes also cries out "O Earth, send my father to direct my sword" (121). Simon Goldhill finds that in *The Libation Bearers* the presence of the absent father is clearly established in the *kommos*, that part of Greek tragedy which displays a climactic and lyrical exchange between chorus and characters. Goldhill argues that "The *kommos* in its literal 'summoning' of Agamemnon attempts to assert the word of the father in the discourse—the missing signifier being precisely the father" (139). Orestes explains clearly why he must avenge his father's death and take his father's place. He gives the following reasons: "the god's command; grief for my father; and with these loss of my patrimony, shame that my proud citizens" are "enslaved" (114). Not only is Orestes acting under divine command, but he personally is trying to regain a father he could not mourn. Also, as rightful heir, he must reclaim his father's place as king. Finally, he must double his father as king and rescue the people from the clutches of the Terrible Mother, Clytemnestra, and her lover whom he considers womanly. Thus, the kingdom of Argos is ruled by cruel and treacherous women. Orestes must restore the Father to his kingdom and bring back the "lost lord" (109), the true paternal authority.

Orestes will also reenact the father in the symmetrical or reciprocal nature of his revenge. The chorus has already cried out for "death for death" and "wickedness for wickedness" (109). Since Agamemnon was killed by treachery, so too will Aegisthus and Clytemnestra be detroyed by treachery in "the self-same snare" (124). Eventually, Orestes enters the house with Clytemnestra the way Agamemnon did. In his act of vengeance, Orestes doubles the father and carries out the father's will.

Before killing Clytemnestra, the chorus tells Orestes he must remember his "father's killing" (133). When Orestes kills her he says "the wind of fate blows straight from my father's death to yours" (137). Orestes then resurrects the father by bringing the "strait jacket" (140) that trapped his father, the "robe dyed red" with the father's blood. Since he could not mourn his father, Orestes now offers his lament "to the treacherous web that caught and killed" (141) his father. Through metonymic substitution the father is present in the form of his death garment while Orestes' speech over the bodies of Clytemnestra and Aegisthus is a mimetic reenacting of Clytemnestra's speech over Agamemnon and Cassandra. Brooks Otis notes about the similar scenes "the wheel of justice has come full circle" or "the whole thing is beginning again" (79). The drama of *The Libation Bearers* does not end the cycle of revenge, but in it the absent father has made his presence known. After Orestes murders Aegisthus and before he murders Clytemnestra, a servant exclaims "the dead . . . come to life to kill the living" (135). The servant is referring to the supposedly dead Orestes, but the reference clearly points to the dead father.

The Libation Bearers is overdetermined with the presence of the absent father not only in the form of the biological or royal father but also in the form of the transcendental father. Orestes implores Hermes, the guide of "dead men's souls" (103) and "Son of Zeus, the Deliverer" to fill the office of his father and be Orestes' "deliverer" (103). Orestes invokes Hermes as the guide of the dead, thus connecting him with the dead father and also as a son of Zeus, the Father God and deliverer. Zeus, the "Father of the Olympian Gods" (131) is the absent father beyond Hermes and Agamemnon. Orestes pleads, "Great Zeus, grant me vengeance for my father's death" (104). He also implores Zeus to "behold the eagles' brood bereaved" who are "daring to claim their father's spoils." If the "eagle's brood" perishes, no one will be left to guard Zeus' shrines. Zeus, the absent father, is connected to Agamemnon. Goldhill notes that the eagle is connected to Zeus, thus connecting Zeus to Agamemnon (135). Also, Zeus, the father, must protect the patriarchal line. For without the ruling fathers, Zeus will be left with no representatives or worshipers. The chorus even notes that the fulfillment of Orestes will be brought about "by Zeus our Father's hand" (114). The absent transcendental father is behind a series of absent fathers. The absent Zeus is behind the Atreid line of fathers and behind Agamemnon. The hand of Zeus will be behind the hand of Agamemnon, who is behind the hand of Orestes, who makes present the absence of the father. Zeus of the Lower Earth and Hermes of the underworld are all connected to the dead. They are all in a liminal state in this drama of mourning, all absent yet their presence is felt.

According to Goldhill the *kommos* ends "with the assertion of a prayer for victory with the help of Agamemnon, the father, in terms recalling Zeus the father of the gods" (150). Goldhill notes that "throughout the *kommos* the terms of the prayer of invocation of the male force of the father in the house recall the vocabulary and images of the earlier transgressions in the house of Atreus. So

the conjuration/invocation/mourning of Agamemnon asserts and presents the role
of the father" (150). In other words, through language referring to the gods and
to the genealogy of the house of Atreus, the mourning of Agamemnon becomes
an attempt to go back to the father as a point of origin.

The other absent god in *The Libation Bearers* is Apollo, who as in *Oedipus
Tyrannus*, speaks for the Law of the Father, a law which cries out for the
avenging of the dead, unmourned, and displaced father. Orestes points out that
Apollo's voice "drives me to dare this peril / Chilling my heart's hot blood with
a recital of threatened terrors / If I should fail to exact fit vengeance" (113).
Apollo threatens repercussions and plagues if the father is not avenged. Just as
in *Oedipus Tyrannus*, the physical and moral order is threatened with chaos.
Apollo mandates "a father's blood lies unavenged and time grows ripe" (113).
If he does not act, Orestes "the neglectful son" will be attacked by "Furies,
roused by blood guilt" (113–14) and driven to madness. Apollo speaks for the
wrath of the father. If Orestes does not avenge the father, he is to be left
accursed. Even though he is not certain whether he can trust the oracle, the
voice of the absent father with the weight of patriarchal law is so strong that
Orestes feels compelled to act. Even when Orestes hesitates to kill his mother,
Pylades reminds him that he must not anger Apollo, the absent god who speaks
for the absent father.

Following the paths of the absent father and listening to his command leads
Orestes to tragic consequences as he is driven to madness by raging Furies sent
to avenge matricide. Orestes, like Oedipus and other lost sons, finds himself in
a double bind. Compelled to follow the path of the absent father, the sons are
inevitably led toward self-destruction.

Unlike *Oedipus Tyrannus* and *The Libation Bearers*, *Hamlet* is not a clear
example of a drama of the absent father because the father of Hamlet is present
on stage in the form of a ghost. Granted, some critics see the ghost as a
hallucination or a spirit that embodies the likeness of Hamlet's father and not as
an actual presence. Still, he manifests himself before the audience and speaks
directly for himself. He clearly occupies the space of performance not the space
of narrative that is outside of performance. However, because of *Hamlet*'s
important status in the canon of English literature and because it stands as the
precursor of modern psychological drama, it bears mentioning as a drama with
some characteristics of the dramaturgy of the absent father.

Of course, Hamlet's father is absent through his death. However, he is not
only absent as father to Hamlet, but he is also a kingly father. His death, or
rather, his "murder foul and most unnatural" (27), has left the entire kingdom
of Denmark in a state of rottenness. Life is composed of feigning and illusion.
In this world, true feelings like grief only seem like grief, and Hamlet finds
himself alone in a grief "that passeth show" (11). Honor and goodness are cast
into doubt in a world of the "seemingly virtuous" (27). The world has become

a wasteland where life has lost its authenticity.

The absence of the father has not only diminished the social order but also has left Hamlet, the lost son, in a profound state of mourning, a mourning which he projects onto the very cosmos. To him, all things of this world become "weary, stale, flat and unprofitable" (12). The Earth itself becomes a "sterile promontory" (49), and the glorious firmament is turned into a "foul and pestilent congregation of vapors" (50). Humankind is reduced to a "quintessence of dust" (50).

Just as in *Oedipus Tyrannus* and *The Libation Bearers*, the world in *Hamlet* is in confusion and chaos because a father and king has been murdered and his mourning rites have been neglected or aborted. In *Hamlet*, the absent father has not only been killed without obtaining the last rites of the church, but his mourning rites have been cut short by the wedding feast of his murderer. Even Hamlet is urged to cut short his mourning of the absent father and told by Gertrude and Claudius that life itself is no more than an endless chain of absent fathers. According to Claudius, "Nature's common theme is the death of fathers" (11). This regressive chain reduces the mysterious power of genealogy with its ascending mimetic links that lead back to a transcendental father to the corrosive status of diminishing mimesis that views fatherhood as part of the process of human transitoriness. Hamlet is sickened by this reduction of the sacred aura of fatherhood to commonness.

In his grief Hamlet has idealized the father. He sees his father as the pinnacle of manhood: "He was a man, take him for all in all, I shall not look upon his like again" (14). Hamlet's father represents a world of stability. Like Agamemnon who conquered Troy, Father Hamlet is a military hero who has conquered the Poles and killed the Norwegian King, Old Fortinbras, in single combat. Yet there is still ambivalence about the heroic father. Is he a man of exemplary virtue or is he a man who died bearing the burden of "crimes broad blown" (85). Is his ghost a "spirit of health" or "a goblin damned" (23). Is the absent father a heavenly guide or is he the devil in a pleasing shape? This father who is supposed to be the center of Hamlet's life was absent at Hamlet's birth, a warrior hero admired at a distance, a man like Agamemnon, both inside and outside of the family. Also like Agamemnon, he is a warrior killed by treachery, not slain in the field. His death was not only untimely but inappropriate to his stature.

In the absence of the father, Hamlet is compelled to double the father. Physically, he takes on the character of his ghostly father. Susan Cole finds that "Hamlet comes to Ophelia as the ghost came to the sentinels guarding the castle—pale, silent, sorrowful, lifting his head and fixing his 'fear surprised' audience with a constant look that seems to speak of hellish horrors" (45). As an avenger, he doubles the father and acts on the father's injunction. Like Orestes he is bound by the Law of the Father. The father commands: "Duller shouldst thou be than the fat weed / that rots itself in ease on Lethe wharf / Wouldst thou not stir in this" (27). Also, his revenge must be symmetrical or reciprocal. He must murder Claudius when Claudius' soul is in a state of sin, just like Claudius murdered Hamlet's father before the father could confess his sins. Hamlet is also suicidal and will put his life in jeopardy, just like Orestes, who was willing to "cast away" (119) his own life. According to James Redfield, "the most perfect mourning would be suicide" (179–81), for in suicide the mourner doubles the absent one. Hamlet as prince has the public duty to restore the father's kingdom. Like other lost sons, Hamlet is compelled by his very status and birth to restore the father and the father's world. He, like Orestes and Oedipus, is the designated savior. Realizing his mission, Hamlet cries out: "The time is out of joint. O cursed spite / that I was ever born to set it right" (33).

Hamlet also searches for father substitutes. Avi Erlich finds numerous father substitutes in Hamlet—all who fail Hamlet because they represent the weak father Hamlet is trying to supplant. Erlich cites Priam in the player's speech as a mighty king who like Father Hamlet in his death became "a weak, defenseless father" (116). Hamlet also sees the First Player, the elder member of the company as a father figure worthy of emulation, but "the first player's heroism is quite ambiguous, he would be capable of nothing more assertive than horrid speech" (121). Even Horatio, who is associated with Father Hamlet's ghost, becomes a "father who sucks Hamlet into the vortex of the past" (130). Erlich demonstrates the recurring theme in Hamlet by which "ambiguous fathers are models for their sons who become indistinguishable from them" (139).

In *Hamlet*, the theme of the absent father and the son avenger runs through other threads in the play. Fortinbras has set up an army to regain his dead father by invading Denmark and avenging the murder of Father Fortinbras by Father Hamlet. Fortinbras tries to bring back the father and restore the father's name by regaining lost land. Diverted from conquering Denmark, he still tries to redress the loss of the father by attacking worthless territories in Poland. He is capable of finding "a quarrel in a straw when honor is at stake" (103). Laertes also seeks to avenge an absent father. Like Father Hamlet's shortened mourning period, Polonius' mourning rites have been cut short. Like a true lost son, Laertes will double the father and revenge the father's death by killing Hamlet. Like Fortinbras, Laertes is relentless in revenge. He is willing to cut Hamlet's "throat in the church" (118) to restore his father.

In the final act, the threads are brought together as Hamlet reenacts the path of his father. Cole states "In the last act he [Hamlet] repossesses the name with which he first addresses the ghost; he engages in (mock) single combat with a rival as his father did with Fortinbras, and dying—like his father—poisoned by Claudius—he becomes in his final passage the military royal presence prefigured by the ghost" (43). The plot lines in Hamlet weave together in a mimetic chain of father murders. Father Hamlet kills Father Fortinbras; Claudius kills Father Hamlet, and Hamlet kills Claudius. Hamlet also kills Polonius then Laertes kills Hamlet. In the end, the kingdom goes to Fortinbras, who restores the name of his father without provoking an endless chain or reciprocal vengeance. Following the path of the father has left Hamlet tormented and caught in a trail of bloody murders. Like Orestes at the end of *The Libation Bearers*, Hamlet has lived on the brink of madness.

Hamlet's world is also the world of the the absent father god. The gods Apollo and Mars are connected to Father Hamlet, whose likeness will not be seen again. But more important than the absence of the pagan gods is the absence of the Christian God. Erlich notes how Hamlet "wishes to see Claudius punished not by himself but by God, the universal father figure" (29) and argues that Hamlet's "profession of belief in a 'divinity' that shapes our ends can be a convenient sublimation for someone in desperate need of a strong father" (30). Sublimation or not, the voice of God is an uncertain one. Although Hamlet sees himself as God's minister, he has no assurance that he is hearing God, the Father, and not the Devil in a pleasing shape.

Combing the plays and source materials, Gilbert Murray sees two mythic patterns behind the Orestes/Hamlet sagas. The king is "dethroned and slain by a younger kinsman, who is helped by the Queen, and his successor tries to destroy the next heir to the throne who comes home secretly and slays both him and the Queen" (19). He even connects this pattern to the myth of Oedipus which is different from Sophocles' play. Murray sees in this pattern the ritual story of the "Golden Bough Kings." In this ritual, the year-king "comes first as a wintry slayer, weds the Queen, grows proud and royal, and then is slain by the avenger of his predecessor" (20). This pattern fits Hamlet and *The Libation Bearers* and even *Oedipus Tyrannus* if we consider Oedipus as both the slayer and the avenger and substitute his self-mutilation for his death. Murray connects these myths to the dying and rising gods. They are also connected to the pattern of the absent father.

All three dramas, *Oedipus Tyrannus*, *The Libation Bearers*, and *Hamlet*, show how the absent father can become a dynamic force in drama and how he can not only propel the dramatic action but also become the element embedded in the dramatic structure that determines the fate of the characters as well as the status of the dramatic environment. All three plays show how a profound sense of longing brought about by the loss of the father establishes a need to reestablish his presence by opening the way for a dizzying chain of substitutes and doubles. Certainly, to argue that the absent father stands at the origin of all dramatic discourse would be a gross overstatement and essentially unprovable. However, to say that there are a series of dramas from *The Libation Bearers* to *Waiting for Godot* that center on the absent father could lead to a plausible and provable thesis.

But the focus of this study is on modern drama and its unique method of enacting a mourning ritual for an absent father. In modern drama, the absent father creates a similar but more elaborate pattern than in the classical dramas. The dead or missing father is no longer a sacred king, but his absence becomes a haunting presence for his sons and daughters beginning with dramas of the early modern period, the plays of Henrik Ibsen and August Strindberg.

CHAPTER 3

QUESTIONING THE FATHER'S AUTHORITY:
Henrik Ibsen's *A Doll House*
Henrik Ibsen's *Ghosts*
August Strindberg's *Miss Julie*
August Strindberg's *The Pelican*

In the modern period Henrik Ibsen and August Strindberg make use of the absent father as one means of adding psychological depth to their dramas and presenting a sociological critique of their times. The plays of Ibsen and Strindberg that focus on the absent father are structured specifically around the father's absence and his symbolic function as a representation of cultural values. But at the same time as the Absent Father represents abstract cultural codes, he also puts into question the validity of such codes. Marjorie Garber points out that "the father is always a suppositional father, a father by imputation, rather than by unimpeachable biological proof. . . . This doubt upon which paternity, legitimacy, inheritance, and succession depends is the anxiety at the root of the paternal metaphor" (133). Doubtful paternity is certainly an issue in the plays of Ibsen and Strindberg where paternity is associated with weakness, uncertainty, death, and above all, absence. In discussing cultural conditions during Ibsen's time, Wolfgang Sohlich describes a society built on the concept of a fatherless family "characterized by the erosion of paternal authority due to the historical developments which displaced the economical and societal functions of the bourgeois family onto corporate and educational oligopolies" (88).

In fact, in the world of Ibsen and Strindberg, the legitimacy of the paternal metaphor itself is questioned. Nowhere is this situation more obvious than in Strindberg's *The Father*. In the play, the Captain tries to exert his patriarchal right to determine the education of his child and to show his wife that she has no rights over his progeny. However, the play undermines the Captain's position. From the very first scene in which one of the Captain's recruits refuses to take responsibility for impregnating the kitchen maid, to the crazed Captain's quotations of Homer and Ezekial on the inability to determine one's father, paternity is questioned and, with it, the authority of the father.

In Ibsen's *A Doll House* and *Ghosts* and Strindberg's *Miss Julie* and *The Pelican*, the questioning of paternity comes out in the figure of the absent father, a central figure that controls the plot, influences the trajectory and configurations of the characters, and projects his presence, often menacingly, upon the dramatic environment. In these plays, a symbolic father is usually a sick or wounded father, a deposed paternity, a god-like figure in a state of decline. He is connected with the patriarchy and its Law. However, he is both a representative of and a transgressor against the patriarchal order, an ambiguous figure who is both within and without the dominant social structure. He represents both the power of the patriarch as well as the erosion of that power. His name, which represents his paternal authority, is either used ambiguously or is absent from the text. The dramatic structure of these plays focuses specifically on a crime committed either in the Name of the Father or against that name. Thus, the person who commits the crime, be it mother or child, is condemned under the Father's Law. Also, the father's absence brings forth the need to recreate or mimic his presence. In other words, the father's absence is foregrounded by metonymic representation of him or by his doubles. The father's children, who are alienated and debilitated, seek to reconcile themselves with the loss of the father by rediscovering him, rehabilitating him or exorcising him. But all attempts to reincarnate the father only point out more clearly his absence, and the general absence of fatherhood itself.

In *A Doll House*, Nora's father is the central figure in Nora's life. No mention is made of her mother or any of her siblings, if there are any. Nora's father is depicted as sick, both physically and morally. Nora remembers her father on his deathbed and her inability to be with him. Like Orestes and Hamlet, she is absent at the death scene of the father. At the same time as her father is dying, her husband is gravely ill. Nora finds herself utterly alone, unable to trouble a dying father who might help her obtain the money to save her husband's life. At a crucial moment in Nora's life, her father is absent. She might have confided in him, "but he was too sick at the time—and then sadly it did not matter" (136). At this point, Nora makes a decision that will be crucial to the plot of the play. By acting on her own and securing the money to save her husband's life, she commits the crime of forging her father's signature to a loan agreement. The absence of the father compels Nora to act, and, in her action, to break the Law of the Father, the cultural code that prevents women from acting in financial matters without patriarchal authorization. This law is central to the issue of *A Doll House*. Ibsen notes: "There are two kinds of moral law, two kinds of conscience, one for men and one, quite different, for women. They don't understand each other; but in practical life, woman is judged by masculine law" (qtd. in Meyer 466). Nora's actions will be judged by the Law of the Father.

Nora's father is clearly a representative of patriarchal values, which he has inculcated in his daughter through his attempts to "improve" (166) her, but he is also a transgressor against these values, a representative of the law, but a breaker of that law. His financial dealings are questionable, if not illegal, and according to Torvald, his "official career was hardly above reproach" (160). His values both reinforce the system and expose it to corruptibility. In fact, as the symbolic father, he is seen as an outcast who had to be saved from destruction by Nora's husband, Torvald, an action which Torvald will bring home to Nora when she too is implicated in criminal financial dealings.

As her father's daughter, Nora is debilitated. She is a childlike creature who has inherited her father's knack for making everything around her charming. She is thus reduced to the status of a trained animal. Her father has left her helpless and alienated from herself. Yet in the absence of her father and to spare him at his hour of dying, Nora performs a courageous but criminal action. She forges her father's signature and dates the forgery three days after her father has died. Thus, it is around the name of the dead and absent father that the crux of *A Doll House* revolves, for the revelation of this crime threatens the security of Nora's doll-like existence. However, it is crucial to note that Nora's crime of impersonating her father through the use of his signature is a crime against the Name of the Father as well as the Law of the Father, both of which seem absent or remote to Nora, but which are very present in the world of *A Doll House*. Krogstad asks Nora, "It really was your father who signed his own name here, wasn't it?" To which she replies, "I signed Papa's name" (148). Nora shuns the law by claiming her "right to protect her dying father from anxiety and care" (149). Nora has put herself above the Law of the Father and taken on the power of his name in the very act of saving him from anxiety.

In *A Doll House* the father's signature is not the only haunting presence of the absent father. As both Torvald and her friend Kristine tell her, Nora is also a double of her father and her crime mirrors the crime of her father, irresponsibility with money. The daughter thus becomes the representation of the dead father, compelled to reenact the crime of the father. However, she is not the only representation of the absent father. She considers Torvald, her husband, like her father, and she loves him like her father. For her, "with Torvald it's just the same as with Papa" (167). In essence, Nora has married her father. The exchange of the daughter from one paternal home to another has kept her helplessly imprisoned in the childhood world of the father. This unhealthy attachment is a form of psychological incest.

Unaware of her entrapment under the Name of the Father (ironically, the script identifies her only as Nora while all the other characters in the play are subsumed under the Name of the Father), she seeks an escape by creating an imaginary father, a rich old admirer who will endow her with the gift of money that her father never endowed her with. Thus, she again attaches a father to money and the need for it. This fantasy father turns into a reality in the person of Dr. Rank, a friend of the Helmers, whom Nora uses as an ideal father, who, unlike her real father and her husband, will listen to her. However, she cannot use him as a beneficent father because he is romantically in love with her. Here she is unwilling to turn a paternal relationship into a romantic one and risk psychological incest. Her second fantasy father is embodied in Torvald, whom she thinks will rescue her and assume the burden of her guilt. In her fantasy, she plans to become a romantic heroine and a sacrificial victim by committing suicide. These romantic notions, however, come from her father. In her suicide threats, she reenacts her father. Torvald scorns her noble suicide speech: "Your father had a mess of those speeches, too" (188). When Nora becomes aware of who Torvald really is, she finds herself demeaned, for in discovering Torvald, she really discovers an emotionally incestuous relationship with her father and her fragile position in the world of the father: "I went from Papa's hands into yours" and "I've been your doll wife just as I was Papa's doll child" (191). She becomes aware of the crime that her father committed against her. "It's a great sin what you and Papa did to me. You're the blame that nothing has become of me" (191). Nora commits a crime against the Law of the Father in order to spare her father and save her husband, a father substitute. However, she is already a victim of the father's crime of keeping her a child, obedient and attached to the father forever. Her final exit is a break away from the father. Clearly, Nora's actions are controlled by the absent father. In essence, her fate is determined by the search for and escape from an absent father.

Nora is not the only character in the play who is touched by the absent father. Nora's absent father becomes a symbol for other absent fathers who are inscribed across the text of *A Doll House*. All these absent fathers are either absent in times of need or are defective in some way. Dr. Rank's father has left him with a congenital venereal disease. He is a son who is paying his father's debt by dying for his father's sins. Just as Nora's father left her emotionally undeveloped, Rank's father has left him physically deteriorated. Then, there is the case of Kristine who has "no father to give [her] travel money" (134). Her own father, who should have taken care of her mother and two brothers, is absent (presumed dead); so she is forced to marry a father substitute, someone to support her family, but like other fathers in the play, he becomes ill and leaves Kristine to work on her own. Kristine, like Nora, marries a man to replace a father, but finds him incapable of fulfilling the role she wants him to fulfill. The father of Anne Marie's child, whom she labels "a slippery fish" who "didn't do a thing for" her, abandons his family and forces Anne Marie to give up her child in order to become Nora's nursemaid. In the end, Nora, too, deserts her children and her husband to situate herself in the world of the father. Thus, absent fathers either abandon their children or leave them debilitated. In fact, fathers as representations of the ideological symbol of the Ideal Father are inevitably absent or deficient.

In *A Doll House*, the absent father is a driving force in the dynamics of the drama. Nora commits a crime in the Name of the Father. The forged document then becomes a central plot device that pushes Nora to create imaginary fathers who are also absent to Nora. In the end, Nora finds her father in her husband who is a double of her father. She rejects both of them and goes out to learn about the other symbolic fathers that surround her. Ironically, she will begin her education by taking with her only those things which she brought "from home" (196), the home of the father, the absent father whom she sinned against and who sinned against her. Nora, bereft of the father, finds herself doubling him. Like most lost children, she is caught in the romantic vision of the father. Ironically, in order to find herself, she returns to her home town, the very place that has been marked by the presence of the absent father.

Just as the specter of the absent patriarch with the tarnished reputation haunts *A Doll House*, it also looms heavily over *Ghosts*. Captain Alving has been dead for ten years, and the play opens the day before the dedication of his memorial, the Captain Alving Memorial Orphan's Home. Captain Alving's son, Osvald, has returned home from abroad. Like Nora's father, Captain Alving represents the social order at the same time as he displays a reaction against it. Captain Alving, the symbolic father, is supposedly a model citizen and public benefactor, but underneath this public facade, he is revealed to be a drunkard and a lecher who has contracted venereal disease. Thus, he is depicted as a sick father who has degenerated both physically and mentally. At the same time as he upholds the Name of the Father and the Father's Law, he is also a transgressor of this Law. He has consorted with prostitutes, neglected his civic and home duties, and impregnated his maid, bringing his debauchery into his own home.

Because of his transgression, Captain Alving becomes a deposed father, stripped of his authority. After Captain Alving brought the pollution of his life into the sacred realm of his home and sired a child by his maid Joanna, he left himself open to the power of his wife who used his crime against him and stripped him of all authority. She not only sent his son away from him, but she also deposed him and took over his estate, building it up in his name while he lounged on a couch. She rendered Captain Alving absent from his role as both father and patriarch.

Ghosts revolves around the issue of the absent father not only because Captain Alving does not appear in the play but also because the ideal or symbolic father is absent from society. Captain Alving is both a Captain and a Chamberlain, holding the position and status of the father in the military and the government. However, he has failed to execute his affairs and allowed his wife to fulfill his social obligations. Because he is being memorialized, he becomes the symbolic father to the poor and fatherless in the community. Yet he himself has been separated from his two children. His legitimate son Osvald is sick and confused. Tormented by headaches and unable to work, Osvald is diagnosed as having a softening of the brain. Though physically healthy, the Captain's illegitimate daughter Regina is morally flawed. Both children have suffered from the absence of the father. Osvald was removed from the pollution of his dissolute father, and Regina was never told who her real father was. For them, the father has always been absent.

The ghost of the absent father haunts the whole play. The disparity in Captain Alving's position as father leads to the questioning of the symbolic or ideal father. The play opens with the preparations for Captain Alving's memorial and the memorial ceremony is one of the reasons for Osvald's return home. Osvald says about his return, "It's the least I can do for Father" (122). However, the occasion for memorializing the absent father brings forth the ominous presence of the father in a series of reconstructed, but illusory, fathers. First, Osvald has been given an image of his father as an ideal father, a narrative fiction created in a series of letters sent to him by his mother. Thus, the absent father that Osvald has come to memorialize is really an illusory father created by Mrs. Alving, a father that never was, an empty reconstruction. Later, when Mrs. Alving wants to reveal to her son the truth about his father, Pastor Manders urges her to let her son hold onto a false ideal. Manders holds that "a child should love and honor his father." He insists that the image of the father fabricated through Mrs Alving's letters creates an ideal father. He feels that the "father is some sort of ideal" to Osvald and Manders "does not want to abolish ideals" (237). Manders, of course, is talking about a symbolic or ideological father. Mrs. Alving, who has become disenchanted with such notions of fatherhood replies, "Don't let's talk abstractions" (236). Thus, fatherhood becomes a concept, a disembodied and illusionary metaphor against which the real Captain Alving is a pale reflection.

However, Captain Alving is not the only father under attack for not being a representative of the Ideal Father. At one point in the play, Manders' perception of respected fatherhood is pitted against the perception of Osvald who has witnessed the actions of other absent fathers. Mirroring the image of Captain Alving are the good fathers of Norway, who, absent from the confines of their respected domains, visit the bohemian world of Paris and shed their veneer of respectability to engage in a depravity that shocks the innocent paradise world of Osvald's artists' commune. These absent fathers away from home are clearly depraved fathers who at home mask their depravity behind moral outrage. Like Captain Alving, they are the promulgators of the Law and also its most flagrant violators. Thus, the play shows a clear break between the transcendental signifier (Father) and the signified (those who are supposed to be model fathers). In fact, the term father is becoming an empty signifier that cannot attach itself to any representative. The Symbolic or Ideal Father thus becomes an absence.

Just as the absent father is hidden behind several layers of illusion in the case of Osvald, in the case of Regina, Captain Alving's illegitimate child, he is found in a preponderance of bogus fathers. Standing behind all of her other fathers is Captain Alving, her real father who is absent because he does not claim her. Her mother Joanna is given money to keep her daughter's paternity a secret and thus, she creates fictional fathers for Regina claiming that a rich Englishman who visited the Alvings is the child's father, another romantic fantasy. The Englishman is doubly absent not only because he has supposedly deserted his child, but also because he does not exist. When Joanna tells Jacob

Engstrand about her predicament, he marries her for the money and takes on the title of father. Engstrand lies to Pastor Manders and marries Joanna claiming that he is the father of her child. His claim to fatherhood under the rule of law is documented in the parish register, but that documentation is based on a fiction. Engstrand clearly illustrates Joyce's claim that the father is a legal fiction. (2:107–8).

Although Engstrand continuously claims the rights of fatherhood, he is not Joanna's father nor has he treated her as a good father should. Manders at one point defends Engstrand's rights and protests, "He is her father," again invoking the empty symbol of the ideological father. But Mrs. Alving emphasizes "what kind of a father he's been to her" (219). Again, when Pastor Manders tells Regina, who has been living with Mrs. Alving, that she should live with her father, she claims that it is not right for her to live with a single man. Manders is aghast at such a remark. "This is your own father that we're speaking of!" he retorts. Obviously Manders does not see the impropriety of Regina living with Engstrand since he thinks she is protected by the sacred bounds of fatherhood which prohibits incest.

However, in an ironic reversal, she passes over Mander's remark and inquires if he knows a gentleman she might live with, and hints that she wouldn't mind living with Manders "almost like a daughter" (211). Thus, she claims Manders as her father; however, the word almost could have two implications: one that she would claim him as a father and become like a daughter to him, and the other that she would pretend to be his daughter whereas she actually would become his mistress. Around her relationship with Engstrand, her spurious father, and Manders, her surrogate father, are the hints of incest.

Manders, however, rejects the role of surrogate father and becomes another one of Regina's absent or phantom fathers. Regina's many fathers again reduce the concept of father to an empty symbol that is only revealed in the shadowy doubles of unreliable and unholy fathers. Captain Alving, the absent father, has spawned a chain of spurious fathers, each one more removed from real paternity. These fathers are fictionalized, romantic, ideal, symbolic, and always absent.

Other than in the diminishing chain of mimetic and reconstructed fathers, Captain Alving's ghost is seen in the doubling of the father and the compulsion to reenact the father. When Osvald enters smoking the phallic pipe of his father, Manders notes that he is Captain Alving "in the flesh" (220), a reincarnation of the father and that he is the "picture of Alving" (221), a mirroring of the father. Osvald not only inherits his father's appearance but also inherits his disease. Furthermore, he reenacts the sin of the father. Alving seduced Joanna, his servant, and Osvald tries to seduce Regina, his servant. The son of Captain Alving repeats the seduction with the daughter of Captain Alving, implying both fraternal and paternal incest. Manders exerts the Law of the Father against incest, and he and Mrs. Alving try to replay the Captain Alving/Joanna scenario by trying to have Regina sent off and married. Thus, the absent father continues to dominate the action.

The absent father is also present in two structures which represent the house of the father and bear the name of the father. The Captain Alving Memorial Orphan's Home not only bears his name, but also symbolizes all the fatherless children he and other fathers have left behind. The orphanage is not insured by earthly fathers so as to give the impression that it is sanctified by a Divine Father. Since the uninsured orphanage burns down, the implication is that it is not protected by Divine Providence, a transcendental absent father. Thus, the house of Captain Alving, the supposed father/benefactor collapses, and along with it, the sanctified Order of the Father. However, out of its ashes springs Engstrand's brothel, disguised as a home for orphan sailors, a house which will also bear the name of Captain Alving, the Name of the Father. Thus, the same absent father that is behind the social welfare of the community is also behind its social corruption. The absent father again stands between the ideal and its perversion.

The play, however, ends with the revelation of yet another reconstruction of the absent father. Mrs. Alving attempts to rehabilitate Captain Alving as a man full of the joy of life who is driven to depravity because he is forced to live a dull bureaucratic existence and to endure the coldness of his wife. Captain Alving is not only a father who has transgressed against the law of the father, but he is also destroyed by that same law because he could not live up to his duty as a patriarch and "never found an outlet for the overpowering joy of life he had" (267). Now, Captain Alving's failure to represent the ideal bourgeois is seen as a revolt against that whole ideological construction of fatherhood. The degenerate father is now transformed into the victimized father. Thus, by this point, the play has completely deconstructed the concept of fatherhood.

However, Mrs. Alving's picture of Captain Alving as a sacrificial victim does not redeem him in the eye of his children who reject him. Regina wanted to have the status of the real father, "to be raised as a gentleman's daughter" (268). At first she was to work in Captain Alving's orphanage, a job she rejected. Next, she sought Osvald, Captain Alving's son, but when she finds out that he is her half brother and is doomed to become an invalid, she rejects a relationship with him and plans to leave Captain Alving's house. Her last option is to follow Captain Alving's substitute father Engstrand and work as a prostitute in Captain Alving's Sailor's Home, a demeaning return to the house of the absent father in its debased form.

Osvald is also not impressed with the image of the sacrificial father, for he never knew his father. He takes the most radical move against the father by denying the sacred status of fatherhood as an outmoded idea. Ironically, Osvald will become like his father. Already he is drinking like his father and soon he will be helpless like his father. Mrs. Alving must take care of him just like she took care of Captain Alving. She has the option, however, of watching him turn into a vegetable or of giving him morphine and committing euthanasia. She tried to kill the memory of Captain Alving, the ghost of the father. Now she is asked to kill her son, the double of Captain Alving. The play stops before settling this issue and ends with a chant to the sun, a Jungian symbol for light and fatherhood, albeit an ironic one.

In *Ghosts*, the absent father is used to question the very nature of paternity as an abstract concept, as a symbolic disembodied father, represented but always hidden. When Mrs. Alving tells Osvald that "a child ought to feel some love for his father," he replies, "Do you really hang on to that old superstition" (270). Osvald cannot identify with an abstract and absent father, no matter how he is constructed. In the end, the sun, which represents the divine power of the father, seems reachable only through annihilation.

Like *Ghosts*, August Strindberg's *Miss Julie* begins in a world of darkness and ends with the shining of the sun. The rising sun should issue in enlightenment and the dawn of a new day. Instead, as with *Ghosts*, it forecasts impending death that will take place outside of the presentation of the drama. *Miss Julie* comes to closure as Julie is going offstage to kill herself. Similarly, *Ghosts* brings down the curtain before Mrs. Alving can decide whether she should kill her son or not. The drama that focuses on absence often leaves an indeterminate closure. *Miss Julie* also focuses on an absent father, a father who is alive but at the same time absent or hidden from view. Through most of the play he is away, and when he returns at the climax of the drama, he is in a room above, unseen. In his preface to *Miss Julie*, Strindberg presents one motive for Julie's suicide as her "father's absence" (102). Although the Count is alive, Strindberg sees him more as a symbolic father. He notes that the "unhappy spirit of the father hover[s] over and behind the whole of the action" (107). Like Captain Alving, the Count is a forceful presence in his absence.

The play opens right after the departure of the father. Jean, the valet, notes that he "went to the station with his lordship" (117). *Miss Julie* has stayed behind. Similar to Nora, Julie appears to be an only child. Just like Nora liked to escape from her father and mingle with the servants, Julie prefers to stay with the servants rather than stay with her father. Both daughters have physically and socially separated themselves from their fathers. The Count, like Captain Alving, is a wounded father, deposed from his position because, like Captain Alving, he allowed a woman to take over his estate. But instead of making it a productive patriarchal estate, she reverses the socio-sexual order and has the men do women's work and the women do men's work, driving the estate into ruin. Thus, the Count, who represents the order of the father, lets the estate be controlled by the mother. When he attempts to restore order, his wife burns down his patriarchal estate. Just like in *Ghosts*, the house of the father, backed by the father's money, is immolated. Both houses are uninsured. Captain Alving's home is uninsured because it is supposed to be protected by Divine Providence, a transcendental absent father who casts judgment on it instead of protecting it. The Count's estate is not insured because a servant could not make the payment on time. Both patriarchal monuments are fatalistically doomed. The Count must rebuild his estate on his wife's money maintained by his wife's lover. Ironically what is left of the financial worth of Captain Alving's memorial is in the hands of Manders, a man Mrs. Alving once considered her lover. Thus, what is seen in *Miss Julie* and *Ghosts* is the usurpation of the father's powers by the mother, and the destruction of the patriarchal estate built on the father's wealth. In both cases, inheritance comes from the mother so that there is a weakening of the power of the father and the symbolic forces that establish that power.

Miss Julie reflects both the search for the father and his rejection in two of his children, his daughter Julie and his symbolic son Jean. As a servant, Jean considers himself a member of the family who is allowed to pilfer a bottle of wine. Jean says, "When I work in a house, I regard myself more or less as a member of the family, a child of the house" (141). Jean wants to double or imitate the father and the aristocratic power structure based on the lineage of the father. He has become "fussier than his lordship himself" (118). He drinks champagne, likes his dish heated, speaks French, and knows how to tell stories. Yet Jean's relationship to the absent father is an ambivalent one. He worships the aristocracy represented by the Count at the same time that he realizes that it is based on tinsel and flimsy paper evidence. The Count got his title because a miller prostituted his wife to the king. The patriarchal title is based on the crime of prostitution against a woman. The patriarchal power in *Miss Julie* is just as flimsy as the paternity in *Ghosts*, where paternity is depicted by fabricated images created in a mother's letter to her son or proven by falsified documents in the parish register.

From his youth, Jean has always longed to enter the Count's garden, a Garden of Paradise where he could eat the apples of the tree of life. Thus, the Count becomes associated with the Judeo-Christian Father God, quick to punish and expel his children for trying to overreach him. Jean's desire is to double the Count by starting a hotel where, just like the Count, Jean can ring bells to order slaves around. He wants to purchase a Rumanian title, another paper authorization of patriarchal power, so that he can make Julie his Countess and make their children counts. He wants to create a paradise world where he can become the all-powerful father. What is absent in Jean's case, however, is not only a father but also a Symbolic Father that is supposed to uphold the social order.

Miss Julie is also a confused child. Her father made her half-man, half-woman and taught her how to hate her own sex. She tries to exert patriarchal power by having her suitor jump over a whip, then cutting him with the whip, but Julie finds herself weak and splintered inside. Like Nora, she doesn't "have a thought I didn't get from my father" (154). Julie gives herself to Jean then plans to escape with him, a man she hates. Julie's escape is a flight from aristocracy and from the father. She steals her father's money, and when dishonored, she cannot look her "father in the face" (137).

As Julie and Jean try to escape, there is a constant apprehension about the Count's arrival. They must act "before his lordship returns" (147). If *Miss Julie* runs away with her servant, both know "that his lordship'd never live that down" (146). Christine is more concerned about the Count than she is about Julie: "Think of his lordship; think of all the misery he's had in his time" (150). Even Julie begs Jean to help her save the honor of her father's name "Save my honor, save his name" (160). However, in her desire to save the Name of the Father, she also wants to obliterate it. Julie symbolically kills the father by predicting his death. She says that when he finds "his desk broken open—his money gone" ; then "he'll have a stroke and die" (155). Julie not only wants to kill the father but also wants to end the name of the father: "the coat of arms will be broken over the coffin—the title extinct" (155). Julie's death will be her mother's revenge on her father.

In the end, she reenacts the father. Like him, she cannot commit suicide on her own. Julie, like Nora, imitates the father in the threat of suicide, but neither father is able to take the honorable or the romantic course. Jean, like Julie, is also paralyzed by the father. He does not want to die, but he is reduced to a child by the ringing of the Count's bell. The voice from a speaking tube gives Jean mundane orders, and Jean is helpless. The Father is part of an ideological system that Jean cannot escape. Jean realizes, "If his lordship came down and ordered me to cut my throat, I'd do it on the spot" (160). Julie tells Jean to become the Count and to pretend that he is the Count and she is Jean. Jean, who has tried to become the Count in his manners, now becomes the Count in action. Thus, the Count through Jean gives Julie the order to kill herself. In a world controlled by the absence of the father, his drama is acted out through his children who are paralyzed in a state of inertia. The stupefied Osvald, infected with his father's disease, begs his mother to help him commit suicide just as Julie needs Jean to help her commit suicide, but both Jean and Mrs. Alving find it difficult to act.

The absent father has left the world in a state of inertia; the last of the fathers' lines are burning just like their patriarchal estates. Osvald says, "Everything will burn. There'll be nothing left in memory of Father. And here I'm burning up, too" (265). For Julie, "the whole room is like smoke around me" and Jean's "eyes shine like coals when the fire is dying" and "It's so warm and good" (161). The world of the father is a world that is passing on. In both *Ghosts* and *Miss Julie*, the play ends on a sunrise. But in *Miss Julie*, the sun shines on Jean alone, and in *Ghosts* the sun is just out of Osvald's reach.

In *Miss Julie*, the powerful presence of the absent Count and his ringing bell dominates the last scene of the play, but the Count through his mysterious power is working on the lives of Jean and Julie. As if he were puzzling like a character in an absurdist play, Jean says "But it isn't only a bell—there is someone sitting behind it—and something else sets the hand in motion" (161). In other words, behind the Count is a vast network of absence, both metaphysical and ideological, all leading to the world of the Father. The Count is a mysterious figure, a hand behind a bell who rings the alarm for the other characters. In these plays by Ibsen and Strindberg, the absent character is crucial to the drama, especially in his role as absent father. In *Ghosts*, the Name of the Father is over-determined and omnipresent. In *A Doll House* and *Miss Julie*, its power is felt but the name is conspicuously absent. The Name of the Father that Nora has signed is never mentioned. And even though Julie berates Jean for not having a pedigree or a patronymic, the name of Julie's father is absent from the play. He exists only behind his title and she, like Nora, is addressed by her first name to show how the abstract power of the absent father is little more than an empty signifier. In a world in which the True Father is absent, the children are condemned to paralysis or fruitless reenactments.

The theme of the persecuted father is a characteristic motif in Strindberg's plays. In *The Father*, Strindberg shows the destruction of the father and the fragility of paternity. In *The Pelican*, one of his later works, Strindberg returns to the theme of the absent father whose presence dominates the drama. *The Pelican* is more expressionistic than *Miss Julie*, and the presence of the absent father more pronounced. Like Captain Alving and the Count, the Father in *The Pelican* has been betrayed by his wife who abandoned him to go to her lover. In fact, she arranged a tryst with her daughter's fiancee, who is now her son-in-law. The Father has been sinned against. His wife's infidelity and her persecution of him drove him to have a stroke, just like the Count's wife through Julie will supposedly drive the Count to have a stroke. The Father had been forced to eat what he did not like, to read what he did not enjoy and, like Captain Alving, had been driven out of his home to bars. Also like Captain Alving and the Count, he has allowed his wife to control his home and to shut him out.

In *The Pelican*, the father is supposedly a prosperous businessman who earned 20,000 crowns; yet he seems to have left only debts. He also had no friends because he thought for himself. Thus, he is both inside an outside of the social structure. The play is about the settling of the father's estate. Even the couch where Father died cannot be moved until an inventory can be taken. Mother is searching to find out if he left a will. In Strindberg, the capitalist system of debt economy is transferred onto the social and spiritual realm as the paying off of debts becomes a metaphor for the reckoning of sins, much as it did in the medieval morality plays. Actual financial bankruptcy also becomes a metaphor for humanity's spiritual condition. Such is the world in *The Pelican* where the absence of the father has left the family under the domination of the Terrible Mother, and where there is only hunger, coldness and disease.

The Father's children are weak and sickly, not through any inherited traits, but through the neglect of the Terrible Mother, a neglect that the Father tolerated. The Son is weak and dying, probably from some type of consumption. He is unable to finish his law studies and is nauseated with the idea of marriage. As a child, his mother's neglect led him to witness sex acts in a brothel and among his caretakers. The Daughter, a bottle baby, is undeveloped as a woman and is sterile. The children's home is freezing, and their food is rancid and unnourishing.

Like *The Libation Bearers*, *The Pelican* is not only a search for, but an invocation to the absent father. The play begins not long after the funeral of the father whose corpse was kept in the house. The house smells of death and disinfectant. Just as *Ghosts* depicts the memorialization of the dead father, *The Pelican* also presents a house filled with the relics of the Father, who cries out to be heard. His portrait stares at Mother with evil eyes; his rocker screeches like knives being whetted; his death couch stands covered in red, like "gory butchers block" (172); and his presence is felt walking outside in the garden. The Son's moaning duplicates the moaning of the Father who cried outside the window of his runaway wife with a sound that "came from the prison or from the madhouse" (173). He stood in the rain "crying out for his lost wife and children" (173). The Son, who sympathizes with the Father, begins to mirror him. Like Osvald, the Son takes to drinking just like his father did. Sitting in the Father's rocking chair, he becomes a double of the Father. Even the Son-in-Law, once the Mother's ally, turns against her and starts to give her orders. He, too, mirrors the Father. Mother tells him, "How much you're like the old man now, sitting in his rocking chair" (189).

The Father also speaks, but only indirectly, through a letter he left to his son, which Mother finds. The letter is never quoted directly, but only indirectly as the Mother notes that it accuses her of Father's murder. Distraught, Mother exclaims, "He rises from his grave and you can't shut him up. He's not dead" (170). Eventually, the Son finds the torn "letter from [his] dead father" and learns the truth about Mother. Like Osvald and Julie, other children of absent fathers, Son and Daughter feel helpless: "Nothing to look forward to, no one to look up to . . . Impossible to fight . . . Let's live to redeem ourselves and the memory of Father" (183). Since neither is able to reinstate the Symbolic Father, they must be satisfied with avenging their biological father. After he has writhed on the lounge where his father died and made a metonymic connection with the Father, he is ready for revenge and claims he has been "visited by a departed spirit" (184). The Father speaks not only through the letter which is paraphrased, but also through the Son who frequently quotes the words of the Father.

Father is regenerated in the eyes of his children. The Son says that Father was the pelican who "had baggy pants and dirty collars while we went around like little aristocrats" (201), and even the Son-in-Law turns in revenge on Mother, who is left isolated and alone. Like Julie and Osvald, the Son wants to die and his only recourse is to burn down the patriarchal house. "What could I do?—There was no other way" (200). The Daughter says, "Everything has to burn, otherwise we could never get out of here" (200). The burning of the House of the Father along with "Papa's laurel wreath" (201) shows how the image of fire in *Ghosts*, *Miss Julie*, and *The Pelican* is not only a symbol of destruction but also a symbol of purification: "Everything old is burning up, everything old and mean and evil and ugly" (201). However, in the fire, there is a sacrificial offering of the children to an absent father. The absence of the father is overpowering. In *The Pelican*, actions are committed in the Name of the Father, but the Father's name is absent. Even though every other character is given a first name, the Father has no name, not even a title like the Count. In these plays the father who is representative of cultural order is also reigning over the destruction of that order. His absence is not only a sign of his abstract disembodied power but it is also a sign of his descent from the world, leaving the world a modern wasteland populated by shallow imitations of the absent father.

CHAPTER 4

ESCAPE OF THE FATHER AND THE SON'S HOPELESS QUEST - I:
Tennessee Williams' *The Glass Menagerie*
Arthur Miller's *Death of a Salesman*

Although there is a great distance in space and time from the bourgeois culture of Scandinavia at the twilight of the nineteenth century and the big business world of post-World War II America, the figure of the absent father is just as present in both eras. During the forties, America may have been ebullient with post-war optimism; yet for those who had lived through the Great Depression, the ultimate faith in individual initiative and the self-made capitalist was shaken. Just as in the late nineteenth century the aristocratic code of the father was being put into question, in the technocratic society of post-war America, the pioneer image of the father who could rise to fame and fortune through self-determination was giving way to the image of the company man. However, the vanishing of the frontier adventurer as patriarch would not go unmourned. As absent father, he would rise up as a seductive illusion, a mythical and almost transcendent image in a world that had lost its faith in transcendence.

Such an absent father plays a significant part in the dynamics of four major post World War II American dramas: Tennessee Williams' *The Glass Menagerie*, Arthur Miller's *Death of a Salesman*, Sam Shepard's *True West*, and David Rabe's *The Basic Training of Pavlo Hummel*. In these plays the father or father figure follows Leslie Fiedler's pattern for the archetypal hero of American fiction. Fiedler defines the American hero as "a man on the run—hurried into the forest and out to sea, down the river or into combat—anywhere to avoid 'civilization,' which is to say, the confrontation of a man and a woman which leads to the fall to sex, marriage, and responsibility" (xx). Fiedler's American hero is recreated in these four dramas in the character of the absent father. This absent father has deserted or escaped from the family and headed out for unknown territories. His identity is shadowy and mysterious, if not mythical. Although he is gone, symbolic traces of his presence often remain.

In addition, the father is associated with the heroes of a past age, a simpler more Edenic world, whereas his sons live in a present world, which is a wasteland and a prison house, a world of constrictions and confinements filled with artificial objects that are corroding or turning into junk. Lost and alienated, the sons of the absent father are confused, perplexed, and unsure of their identity. They feel compelled to bring back the father or to follow in his path. In their turmoil, they seek to recreate the father through doubling him, searching for him, creating surrogate fathers, and/or restructuring the father through a series of fraternal relationships. In the end, their quest for the father leads to death or aimless flight. This chapter will examine the pattern in two American dramas written during and immediately after World War II by playwrights who have come to dominate the American canon: Tennessee Williams and Arthur Miller.

Much of this pattern of the absent father can be seen in Tennessee Williams' *The Glass Menagerie*, a play which centers around an absent father. The father is an imposing figure in many of Williams' plays from Big Daddy in *Cat on a Hot Tin Roof* to God the Father in *Night of the Iguana*. The overpowering figure of the father in Williams' works can best be accounted for by Williams' early impressions of his own father. Williams recounts: "Often the voice of my father . . . was harsh and sometimes it sounded like thunder. He was a big man . . . And it was not a benign bigness. You wanted to shrink from it" (Williams, E. 26). In Williams, the father becomes a striking figure and in *The Glass Menagerie*, his very absence places him as a central character. Commenting on the play, Nancy Tischler notes that the fact "that the father does not appear directly in the play suggests that Tennessee Williams could not view him with sufficient objectivity to portray him" (96). However, earlier versions of the play which have come to light after Tischler's observations show that the father was at one time present in significant scenes. From examining these early manuscript versions of the play, Brian Parker concludes that the play shows "Williams' ambivalence, particularly his unexpected siding with his father" (18). The ambivalence towards the father is a key theme in the plays about the absent father as illustrated in Ibsen's *Ghosts*, a play which deeply moved Williams as a young man. Williams notes: "It was so moving that I had to go and walk in the lobby during the last act. . . . I suppose the play was one of the reasons that make me want to write for the theatre" (qtd. in Spoto 41). Certainly Williams' image of the father as a charming drinker out to escape the oppressive atmosphere of a bourgeois family could have been partially influenced by Captain Alving in *Ghosts*. Both plays feature a hidden presence of the father in the son and a strong ambivalence towards the father as well as the son's tendency to follow in the footsteps of the father.

This pattern of the quest for the absent father is central to the dramatic structure of *The Glass Menagerie*. In the same manner as *The Pelican*, the father's "blown up" (22) or "larger than life size photograph on the mantel" (23) designates his central position as an ironic viewer and a constant source of reference for other family members. Although absent, he is a "fifth character" (23) who propels the actions of the other characters.

The absent Mr. Wingfield, an elusive character without a first name, has left his family and abrogated his responsibilities. He is a wanderer, "a telephone man who fell in love with long distances" (23). He is not only absent, but he is also in a constant state of flight. His cryptic postcard home says only "Hello—Goodbye" (23). In other words, he acknowledges his presence, then closes his discourse, leaving no message or advice. This absent father who skipped "the light fantastic" (23) leaves no directions for his son. He ventures toward the Pacific coast of Mexico, heading not only south but also westward, the direction of the legendary American hero. He is always out of reach, leaving "no address" (23). His wife Amanda states, "Now he travels and I don't even know where" (83). The absent father has taken a line of flight "as far as the system of transportation reaches" (41). In the world of the absent father, technology is more indicative of flight than it is as a means of binding the community. The telephone only reinforces the separation from family by "long distances," and transportation is used as a means of escape beyond the bounds of civilization.

In *The Glass Menagerie*, traces of the absent father are everywhere. His gallant smile seems to be saying, "I will be smiling forever" (23). The eternal smile of the fugitive father haunts his son and points out the path of escape. His daughter is condemned to "eternally play those-worn out phonograph records [her] father left as a painful reminder of him" (34). Amanda, Tom's Mother, is also caught in the world of the absent father, wearing his overlarge bathrobe "as a relic of the faithless Mr. Wingfield" (40). John Jones notes: "Amanda's life has actually stopped at the time Mr. Wingfield left. She now tries to recreate the past through nostalgic remembrance of her life before Mr. Wingfield disappeared and by forcing her children to play roles that recall to the present an idealized version of their father" (29). The son's fixation on his everlasting smile, the daughter's eternal compulsion to play his records, and the mother's holding on to the relic of his bathrobe keep the whole family bound to the task of reestablishing the presence of the absent father.

The absent Mr. Wingfield is connected to two kinds of Edenic worlds: one in the pastoral past and the other in the adventurous future—a future, however, which is no more than the recreation of the past world of the romantic warrior. Judith Thompson shows how Williams' plays focus on a memory story which "recalls archetypal myths of primordial wholeness, evoking nostalgia for a once perfect human condition and a unified cosmos free of antimonies" (1).

Mr. Wingfield, a charmer, comes from such a world of "gracious living" (82), a paradise world of jonquils and gentlemen callers. When he smiled, "the world was enchanted" (64). But Wingfield was not a son of planters. He moved outside of the world of the agrarian aristocracy and became a part of the fast-moving world of modern technology: "a telephone man who fell in love with long distances" (23). It is this mobile father that Tom transforms into another mythic image from out of the past. Tom sees his father as he is in his picture, "a very handsome young man in a doughboy's First World War cap" (23), a soldier of fortune seeking adventure on foreign shores. No one, however, knows what happened to Tom's father. According to Thompson the father's name which juxtaposes "wing" and "field" shows how "a symbol of transcendence is fused with an image of mundane reality" (16). However, his name might also indicate the contrast between a pioneer world of flight and the settled world of agrarian life. In an earlier draft, *Description of the Gentleman Caller* (1944), Williams saw the Wingfields as "Pioneers, Indian fighters, trailblazers" (qtd. in Parker 15). However, Mr. Wingfield's flight points his son in the direction of the sea, the other American wilderness. In any case his trajectory is vague and undisclosed, which opens him up to multiple readings. Yet it is his absence that moves both Amanda and Tom to seek him out or replace him.

In the absence of the father, the world itself is dead. Tom lives in a wasteland where the city itself becomes a metaphor for entrapment. People live in "hivelike conglomerations" located in "overcrowded urban centers" (21). They exist as the "enslaved section of American society" functioning as "one interfused mass of automatism" (21). The world is an ironic parody of the open land. Narrow alleys "run into murky canyons of tangled clothes lines, garbage cans, and the sinister latticework of neighboring fire escapes" (21). The canyons of the promised land are seen only in tangled clothes lines. The view of the outside world exposes only its garbage, and the fire escapes provide relief for those burning with the "implacable fires of human desperation" (21). Like those who surround him, Tom is boiling inside. He is forever trapped in the artificial world of the shoe factory with its "celotex interior" and its "fluorescent tubes" (41).

Amanda, of course, can escape this world by going back to her moment of love when she met Mr. Wingfield. She remembers: "Malaria fever, jonquils, and then—this—boy" (72). The word "boy" indicates a childhood paradise. Tom, however, has no nostalgic world to return to, so he escapes through fantasy. Like other sons of absent fathers, he becomes involved in mythmaking. And many of his myths come from the movies, for they open up to him the world of adventure: "Adventure is something I don't have much of at work, so I go to the movies" (51). In a rage, he fabricates a story which describes his situation: "I'm leading a double life, a simple warehouse worker by day, by night a dynamic czar of the underworld" (42). The lost son seeks a fantasy life that points in the direction of the father. His sarcastic remarks to his mother represent the split in himself between the dark father, who has enemies who will dynamite his mother's house and the good hard-working father that he is asked to become. His portrayal of himself as a gangster links him with the romantic world of outlaws perpetuated by the American cinema. The restless sons of absent fathers often see themselves as rebellious outlaws or compulsive petty criminals trying to beat the system. Tom also becomes a fabricator, fascinated with illusionists, like Malvolio, the Magician, who can get a man out of a coffin without removing one nail. Tom sees himself as a member of the living dead and seeks a way out. But when Tom questions whether anyone can escape from a coffin without removing a nail, "The father's grinning photo lights up" (46). Tom's fantasies point him in the direction of the absent father. As Amanda tells him, "You live in a dream; you manufacture illusions" (112).

Like other lost sons, Tom becomes a double of his father. He drinks and stays out late like his father. Amanda tells him, " More and more you remind me of your father. He was out all hours of the night! Then left Good bye!" (52). Like Osvald, Tom drinks to relieve himself of the burden of the father. His mother expects him to sacrifice his life in order to become a double of the ideal father who will support mother and sister. Yet he seeks to follow the path of the romantic father who escaped this burden. Amanda gives Tom permission to leave, "But not till there's somebody to take your place" (53). In other words, Tom must find another father figure to replace him as the ideal father. The absence of the father leaves a vacuum that propels the dramatic action to create doubles for the father. Such a double comes in the form of a savior figure, the miracle that will replace the father, the new gentleman caller, the "long delayed but always expected something that we live for" (23).

Jim O' Connor, the promising high school athlete who played the lead in the *Pirates of Penzance* becomes the romantic gentleman caller, straight out of the world of the ideal father. However, Amanda must make sure he does not drink so that he bears no resemblance to the real father. For him, Amanda recreates the meeting of the father. She tells Laura that she is wearing the dress she wore on "the day I met your father" (71). She brings out her wedding silver to serve the new father figure. But Jim, the new father figure, must also abandon the Wingfield family. Thompson also points out the resemblance between Tom's father, Jim, and Tom: "All three embody the romantic concept of war as adventure in their respective roles of World War I doughboy, make-believe pirate, and merchant seaman" (15).

Tom must follow the father into this world of adventure, to become "a lover, a hunter, a fighter" (52). He wants to escape to the romance of the primitive world. The impending war (World War II) will make adventure "available to the masses" (79). Tom has now replaced the fantasy of the movies with the world of moving. The war will take him to that Melvillian paradise, the last outpost holding back the tide of civilization—the South Sea Islands. Tom admits, "I'm like my father. The bastard son of a bastard" (80). Tom sees that the father has been "absent going on sixteen years" and he is still "grinning" (80). For Tom, he is grinning because he has found a way out of the confines of family life, the same way out that Tom seeks. But Tom's quest is futile. He follows "his father's footsteps attempting to find in motion what was lost in space" (115). Instead of reaching paradise, he becomes an aimless drifter haunted by the memory of home and of his sister Laura. His position as the narrator of a memory play leads him back to the continual reenactment of the visit of the gentleman caller. As Tom looks at his mother and sister from a distance, he sees his mother "glance a moment at the father's picture" (114). He "is as lost in the supposed present as in the recalled past" (Bigsby 47-8). The son has followed this absent father, but he has never found him, for the path to the absent father is an endless road. Tom's "dreams of life as a meaningful voyage (a 'sea change') end up in aimless wandering" (Thompson 14).

Like Tennessee Williams, Arthur Miller also focuses on the symbolic father. Many of his dramas center on the conflict between father and son. O. P. Dogra says about Miller: "In all his major plays, the prime authority and guidance of the father is of primary importance" (58). Harold Clurman also notes: "The father in Miller's work is a recurrent figure regarded with awe, devotion, love, even when he proves lamentably fallible and when submission to him becomes particularly questionable" ("Introduction" xiii). However, Miller, like Williams, is ambivalent about the father. Heavily influenced by the failure of his own father during the Depression, Miller has split the father in two. He acknowledges: "I had two fathers, the real one and the metaphoric, and the latter I resented because he did not know how to win out over the collapse" (*Timebends* 114). The metaphoric father and the resentment towards him reverberates throughout Miller's works and becomes a dynamic symbol in his plays. Commenting on his own Oedipal crisis, Miller posits, "Regardless of how the game is played out, it had to end in some way, in confrontation with the father." But this father is always a powerful force looming behind the scenes: "The father could move in all directions and his decree of punishment was death" (*Timebends* 145). Thus, the all-powerful mythic figure of the symbolic father as an ambivalent figure stands behind much of Miller's dramas. Miller comments: "The father was really a figure who incorporated both power and some kind of moral law which he had either broken himself or had fallen prey to. He figures as an immense shadow" (Carlisle and Stryan 267-8). This shadow looms large in *Death of a Salesman*.

In *Death of a Salesman* this symbolic shadow is seen most clearly in the figure of the absent father. Willy Loman is searching for his lost father and trying to duplicate him. The play opens and closes with flute music associated with the father who sold flutes. Willy's earliest recollection of his father contains the sound of "some kind of high music" (48). Willy's father, like Tom's, is a mysterious figure without a first name. The father was a "great and wild hearted man" with a "big beard." He was a true American patriarch "sitting around a fire" (48) in the wilderness. Willy's father, like Tom's, is a wanderer. As a true American hero, he would head out from Boston, the cradle of American democracy, and "He'd toss his whole family into a wagon and then he'd drive the team right across the country; through Ohio and Indiana, Michigan, Illinois and the Western States" (49). Willy's father, a real frontiersman heading West to seek his fortune, is also a peddler and an inventor. Ben notes: "Great inventor, Father. With only one gadget he made more in a week than a man like you can make in a lifetime" (49). Thus, the father is mythologized as an incredible salesman, making money selling an item with questionable profitability. Willy's father, like Tom's, abandons his family and heads out to seek adventure and a fortune. The father heads northwest to Alaska, the last frontier, in order to find gold. He has no name and he vanishes into the wilderness without a trace as neither of his two sons ever acknowledges hearing from him. Thus, the absent father reenacts the journey of the archetypal American hero.

As a lost son, Willy is trapped in a gloomy world. Like Tom, Willy lives in an urban inferno. His one-time suburban house is surrounded by "towering angular shapes." It is "small and fragile-seeming" amidst "a solid vault of apartment houses" (11). Like Osvald, Willy lives in a sunless world and cannot plant his Edenic garden in his yard because "not enough sunlight gets back there" (72). Willy feels boxed in by "bricks and windows." The street is "lined with cars." "There's not a breath of fresh air in the neighborhood. The grass don't grow anymore" (17). Using a term that describes the peril of the western hero, Willy notes that city builders have "massacred the neighborhood" (17). Willy is lost. His whole world is turning into junk: "I'm always in a race with the junkyard! I just finished paying for the car and its on its last legs. The refrigerator consumes belts like a goddam maniac" (73). In this overcrowded world, the competition is stifling, business is bad, gratitude and comradeship are gone, and no one knows who Willy is anymore. In other words, Willy lives in a wasteland of deterioration and desolation where nothing can grow or prosper.

Willy tries to escape this nightmare world by searching for his father. Willy admits, "Dad left when I was such a baby and I never had a chance to talk to him and I still feel kind of temporary about myself" (51). Like the characters in *Waiting for Godot* and other absurdist dramas, Willy lives in a world of uncertain appointments and yearns to grasp something permanent like a diamond. Deeply in need of a father, Willy asks his brother, "Where is Dad?" (47). Willy, at one time, was going to search out his father. He tells Howard, "I thought I'd go out with my older brother and try to locate him and maybe settle in the north with the old man" (81). But Willy abandoned that quest for new frontiers and has spent his whole life trying to reenact it within in his own space.

Willy tries to recapture the wilderness life of his absent father by creating a wilderness in his backyard, a suburban frontier where he can hunt "snakes and rabbits" (50). Later, he tries to go back to this paradise world. The boy who sat by his father and held a flower in his hand dreams of the garden world and the smell of "lilac and wisteria" (17). Willy also yearns for "a place in the country" (72) where he can raise chickens. Obviously, Willy is being lured by the call of his father's flute music which evokes images of "grass and trees, and the horizon" (11).

Willy has always tried to gain security by reenacting the father. Like an explorer he opens up "unheard of territories" (56) for the Wagner Company. He supposedly brings the company's business north to New England, thus following the direction of his father who headed north to Alaska. Willy, however, does not immediately abandon his family like his father did; yet he has doubts about his decision. Tom left his family, but is constantly being drawn back to them in his memory. Willy stayed and did not follow his father, but has his doubts as to whether or not he has made the right choice. In either case, the lost son must live in a double-bind situation. However, even though he does not completely abandon his family, Willy is constantly on the road, leaving his son Biff feeling "lonesome" (30). He promises Biff, "Someday I'll have my own business and I won't have to leave home anymore" (30). But Willy is a "road man" working for a company who does a "road business" (80). Willy's brother Ben pointed out the path of the father as an "open road" (48), the road to flight and adventure, and by the time Willy is eighteen, he is "already on the road" (51). Leah Hadami finds that "the ideas of being in close touch with nature and taking to the open road that are inspired by Willy's memory of his father are diminished in his own life to puttering around the garden . . . and making routine rounds as a travelling salesman" (160). But the open road of the father is not only diminished, but it is also an uncertain place for Willy, and he cannot seem to stay on it; so he winds up deliberately driving himself off of the road. Like Tom Wingfield, Willy cannot find a clear path to the father, for he is in search of a chimerical figure.

Lost, bewildered, and always searching for answers, Willy turns to a series of surrogate fathers who duplicate his father. The first father he turns to is his brother Ben, "success incarnate" (41). Ben is the only man "who knew the answers" (45). Significantly, Ben has just died a couple of weeks before Willy undergoes his final crisis in the last two days of his life. Ben's death propels Willy to return to the father. Like the father, Ben is a mysterious figure. He not only appears to Willy in flashbacks but also as an hallucination or ghost, the only known dead person that Willy conjures up. Ben is very much like Willy's absent father. He too was following the path of the father down the "open road" (48), but lost sight of his direction and headed south to Africa and diamond mines. Like the father, Ben has disappeared from Willy's life with the exception of a few visits. Instead of following the father in his hunt for gold, Ben recreates the father's quest in a territory of his own and finds diamonds. Both sought an instant fortune. Ben went into the jungle and came out rich. His wilderness is different and more vicious than his father's open frontier. In fact, Ben does eventually wind up in Alaska and again his timber business is associated with the forest. However, he makes no mention of ever seeing the father in Alaska.

Willy, who decries the cutting down of trees, does not belong in the timber business and when he finds himself trapped in the business jungle, he can only cry out that "the woods are burning" (107). The jungle wilderness is obviously no place for Willy. Like the father, Ben shuns the city and tells Willy, "Get out of the cities, they're full of talk and time payments and courts of law" (85). Ben, like other American frontier heroes, wants to stay out of the reach of the law. Like the father, Ben is constantly on the move, looking at his watch and hurrying to catch a train or ship.

As an older brother who knew the father, Ben is sought after by Willy. Willy wants Ben to stay with him a while so that he can rediscover the father. Like a lost son, Willy turns to Ben for answers: "Ben, I've been waiting for you for so long! What is the answer? How did you do it?" (47). He also asks Ben for fatherly advice about raising his children. "Ben, how should I teach them?" (52). Ben's answer is cryptic and indicates following the path of the father into the wilderness. "When I was seventeen, I walked into the jungle and when I walked out, I was twenty-one. And by God I was rich" (48). This route to success is just the path that Willy has been unable to follow.

Ben represents the father as adventurer and frontiersman while Dave Singleman, another father figure, represents the father as salesman. Dave is also a man on the move, an eighty-six year old salesman who rides the trains and sells on the telephone. The train and the telephone are powerful extensions of the road. Just as in *The Glass Menagerie* symbols of transportation and communication represent movement and distance. Dave died on a train going to Boston, counterpointing Willy's father who started out in Boston. Thus, by focusing on Dave's funeral, Willy completes the cycle of the father and brings the father home to mourn him. Ben's death provokes Willy's sense of loss for the father and the image of Dave's funeral allows for the heroic mourning of a dead father. Willy raises Dave to mythical status through the spectacle of his mourning. Dave had hundreds of people from miles around attend his funeral and "things were sad on a lotta trains for months after" (81) his death. In Dave, Willy sees both the model of a successful father and a way of mourning the loss of an absent father. In examining the father figure in *Death of a Salesman*, David Bleich observes: "The psychological tragedy of the play is the destructiveness of the wish to be loved by some older man—an older brother, an 'older son,' an older salesman: a missing father" (32).

Finally, Willy uses Frank Wagner, "a prince" and "a masterful man" (14) as a father figure. Whether it is true or not, Willy sees Old Man Wagner as a man who will take him in and make him a partner in the Wagner firm. Willy reminds Frank's son Howard about "promises made across this desk" (81). When the son will not make good on the father's promises, Willy cries out, "Frank, Frank, don't you remember what you told me that time? How you put your hand on my shoulder" (82). Through his death, Frank has also deserted Willy and left him in the hands of Howard, who fires Willy.

Both Dave and Frank are leading Willy towards reconstructing the frontier in the business world by diminishing its territory. The frontier enterprises of self-reliant heroes are reduced to the business lunches of entrepreneurs and financiers. For Willy, "The whole wealth of Alaska passes over the lunch table of the Commodore Hotel" (86). Just like Willy tries to recapture the wilderness in his suburban backyard, he also tries to shrink frontier enterprises into business meetings. Whether following Dave or trusting in Frank's promises, Willy seems to be looking for a way to conquer Alaska like his father supposedly did, but without leaving home. Willy's dilemma illustrates the ambiguous nature of the absent father. The dichotomy between Ben's image of the father as a ruthless exploiter with a "get rich quick" scheme and Willy's notion of the father as an influential business broker with contacts reflects an internal conflict in American culture itself.

Like other children of absent fathers, Willy is hopelessly lost and in search of a miracle or a savior. In a world empty of the power of the father, the hope of salvation lies in pulling off some kind of big deal. Ben is winding up the Alaska deal and Willy is pushing Biff to approach Bill Oliver to back Happy's "Florida idea" to start the Loman Brothers sporting goods business. Biff and Happy will start a sporting goods chain by going on the road and playing exhibition games. The Loman brothers will make a million dollars not as businessmen but as two boys recreating their youth, "out playing ball again" (64). In other words, the Florida idea is another search for gold, a duplication of Old Man Loman's trip to Alaska. Also, Willy wants Biff to walk into Oliver's office like Ben walked into the jungle and to come out rich. This deal, like all the other fantasy schemes of lost children, falls apart. Oliver, the savior father, walks away from Biff, and, by extension, from Willy, who has put all his hopes in Biff.

Willy, like Tom, has lived in the world of illusions and has tried to construct his identity on lies: stories of fabulous commissions and prestigious contacts. In the end, Willy "hasn't got a story left in [his] head" (107). Willy is a man who "never knew who he was" (138). Unable to duplicate the world of the father himself, he turns to his sons as his last hope. Thus, the trajectory of the absent father is passed down to the next generation.

The Lomans of the third generation, Biff and Happy, double the situation of Ben and Willy. Ben is the older brother who achieves success through prowess while Willy tries to do his best as a salesman. Similarly, The young Biff is a football hero destined to go to the University of Virginia while Happy is satisfied to carry Biff's gear and brag about losing weight. Ben ventures forth into unknown territories while Willy stays at home with his mother and tries to establish himself in the business world. Biff, like Ben, abandons the city to seek his fortune in the great outdoors, while Happy, like Willy, stays in the

city trying to establish himself in business. Biff, however, is "not bringing
home any prizes" (132). Like Willy, Biff is a failure in the business world
who just "can't take hold" (54) of anything. In the end, Biff goes back to the
West and invites Happy to go with him, just like Ben invited Willy to join him
in Alaska. But Happy will stay home like Willy and recreate Willy's dream.
The motif of the two brothers recreates the world of the absent father, the
great peddlar who headed West to seek his fortune. One brother heads out in
the direction of the father and the other tries to recreate the world of the father
in the city. Happy states about Willy, "He had a good dream. . . . He fought
it out here, and this is where I'm gonna win it for him" (139). The sons
continue to follow the path of the father. Thus, the whole play becomes a quest
for the absent father.

Even in his final action, Willy reenacts the trajectory of the father. Willy
wants to pull off the biggest deal of his life by killing himself and cashing in
on his twenty thousand dollar insurance policy. Like his father before him, he
too will abandon his wife and family to gain a quick fortune. He will establish
his success, but through his son: "We're gonna make it, Biff and I" (134). In
his death, Willy can become a better salesman than his father. He can also
duplicate Dave Singleman and have hundreds of people at his funeral. He will
also walk into the dark wilderness like Ben and fetch a diamond. Barry Gross
states, "In committing suicide Willy is still the peddler selling his life for a
profit . . . but he is also the pioneer penetrating unknown and dangerous
territory" (409). Willy believes that he will finally double Ben and follow the
path of his father. As Kay Stanton points out: "Although he had missed the
'boat' of Ben's success, Willy can catch the 'boat' of death to join the recently
dead Ben and, through him, the father" (88). Willy is "his father's victim and
must perpetuate that hollow deal that is his father's legacy" (Dogra 58).
Pursuing the absent father has inevitably led to Willy's tragic downfall. In
Death of a Salesman as in *The Glass Menagerie*, the lost son is unable to reach
or recreate the absent father.

In *The Glass Menagerie* and *Death of a Salesman*, the father is a focal
figure that draws the son toward a timeless world, one that conflates the past
and present. This world is withdrawn beyond the bounds of time and distanced
by a space that is not only an indeterminate geographical territory, but also a
mythological cosmos. Tom seems condemned to reenact the memory of the past
and to watch himself forever trapped in time. Willy has ceased to distinguish
between present and past, myth and reality. He goes to his death coaching his
son at football and looking toward the discovery of diamonds. Bigsby states,
"Like Miller's Willy Loman, [Williams'] characters find themselves hopelessly
stranded in a kind of temporal and spatial void" which "they fill with distorted
memories of the past or wistful dreams of a redemptive future" (2: 45). This
absorption with the Edenic past is part of a longing to recapture the absent

father, a longing that leaves an emptiness so expansive that it leads the lost son into a frontier from which there is no return.

CHAPTER 5

ESCAPE OF THE FATHER AND THE SON'S HOPELESS QUEST - II:
Sam Shepard's *True West*
David Rabe's *The Basic Training of Pavlo Hummel*

Miller and Williams are not the only American playwrights obsessed with the father. The father is also a haunting figure in the plays of Sam Shepard. According to Richard Stoner, one consistent character type in Shepard's plays is "a distant father in conflict with a dominating mother" (1663). Shepard's plays, like those of Miller, focus on the tensions between fathers and sons. After analyzing the generational conflicts in Shepard's early plays, Gary Grant discusses the role of the father in Shepard's major work:

> His father moves beyond generational conflict to images of continuity or . . . psychological conflict. Shepard finds a shared identity between father and son in *Curse of the Starving Class*, a ritual return of the son to the grandfather's heritage in *Buried Child* and a gestalt-like image of dynamic balance of two siblings' psychic states influenced by contrasting parental forces in *True West*. (559)

Grant notes that at the center of Shepard's plays is the father/son conflict which focuses on identification with the father and the quest to find him, two key factors associated with the drama of the absent father. Similar to Williams and Miller, the father in Shepard is seen as an ambivalent, but haunting symbol. Esther Harriott notes that in Shepard's works the quest to establish a sense of identity is "characteristically dramatized in ambivalent relationships of sons to their fathers. . . that oscillate between dreams of parricide and reconciliation" (3). This image is central to *True West*. Ron Mottram explains: "Particularly prominent is the never-seen father of the estranged brothers of *True West*, who is the center of many conversations. Like this absent character and for similar reasons, Shepard's own father lived the life of a recluse" (65).

In *True West*, Shepard creates a drama of the absent father. After not seeing each other in five years, two brothers, Austin and Lee both happen to appear at their mother's house, which Austin is watching. Their mother, like Willy's father, has gone to Alaska, the last frontier, and their father lives on the desert, a wilderness world outside of the bounds of society. Austin, who has become a conventional success as a screenwriter, is the caretaker and protector of the mother's house and Lee, an aimless drifter, is the intruder. Both are in a quest to find the absent father and to retrace his path.

In *True West*, the father is a mysterious figure. His name is never revealed and no mention is ever made of his patronymic. He is simply known as the "old man." Like the absent fathers in *The Glass Menagerie* and *Death of a*

Salesman, the old man has abandoned the family, escaped society, and fled to the desert. He is an elusive character who hitchhikes his way to Mexico and drifts from bar to bar. Although he does not represent the mystique of the pioneer or soldier of fortune, he does embody the romance of the loner, the man who has fled from society. The father is holding onto the last vestiges of the Western pioneer spirit. Commenting on the absent father, Richard Wattenberg states: "His existence only in other character's speeches conveys Shepard's sense of the place of old western individualism in modern America" which "has been undermined and devitalized, and, at last, banished to the desert" (235). The choice of whether to settle down and become a success or to abandon the restrictions of the civilized world haunts his two sons.

Both lost sons are longing for the paradise world of their youth, a world connected with a suburban wilderness associated with the father. Both are trying to create "fantasies of a long lost boyhood" (40). Lee recalls the times when he and Austin "used to catch snakes" (12), and Austin used to play Geronimo. Lee reminisces over the pastoral or garden world. Like Willy, he remembers a rustic suburb that was close to nature. Austin also returns to his youth and cries out in desperation, "When we were kids here it was different. There was life here then" (49). The nostalgia for the pastoral Eden becomes an obsessive longing to return to the father, for the present world that the sons live in is lifeless and artificial.

The world represented by mother's house and the Los Angeles suburb where she lives is a wasteland. Lee notes that his mother's house has "the same crap" that was always around, "plates and spoons" (10). Lee scorns mother's personal "antiques" and calls them "a lotta junk" (10). He cannot eat off of her plates with the state of Idaho painted on them. A Western state has been reduced to a cheap imitation on a plate, a souvenir deprived a of its symbolic aura. Even the wildlife in the area is diminished. The "city coyotes" can only yap instead of howling like those on the desert. Looking at the world around his mother's house, Lee experiences alienation. To him the world is "different" (10). He rejects Austin's idea that "it's been built up" (10). Almost echoing Willy's appraisal of his Brooklyn neighborhood, Lee replies, "Wiped out is more like it. I don't even recognize it" (11). To Lee, the place even smells funny. Later, the silence and confinement of mother's house will close in on him like "a rest home" (22).

Lost in the world that the father has abandoned, both sons are disoriented and confused. Although repulsed by the artificial world, Lee cannot help admiring the houses with the "yellow lights" and the "copper pots hangin over the stove . . . like they got in the magazines." To him, this world is "like a paradise" and represents the "kinda place you wish you grew up in" (12). Lee looks at the imitation world as a paradise, but it is the world of slick magazine ads. A pioneer world of copper pots is no more than the cheap creation of

Madison avenue. Austin, too, is confused about the artificial world. At one point, he believes that as a writer he can keep in touch in with his audience. He says, "I drive on the freeway. I swallow the smog. I watch the news in color. I shop at the Safeway. I'm in touch" (35). But the more Austin becomes aware of his situation, the more he begins to doubt whether he is in touch with the world around him. He mocks Lee's paradise as a false paradise. He mocks the sanitized world, "The bushes. Orange blossoms. Dust in the driveways. Rain bird sprinklers. . . . Everybody else is livin' the life. Indoors. Safe. This is a Paradise down here" (39). Lee replies to these remarks, "You sound just like the old man now" (39). The decorated artificial world that attempts to duplicate the wilderness paradise is just the world that the father has abandoned.

The escape of the father has prompted both sons to search him out. Unlike Willy, who never sought the father, and Tom, who left home but never came in contact with him, the two sons in *True West* have seen the father. Both have searched him out. Lee was driven to the desert by the archetypal quest for the father. He went to "see the old man" (12). Austin went to the desert too, but Lee sees Austin's attempt to save the father as an attempt to "buy him off" with "Hollywood blood money" (8). Austin, however, cannot reach reconciliation with the father: "I went all the way out there. I went out of my way. I gave him money and all he did was play Al Jolson records and spit at me!" (39–40). Austin cannot communicate with his father, who is not only removed in space, settling in the desert, but also in time, living in the world of Al Jolson records. He is the embodiment of the past, a man adrift in the desert wilderness and absorbed in the sentiment of Jolson's records.

Both sons try to double the father. Like the father, Lee finds himself compelled to abandon civilization: "I'm livin' out there because I can't make it here" (49). Lee, a drifter out on the desert who earns money setting up pit bull fights, is also an outlaw who breaks into houses and steals people's televisions. Like Ben Loman, Lee is a restless wanderer who "can come through the window and go out the door" (31). A man in perpetual motion, Lee needs to do a job then leave. When Lee tells Austin, "I'm not like you. Hangin' around bein' a parasite offa other fools. I gotta do this thing and get out" (22), Lee sounds like Ben urging Willy to abandon the city. Both Lee and Ben display the restless mobility of the American son. Shattered by loss and instability, the lost son is forever moving on to the next stop on the road to nowhere. Whether he seeks his fortune in dog fights or diamonds, there is always something unsettling in his frenetic attempt to conquer space and time.

Austin also doubles the father. For one, he works by candlelight, like the "forefathers," the pioneers who had "cabins in the wilderness" (6). Early in the play, Lee is drinking heavily; later Austin starts drinking and mocking the false paradise they live in. When Lee accuses him of sounding like the father, he says, "Well, we all sound alike when we're sloshed. We just sorta echo each other" (39). Both sons mirror the absent father.

Also, the motif of the older brother as father substitute which is found in *Death of a Salesman* repeats itself in *True West* as Austin treats Lee like a substitute father. Austin has always wanted to be like Lee who was "always on some adventure" (26). Austin confesses, "I used to say to myself, 'Lee's got the right idea. He's out there in the world and here I am. What am I doing?'" (26). Adventure is what the wandering American hero seeks and adventure is in the path of the father, the man outside of civilization and beyond confinement, somewhere "out there in the world." Austin also wants to make contact with Lee. Just like Willy wanted Ben to spend time with him, Austin wants to spend time with Lee. He invites Lee to live with him in the North and tries to "take care of" (47) Lee since he is unable to take care of the old man. But Lee, like the father, is too restless to settle down and is beyond reform. Eventually, Austin asks Lee to take him out to the desert. Like Willy, Austin wants to follow his brother and his father out into the wilderness. Just as in *Death of a Salesman*, the wandering brother seems to explore the world of the father while the settled brother longs to break free and follow his older brother on the path of the absent father.

However, before escaping the world, Lee wants to pull off a big deal and Austin encourages Lee to sell his story idea to the Hollywood producer, Saul Kimmer. In the world of the absent father, there is often the concept that one big deal will transform a person's life. Selling the movie script becomes another salvation scheme that will replace or redeem the father. Like the sons of Willy, Lee believes that pulling off this deal could "get the old man outa hock" (25). Austin, however, realizes that the old man is "different. He's not gonna change. Let's leave the old man outta this" (25). But the father cannot be left out. Lee sells his idea for a stock western to Saul who buys the flimsy idea. In the world of the absent father, all one needs is a magical scheme to gain success. Both Saul and Lee see the money from the script as a way to rescue the father who is "destitute" and "needs money" (33). Austin states, "And this little project is supposed to go toward the old man? A charity project. Is that what this is?" (33). Austin has already failed to help the father: "I already gave him money. He drank it all up" (33).

In *True West*, the absent father is again connected with the alcoholic father who escapes the world through the magic elixir of drink much as the father did in *Ghosts*, *The Pelican*, and *The Glass Menagerie*. Saul also acts as some kind of savior figure who is going to "set up a trust" (33) for the father which Lee will oversee. Lee, who is a double of the father, will become the father's custodian. In this deal, Lee will win out over Austin and redeem the father. This deal made in the name of the father, of course, is another sham like Captain Alving's Home or Loman Brother's Sporting Goods. There is no "trust" or insurance that can save, redeem, or remake the image of the father.

Like Biff and Happy (who are supposed to reenact what Willy and Ben might have been), Austin and Lee join together on an unworkable project to save the old man. Lee says, "Maybe if we could work on this together we could bring him back out here. Get him settled down some place" (39). At the mention of the absent father "Austin turns violently toward Lee" and "takes a swing at him" (39). Austin is swinging at the father who is out of reach and who is beyond redemption. "I've had it with him" (39), Austin shouts.

But Austin cannot rid himself of the father and is compelled to follow the father's path, so he agrees to write the screenplay for Lee's idea if Lee will take him out on the desert, the path of the father. But all projects to save the father are doomed. Lee and Austin, like Willy, become mired in a world of junk: smashed typewriters, empty beer and whiskey bottles, broken toasters, and dead house plants. Outside, coyotes are killing cocker spaniels as the savage world encroaches on the civilized one and the world of the two lost sons becomes like a "desert junkyard at high noon" (50).

Caught in an unworkable project, the brothers become disoriented. Lee cannot create, burns his writings, is unable to determine the time, and cannot remember phone numbers and names. Austin cannot remember what county he is in. Lee rips the telephone off the wall and cries out "Who lives in this house anyway?" (47). Lee realizes that he is lost outside of the world of the father: "I would never be in this situation out in the desert" (47).

And the desert becomes the final destination of both sons. When mother returns home from Alaska and Austin tells her he is going to live out on the desert, she tells him: "You can't leave. You have a family" (55). But Austin, doubling his father, is abandoning his family and "getting out of here" (55). Lee also wants to flee so that the civilized world does not alienate him "like it done to Austin" (57). His journey will take him into the unknown wilderness: "No sir, I'd rather be a hundred miles from nowhere than let that happen to me" (57). The path seems clear. Mother tells Austin "You gonna go live with your father?" (53). When he tells her that he is going to another desert, she perceptively replies, "You'll probably wind up on the same desert sooner or later" (55). All paths converge in the direction of the absent father, the archetypal wanderer outside the bounds of confined space.

But Lee wants to travel alone and refuses to take Austin, who will not be abandoned. The brothers engage in a violent conflict which leaves them frozen in time. As they face off ready to attack one another "The figures of the brothers appear to be caught in a vast desert-like landscape" (60). The play closes on the world of the father. Like the father's flute music which closes *Death of a Salesman*, the image of the desert-like landscape sets up the world of the father which is both seductive and treacherous, a desert wilderness always shy of the promised land.

The deadly search for the lost father and the juxtaposition of two brothers in *Death of a Salesman* and *True West* are motifs that are repeated again in David Rabe's *The Basic Training of Pavlo Hummel*. As in the case of Miller and Shepard, fathers and father figures play a significant role in the dramas of Rabe. Speaking of *Streamers* in particular, but applying his insights to other plays in Rabe's *Viet Nam Trilogy*, Philip Kolin states: "An essential character in the drama of manhood is the father or (father figure); and multiple examples in *Streamers* underscore Rabe's message about the failure of fatherhood for a Viet Nam generation. The sons in the barracks are abused, betrayed, and deserted by fathers who are alcoholic, diseased, self-destructive, and malicious" ("Rabe's *Streamers*" 63).

Apparently, not only the father, but the absent father struck Rabe as an effective plot device when he was writing plays in school. Using reviews from local papers, Philip Kolin describes Rabe's first play "The Chameleon" as a story about a young boy who is told by his mother that the father deserted the family. However, letters found behind a picture show that the father went off to fight in World War II against the mother's wishes. Another letter reports the father's death. This scenario bears a resemblance to *The Pelican*. Also, Rabe's teacher pointed out the play's similarity to *The Glass Menagerie*. Kolin concurs with her comparison: "There is a lot of Tennessee Williams in "The Chameleon"—the mother/son conflict, the apartment setting with its imaginary wall and fire escape, the highly symbolic photograph and letters, and the absent father" ("Notices" 100). The mother/son conflict, the supposed letter revealing the father's identity, and the absent father connected to a military hero reappear in *The Basic Training of Pavlo Hummel*. Kolin holds that the damage caused by the father in Pavlo Hummel is "not as extensive" as in the other Viet Nam plays because Pavlo's father is absent. ("Rabe's *Streamers*" 64 f3). One might easily disagree with Kolin and state that the damage is extensive primarily because the father is absent.

Like *Death of a Salesman* and *True West*, *The Basic Training of Pavlo Hummel* also focuses on the search for an absent father. Pavlo Hummel is an alienated son who does not know who his father is. Like Willy, he tries to compensate for his lack of a father through a desperate effort to make himself part of a fraternal order where he can be accepted. Wanting to be "regular army," Pavlo tries too hard to be accepted and pursues a suicidal quest to double the heroic father. Just like the opening of *Death of a Salesman* begins with the flute music of the father, *The Basic Training of Pavlo Hummel* starts out with an outcry to the father. Bragging about his prowess as a fighter, Hummel shouts, "Can you hear your boy?" (7). Then he demonstrates his punches and proclaims, "Ain't I bad, Man?" (7). Pavlo feels that he has proven his manhood before his imaginary father, and freed himself from the bonds of his mother. He notes that his "mudda" would be aghast to see him with an "odd-lookin' whore, feelin' good and tall, ready to bed down" (8).

Like Willy and Austin, Pavlo needs to prove himself before the father. In his case, however, the father is a complete absence. Willy at least had a vague image of his father when Willy was three. The name of Pavlo's father is unknown and forgotten. The only thing Pavlo knows of his father is that his crazy mother whispered his father's name into his ear when Pavlo was three. Pavlo is an illegitimate child who has never seen his father. His mother slept with many men and Pavlo's father is only seen as one of the many "ghostly pricks" who were "humpin' the ole whore" (69). The father is no more than a series of mysterious phalluses, unseen and unrevealed, one of the many "one night stands" (69). In other words men who were on the move, evading the responsibility of fatherhood. As an abandoned son, Pavlo questions his mother: "Who . . . was . . . my father?" (74). But the mother is evasive. She claims to have revealed the father to him in a letter, another bogus documentation of fatherhood. Finally, the mother converts her one night stands into heroic fathers:

> No, you had many fathers, many men, movie men, filmdom's great—all of them, those grand old men of yesteryear, they were your father. The Fighting Seventy-sixth, do you remember, oh, I remember, little Jimmy, what a tough little mite he was, and how he leaped upon that grenade, did you see, my God what a glory, what a glorious thing with his little tin hat. (75)

Just like they did for Tom, Lee, and Austin, Hollywood movies recreate the mythical past of the father for Pavlo. Pavlo never learns who his "real father" (75) is; so he follows the model of the heroic father. The father becomes the mythical warrior of "yesteryear," the World War II heroes created in John Wayne movies. Just as in the other plays about absent American fathers, the father is connected with a heroic age, which is inevitably in the past. He also points the direction of the son to a world of adventure. In Pavlo's case, it is the battlefield, "freedom's frontier" (107), the farthest and most dangerous American frontier of all. This father, like the romantic pioneer, is a fantasy, a dangerous fantasy to pursue. In war, the sons are sacrificed to the ideals of the fathers and then glorified as heroes. Like Tom, Pavlo sees the adventures on the battlefield as the last testing ground of his manhood and his final escape from the mother.

Also, Pavlo, like other lost sons, is alienated and unsure of his own identity. He goes into basic training denying the fact that he has a family because he wants to stand outside of the bounds of family. But he is forced to admit to his family and to give his address, to which he becomes linked. After he gives his address, Ardell says, "Now we know who we talkin' about. Somebody say Pavlo Hummel, We know who they mean" (12). Pavlo is linked to a home that was never his, a home without a father.

Like other American heroes (Ishmael, Leatherstocking, Huck Finn), Pavlo creates his own name and shifts his identity. His change of name is a way of creating an identity for himself that will remove him from the influence of the absent father. His real name is Michael, but he changed it to Pavlo so he could escape the longed-for return of the father. He says, "Someday my father is gonna say to me, 'Michael, I'm sorry I ran out on you' and I'm gonna say, "I'm not Michael, Asshole. I'm not Michael anymore'" (45–6). Unable to find his absent father, Pavlo psychologically reverses the circumstances by having father engage in a fruitless quest for a son who has changed his identity.

Like Austin, who can no longer feel that he is real, and Willy, who can only feel temporary about himself, Pavlo has to deal with the emptiness inside of him. Ardell reminds Hummell, "You black on the inside. In there where you live, you that awful hurtin' black so that you can't see yourself noway. Not up or down or in or out" (46). Like other lost sons, Pavlo has lost his sense of direction. Appropriately, he dreams that he is a drowning man and explains, "I was all confused, you see, fighting to get down thinking it was up. . . . I pounded the bottom. I thought the bottom was the top" (101). His dream is similar to Miss Julie's dream. As victims of the crazy mother and the absent father, both are self-destructive children plunging themselves downward. Twice, Sergeant Tower tells his men to follow the North Star when they are lost: "Once you know north you ain't lost nomore" (97). Ardell later asks Pavlo "You ever see any North Star in your life?" (98). Pavlo only saw other people pointing towards it. Pavlo is like Lee, who cannot orient himself "around the North star." (Shepard *True West* 44). Both are lost in the wilderness and have no sense of direction.

Pavlo's alienation also brings him to the brink of suicide as he swallows a bottle of aspirin. However, Pavlo recovers and seeks his identity by following the path of his heroic fathers, the war heroes that his mother told him were his fathers. Pavlo is recreated as a soldier. He and Ardell climb the phallic tower of the mythical father and Ardell asks Pavlo, "Who you see in the mirror, man? Who you see? That ain't no Pavlo Hummel. . . . That somebody else" (62). Finally, he is able to identify his new self as "PAVLO MOTHERHUMPIN' HUMMEL" (63). With all the Oedipal implications, Pavlo wants to become his own father and to recreate himself in the image of the soldier hero.

Like Willy and Austin, Pavlo also lives in a wasteland world. The furniture in Pavlo's world is makeshift, put together out of containers that have been discarded. "An ammunition crate" is used for a table and an army oil drum for a chair. Symbols of destruction are a part of everyday life. There is a sheet metal wall covered with beer can labels. The labels are an obvious collage of cheap advertisements, a world put together out of junk art that mirrors the junkyard worlds of Willy and Austin. The high viewing tower sets up a prison camp atmosphere while the pit and furnace give an infernal quality to world of the barracks. The temperature in Georgia is always freezing and Pavlo is isolated as "weird," which could have the multiple connotation of meaning not only different but also fated. Facing him is the war, the ultimate wasteland filled with destruction and human carnage.

During his "basic training," Pavlo seeks out father substitutes and creates imaginary fathers to fill the gap left by his absent father. The most mysterious of these father figures is Ardell. Like Ben, Ardell is almost mythical and acts as a kind of springboard for the self-reflections that Pavlo is unable to articulate. Like some type of fairy godfather, he keeps "appearing and disappearing without prominent entrances" (9). Like Ben, Ardell serves as a mysterious brother figure, an alter-ego who preaches the doctrine of the mythical father. When Pavlo is blown to bits by a grenade, Ardell hears his distress call and says, "Don't I hear you callin'" (9). Ardell, like Ben, comes to the rescue of a lost son. He even resurrects Pavlo's spirit from the dead and guides him through the reenactment of his basic training.

Pavlo also seeks leaders as father figures. He stands behind his squad leader, Pierce, as protection. He says of Pierce, "He's my squad leader and I'm with him" (21). He wants Pierce to hear him recite his general orders. "You want to see if I'm sharp enough to be one of your boys" (25), he tells Pierce. Pierce, however, realizes that all Pavlo wants is a sympathetic father "to pat [his] goddamned head for bein' a good boy" (26). When Pavlo is beat up he expects Pierce to protect him. In a cry for help, he even tells Pierce, "I'm gonna kill myself" (55). But Pierce cannot identify with Pavlo. Even though he feels he "oughta do somethin'," he cannot help finding Pavlo "unbelievable" (48). Thus, just like Pavlo's father, Pierce abandons Pavlo.

If Pierce is supposed to be the protective father, Sergeant Tower is seen as the heroic father that Pavlo wants to double. Pavlo wants to know how long it will take him before he can do as many push-ups as Tower. Tower tells him that identification is impossible: "You'd be an ole bearded blind fuckin' man pushin' up all over Georgia" (29). He even asks Tower for fatherly advice about whether he was right not to let his mother hug him when he left. But Tower gives him no advice. Pavlo wants the heroic father's permission to break away from his mother, and asks Tower "Was I wrong?" (29). But Pavlo will never be able to double Tower, nor can he depend on Tower to give him advice about anything other than obeying orders.

Pavlo also tries to fabricate an image of his real father whom he sees as a disciplinarian: "My mom used to tell my Dad not to be so hard on me, but he knew" (26). Pavlo's imaginary father, however, projects Pavlo's own desire to set himself up for abuse and to justify his abusers. The father he creates in his imagination disciplines out of love. Pavlo explains, "He was hard on me because he loved me" (26). This imaginary father only reinforces Pavlo's victimization.

Pavlo's surrogate and imaginary fathers are not the only father figures that lead him toward his own self-destruction. He also creates fictional fathers. Like Biff and Lee, Pavlo is a petty thief, a cheat, and a liar. Like other lost sons, he engages in "storytelling" (26) and creates for himself a world of imaginary adventures. Even his brother calls him a "mythmaker" (66). Similar to the other lost sons, he creates an adventure world from the movies. Like Tom and Austin, he fashions himself as an outlaw. He creates a life for himself out of gangster movies and describes his exploits as a car thief engaged in high-speed car chases. Rabe finds that Pavlo "has romanticized the street kid tough guy and hopes to find himself in that image" (110).

Even though he is told people are laughing at his lying, he continues to romanticize his life. Out of his fantasy, he creates a father figure in Uncle Roy, who died in San Quentin for killing four people in a barroom brawl. Pavlo tells the story of how Uncle Roy was mean and rotten and how his family was afraid that Pavlo would pick up Roy's traits. Pavlo brags "I got that look in my eyes like him" (24). Ironically, Pavlo lives up to the fabricated image he set for himself by becoming mean and brash and engaging in a barroom brawl that leads to his death. Again the absence of the father leads to the creation of a destructive father image that the son is compelled to reenact. The traits Pavlo supposedly inherited from his fictional father figure lead to his death, thus he follows the path of the father to destruction.

But before he leaves on his tour of duty to ultimately follow the path of the father hero, Pavlo goes home to visit his brother. In the same manner as in *Death of a Salesman* and *True West*, the brother motif works itself out into a dichotomy. Mickey is the legitimate son who has stayed at home and has become materially successful. He has "brains," "wit," "charm," and earns "eighteen thou a year" (66). He has women falling all over him. Pavlo is an illegitimate child who left home and failed to become a success. Yet there is a strange mirroring in their activities. Craig Werner considers Mickey as "a civilian double of Pavlo" (519). At the end of Act One, Pavlo looks into a mirror and proclaims his identity as PAVLO MOTHERHUMPIN' HUMMEL. When Act Two opens Mickey is in front of a mirror too. Again, the subject of incest is brought up and Pavlo connects both sons to mother incest. They both agree that their mother is a psychotic old witch and a whore. Yet like Pavlo's father, they both pride themselves on whoring, thus doubling the absent father. Yet Pavlo brings up the question of incest when he implies that he too could be sleeping with the mother. Mickey reminds him that only "nonfamily" have sex with her. Pavlo replies "THAT'S YOU AND ME NONFAMILY MOTHERFUCKERS" (66). Pavlo has again intimated that he has become the father and assumed the place of the father.

If Pavlo is to be believed, his real name is Michael. His brother is called Mickey, which is a nickname for Michael. Knowing the mother, it is not unfathomable that both brothers were given the same name, leaving Pavlo an illegitimate copy of the legitimate brother. Thus, he not only wants to displace his father but also his brother. Apparently, Pavlo has chosen to renounce Mickey. Pavlo tells Mickey, "I come here to forgive you. I don't need you anymore" (69). Making the choice he always wanted to make, Pavlo renounces his family and accepts the world of the army as family, following the path of the hero father. He says, "I don't need you anymore. I got real brothers in the army now" (69). Like Willy, Pavlo, the lost son, creates a fantasy world of true brotherhood. He was beat up by a group of trainees who considered him an outcast. However, he fabricates a story which has his enemy along with the other soldiers hug him. Like Willy, Pavlo knows people are laughing at him, yet he continues to see the army as a place where he can enjoy a family. Mickey, however, does not believe Pavlo and accuses him of faking his whole army experience. "For all I know you been downtown in the movies for the last three months" (66). In one sense, he has been to the movies, for he is following the path of the movie war hero that his mother has set for him.

Even though he is told by his mother, Ardell, and his Captain that he has a death wish and is following a path of self-destruction, Pavlo follows the romantic path of the father hero, for he is set on a path of doom. Carol Rosen considers him "a misplaced Everyman figure and, like all Everyman figures, this Willy Lomanesque boy is doomed from the start" (239). Both Pavlo and Willy are doomed to the quest of recapturing the father. Pavlo is not satisfied being a medic and wants to be with "a unit Victor Charlie considers valuable enough to get it" (91). In his heroics, Pavlo drags dead comrades through battle zones, is wounded three times, and wins a Purple Heart. In the end, however, Pavlo, who wanted to be the romantic thug, is killed as a result of a barroom fight over a whore. Pavlo's attempt to take a whore away from Sergeant Wall puts him in direct conflict with the father. He taunts Wall, who becomes the figure of the powerless father: "Old Papasan can do fuck fuck, one time, one week" (105). Pavlo kicks Wall in the groin symbolically castrating him. Pavlo's attempt to possess a whore, a whore like his mother, puts him into direct confrontation with the deadly father. Wall throws a grenade into the bar and Pavlo catches it. Just like little Jimmy, the hero father from the movie that his mother told him about, Pavlo dies by grabbing onto a grenade. He dies reenacting a scene from the life of his imaginary absent father. In the end, it is Pavlo who is castrated. Ardell makes him admit his castration: "It hit you in the balls, blew 'em away" (11). Pavlo's last words echoing in his marching song are a final plea to the father: "Sergeant, Sergeant, can't you see. . . . All this misery is killin' me" (109).

Pavlo Hummel is a trapped man. Like Tom, he becomes a witness to the past. Caught in a repetition compulsion, the dead Pavlo must reenact the events leading to his death without ever reaching insight. He is forever haunted by the father he cannot recreate. Like Pavlo, the brothers in *True West* also reenact a cyclical crisis. Their quiet suburban home is surrounded by images of the desert and haunted by the father. William Kleb points out, "The old man's spirit seems to take over not only Austin, but the house itself. Even Lee is unable to break free" (119). In the end, they are frozen in time, caught forever in the desert landscape.

In comparing *The Glass Menagerie* and *Death of a Salesman*, Bigsby notes how "the tension which holds past and present apart are gone" and how "imagination, a product of paranoia," is "in some degree a primary evidence of the collapse of structure. It becomes a kind of hysterical or neurotic spasm which can no longer be controlled because there is no longer an available model of order or of social or moral imperatives which can command respect or authority" (2: 45–6). In other words, this world, which can be applied to the world of *True West* and *The Basic Training of Pavlo Hummel*, is a fractured world in which the father is absent. Like some fertility god, he has headed to the underworld, leaving the terrain open to blight and destruction. Yet the search for him is a futile quest, one which Northrop Frye describes as part of the final stages of the ironic vision where one searches for "the goal of the quest that is not there" (*Anatomy* 239). From a distinctively American perspective, Fiedler describes this childhood world of the American hero, which could easily apply to the lost son of an absent father:

> The child's world . . . is terrible, a world of fear and loneliness, a haunted world. "To light out for the territory" or seek refuge in the forest seems easy or tempting from the vantage point of a . . . restrictive home, but civilization once disavowed, the wanderer feels himself without perspective, more motherless child than free man. (xxi)

One might add to Fiedler's appraisal the fatherless child lost in the wilderness. In America, the lost son becomes an aimless wanderer who has lost his sense of direction. Whether heading out to the sea, recreating a mythical wilderness, wandering in the desert, marching off to war, or roaming aimlessly across the United States, the son of the absent father always embarks on a futile and self-destructive quest.

CHAPTER 6

THE ROMANCE OF THE DEAD FATHER:
Marsha Norman's *'night, Mother*
Henrik Ibsen's *Hedda Gabler*

Unlike the American son, the American daughter of the absent father lives in a world where there is no possibility of escape through space and distance. The father has set the restricted pattern of the daughters' lives. In Marsha Norman's *'night, Mother* and Beth Henley's *Crimes of the Heart* the absent father creates for the daughters a romantic vision of life that leads them toward self-destruction. Marsha Norman's *'night, Mother* won a Pulitzer Prize in 1983, both catapulting the playwright into instant celebrity and opening the play up for critical debate.

'night, Mother focuses on Jessie and Thelma, her mother. Jessie announces to her mother that she will commit suicide at the end of the play, and the rest of the drama deals with Thelma's desperate but ineffectual attempt to prevent Jessie's death. Leslie Kane places *'night, Mother* squarely in the tradition of the modern drama of alienation. Kane compares Norman's dramas to those of Samuel Beckett, Harold Pinter, Anton Chekhov, Tom Stoppard, and Lanford Wilson, citing Norman's use of "entrapment, illness, pain, solitude, and failed relationships" (256). But as Kane states in discussing the above-cited playwrights, "None of these men focuses sharply on mothering nor offers many portraits of mother and child" (256). In Norman's work, following the mother/daughter conflict is essential to an understanding of her plays' themes. Elizabeth Stone states that in Norman's view the "relationship between mother and daughter is crucial and possibly predictive of how the daughter will experience herself" (59).

In *'night, Mother* critics focus on the ambivalence of the mother-daughter relationship. According to Jenny Spencer, "It is not the mother's mirroring image that can provide the source of originating identity and power. And yet . . . for Jessie, this is precisely the role the mother is asked to play" ("Marsha Norman's She-tragedies" 162). Kane also notes that "in Norman's portrayal of the daughter's need to break free and the mother's to maintain connection, Norman poignantly conveys the agony of a mother unable to help her daughter or let her go" (266). Certainly, the play is a struggle between mother and daughter to come to terms with each other, but whether Jessie's suicide provides her mother with a new sense of self-awareness is also debatable. Katherine Burkman feels that Thelma is "bereft of the daughter she had possessed but ironically at one with the daughter from whom she has derived new strength and life" (255). Harriott, however, feels that Thelma is doubly punished because she "must endure both the suicide and her inability to prevent it" (144).

'night, Mother is undoubtedly about mother/daughter relationships; yet there

is another side of the drama which links it to the drama of the absent father. The structure of *'night, Mother* has been called "linear" (Copeland 11 3:1) and "chastely classical" (Brustein 25). The play takes place in a single setting and holds strictly to the unity of time with on-stage clocks reflecting the same time frame experienced by the audience. Such a drama emphasizes the revelation of past events external to the play. Jenny S. Spencer notes about Norman's women dramas, "Nothing happens in these plays . . . significant action happens elsewhere . . . offstage, in the past or outside the enclosure of the play" ("Marsha Norman's She Tragedies" 148). This kind of drama is often propelled by an absent character, and *'night, Mother* focuses on actions "crucially determined by absent male characters" and "the hopelessness of Jessie's state and the inevitability of her suicide is defined primarily in terms of the absent men to which most of the dialogue refers" ("Marsha Norman's She Tragedies" 156). Sue-Ellen Case also sees the women's relationship "animated by the absent male." (4). Case argues that it is really "the father who animates the mother/daughter relationship in *'night, Mother*" (4). Clearly, the absent father plays a crucial role in *'night, Mother*.

Although Jessie's father has been dead for at least fifteen years as determined by the age of the bullets in his gun, Jessie still misses him because she had a special attachment to her father. Thelma says, "You loved him enough for both of us. You followed him around like some . . ." (46). At this point the text does not reveal Thelma's thoughts. Perhaps Thelma does not complete her statement because the line would be offensive. Did Jessie, who gave her father the love that Thelma could not give him, follow him around like some kind of lovesick woman? Jessie would stay at the table and talk to her father about simple subjects like "why black socks are warmer than blue socks" (48) instead of washing the dishes with her mother. Thelma says, "I was jealous because you'd rather talk to him than anything" (48). There is a closeness in the father-daughter bond that has isolated the mother.

Jessie's father made her "a boyfriend out of pipecleaners" and would "smile like the stick man was about to dance" (49). The father creates a magic world for his daughter out of stick men. Jessie's memory of him is attached to a childhood world of toys where Jessie is safe from hurt. The father would also "sit up with a sick cow all night" (47) and leave Jessie "a chain of sleepy stick elephants" (47). In his absence, he left toys, and he expressed his own sleepiness through the elephants. Apparently, the bond between Jessie and her father was a close one, one attached to a childhood world.

Thelma, of course, focuses on Jessie's sense of loss for the absent father. She says, "He died and left you stuck with me and you're mad about it" (48). Jessie admits that at one time she was angry by saying to Thelma, "Not anymore. He didn't mean to" (48). For Jessie, the father's death left an absence in her life which she has tried to overcome. Jessie says, "I knew he loved me"

(48), and even though his love didn't "change anything" (49) in her life, she feels that "it didn't have to" and says "I still miss him" (49). Jessie has a great longing to be with the father, an unspoken longing to return to her missed father.

Since her father's death, Jessie, the lost daughter, has led a dismal life. She has debilitating epilepsy. In her fits, she becomes "like a puppet" from whom "somebody cut the strings" (64). She slides "down the walls" like someone before a "firing squad" (64). Jessie becomes like a puppet or a condemned prisoner. The only job she maintained was keeping her father's books. Outside the world of the father, she has failed to hold a job. Her marriage has not worked out. Cecil, her husband, wanted an active wife. However, Jessie, like her father, was a slow and reclusive person who tried to please her active husband. She tried "to get more exercise", and "to stay awake and to go out more" (59), but was unable to live up to Cecil's expectations, so he left her even though she begged him to take her with him. Her son Ricky is a thief who according to Jessie will probably be a murderer some day. Jessie has given up on Ricky and knows she cannot get through to him. "If I thought I could do that I would stay" (25). In her son, she can only experience desertion and disappointment. Like her father, the men in Jessie's life have all disappeared, leaving Jessie to return to her mother, a return which Jessie feels is "a mistake" (28). Even King, her pet dog, ran under a tractor and was killed.

Jessie's mother cannot offer her a life, only a way of passing time by working puzzles, putting in a garden, going to the A&P, and buying new dishes. Life has become routine and predictable, a wasteland. Jessie even knows what gifts she will get for her birthday. Her mother is all she has, and her mother is not enough to keep her alive. Jessie says, "I'm tired. I'm hurt. I'm sad. I feel used" (25). She has taken her mourning for her own loss which is centered in the loss of the father, and Hamlet-like has projected it onto the whole world. "I read the paper. I don't like how things are. And they are not any better out there than they are in here" (30).

Pondering her futile life takes Jessie back to the world of the father and the path of escape. Jessie's father is not an adventurer who has headed out for territories unknown. He is a silent man who escapes from his family by going fishing and withdrawing from the world. Even when alive, he was noted for his absence. Father's GONE FISHING sign served only as an excuse. Thelma says, "He never really went fishing . . . All he ever did was drive out to the lake and sit in his car" (49). Instead of fish, he brought home "a whole pipe cleaner family" (49) of "chickens, pigs, and a dog with a bad leg" (49). Father lived in a world of his own. When he wasn't farming, he would just sit "and try to think of somebody to sell the farm to" (49). Jessie's father was not only absent when he left, he was also absent when he was physically present. Thelma notes, "He could have had the GONE FISHING sign around his neck in that chair" (47). Only Jessie could intuit what he was thinking.

Jessie eventually turns to the father's death scene, a recurrent motif in the dramas of the absent father. She alone had to sit through his deathwatch as her mother stormed out of the room, telling Jessie that Jessie could wait it out with him while she (Thelma) watched *Gunsmoke*. When Jessie asks what her father told Thelma, Thelma says, "He didn't have anything to say. . . . That's why I left" (52–3). The father refuses to communicate with his wife and withdraws from the world in silence. Louis Grieff equates the father with the dark archetype of the silent rebel or passive resister who refuses to accept "life's inadequacies" (225). He describes the father as a "Redneck Bartleby" (225) and links him to those existential rebels who "choose 'nothing' in its perfect negativity, as far preferable to the shabby 'something' the world has offered them" (227). Perhaps, Grieff goes a bit too far in projecting the image of the alienated romantic hero upon a poor farmer who contemplates his boots and his crops, but he does pinpoint the father's seductive path towards escape from life.

Laura Morrow goes as far as to make him a sort of homespun artist who uses "silent reflection" to examine "reality" (27) and "fashions original figures according to his whimsy" (28). Morrow contrasts him to Thelma, whose life is based on shallow routines and fixed patterns: "Because she insists on interpreting reality as shallowly and simplistically as possible, Mama [Thelma] resents his indulgence in private reflection" (27). Both Grieff and Morrow follow through on the American archetype of the silent, deep, and mysterious male who has detached, or one might say elevated himself, from the mundane preoccupations of daily life. However, one might see him more as an ironic version of the Thoreauesque recluse who has escaped the responsibilities of family life without ever leaving home. Both critics, however, are partially right in that the father has chosen absence as a mode of life and has bequeathed this heritage to his daughter.

Because of her father's symbolic absence or detachment from the world as well as his actual absence, Jessie, like other lost children, doubles the father. Like her father, she is mostly silent. She even walks out of the room when guests arrive. Although the play necessitates Jessie's ability to carry on a conversation, Norman assures the reader that "Jessie has never been as communicative" as she is during the play and that "she has not always been this way" (2). Even so, Jessie orchestrates her conversation around a series of distracting activities. Because Jessie was shy and withdrawn, Thelma even brought Cecil over to the house. Thelma felt Jessie would never get a husband because Jessie would just "sit like [her] Daddy" (58).

'night, Mother, however, goes deeper into the father/daughter connection than to present only a daughter's imitation of her father. The play has a buried secret that is directly connected to the father. Jessie has apparently inherited epilepsy from her father. Thelma says, "Your Daddy had fits too" (62). Apparently, the father had a series of mini-seizures, and Jessie had signs of

epilepsy since she was a young girl. Mother withheld the information from Jessie because if she told Jessie about her seizures, she would have to reveal the father's epilepsy.

At this point, the drama brings in the issue of inherited disease and in Jessie's case, at least, a debilitating one. The idea of directly inheriting the father's disease puts *'night, Mother* clearly in the tradition of the dramas of the absent father, like *A Doll House* and *Ghosts.* Just like in *Ghosts,* a child leaves home, develops a crippling illness, and returns home to mother only to find that the illness was inherited from the father. Just like Mrs. Alving tries to reassure Osvald, Thelma tells Jessie, "Your Daddy gave you those fits, Jessie. He passed them down to you like your green eyes and your straight hair. It's not your fault" (68). Knowing that the disease came from the father does not deter Jessie from her suicidal quest, just like it does not deter Osvald. Of course, Osvald's disease is different from Jessie's, for it is fatal and bears a heavy moral stigma, yet Jessie's epilepsy has had a debilitating effect on her life and has rendered her freakish. Just as in the case of Osvald, the absent father becomes embodied in the offspring. Thelma explains that Jessie's fits at first were "like your Daddy's" (69). Thelma had to watch both of them "turning off and on like light bulbs" (69).

The idea of turning off seems to be a clear image for describing both Jessie and her father. But Thelma does not leave herself free from guilt. In a moment of anguish, she feels she might be responsible for Jessie's epilepsy because of "how I felt about your father" (71). Now epilepsy becomes a curse to punish Thelma for not loving Jessie's father. Jessie dismisses the notion of a curse and reassures Thelma that epilepsy is simply a disease. The modern realistic drama deemphasizes the tragic curse, but the issue of inherited disease and the mention of curse are already established. Even if they are not given full credence, they do lurk behind the surface of the text. Also, just as in *The Libation Bearers, Hamlet, Ghosts,* and *The Pelican,* the mother's sin against the father surfaces. Thomas Adler even holds that "Jessie will desert her mother by dying and thereby perhaps retaliate against Thelma for never having loved her husband" (8). In Adler's scenario, suicide becomes revenge just as it does from the opposite perspective in *Miss Julie.*

Jessie has not only doubled the father, she has also lived out her parents' life. To Cecil she "never was what he wanted to see" (61), just like her father could not see what he wanted in Thelma. Father wanted and married "a plain country woman," and then "he held it against" Thelma "like [she] was supposed to change" (46). Father died leaving no parting words, just like Cecil left Jessie without saying goodbye. Jessie has a child she cannot reach, just like she cannot be reached by her mother.

None of Thelma's illusions can keep Jessie's hopes up. Jessie cannot see the day when "Ricky will be married . . . and bring . . . grandchildren over"

(74). So Jessie decides upon suicide, but her suicide is also taking her through the path of the absent father and toward a union with the absent father. First, Jessie wants to shoot herself with her father's gun. Spencer notes the fact "that her life will be taken with her father's gun is a detail Jessie finds unnecessary but particularly appropriate. This action, after all, is a highly symbolic one" ("Norman's *'night, Mother*" 368). Spencer, however, never fully elaborates on the symbolism of the gun. Jessie's seventh line in the play ends "Where is Daddy's gun?" (7). The search for the gun begins the quest for the father. The gun is in a shoebox in the attic. The shoes were the ones her father wore to the hospital, but Thelma told the hospital to keep the shoes. Even the shoes are absent like the father.

The shoes are also metonymically connected with illness and death. The gun is not only the father's gun, but it is in the box for the shoes that are directly connected to the father's death. When Jessie asks Mother which shoebox, Thelma replies, "Black" (10). Jessie then asks if the box is black, connecting the box now with the black box of death. The gun is thus connected to the father, to his absence, and to his death.

The gun is also a symbol for a struggle to claim the father and his power. Jessie feels strongly about the possession of the gun. She says, "Dawson better not have taken that pistol" (8). Jessie feels that the gun belongs to her, not to her brother Dawson, who patrimonially would be the rightful heir of the father's gun. And though Thelma thinks that Jessie is going to shoot her own son Ricky, Jessie says the gun is "not for him, it's for me" (11). The "for me" is taken in two ways. One, she is going to use it to kill herself, and two, she is claiming the father's pistol for herself. To Jessie, the gun is hers; it is not to be turned outward toward the aberrant son, another male heir. For a second time, Jessie tells Thelma "the gun is for me" (13); then she tells her mother that she is going to kill herself. Immediately, the mother tries to disempower the gun by rendering it "broken" and saying that it had fallen "in the mud" (14). When Thelma realizes that this tactic will not work, she tries to render Jessie inadequate to handle the gun. Jessie, however, "knows her way around a gun" (14). Presumably, her father taught her. Finally, Mother claims rightful possession of the gun, "You can't use your father's gun either, it's mine now" (19). Jessie is determined to use her father's gun. She had "Cecil's all ready, just in case I couldn't find this one, but I'd rather use Daddy's" (14). The husband's gun can only be used as a substitute for the father's gun.

Perhaps this reading of Jessie's struggle to find and claim the father's gun is blatantly Freudian, but it does illustrate the position of the absent father in Jessie's death. Burkman finds that Jessie's "anticipated encounter with death" is "one that Jessie associates as a merging with her withdrawn father" (260). Except for a vague association of death with Hades in the Persephone myth, Burkman does not pinpoint the daughter's search for an absent father. Adler comes closer to the father/daughter connection when he says that "using her Daddy's gun indicates his continuing grip over her and the way that no other man in Jessie's life could measure up to him as well as how he failed her by dying" (8). Adler might overstate his case. Jessie does love Cecil, and as with the gun, he is an adequate substitute for her father. Also, Jessie's anger at her father for dying seems to have subsided. But what has not subsided is the seductive quest to follow him.

Jessie wants to follow the father in death. "I want to hang a big sign around my neck like Daddy's on the barn. GONE FISHING" (27). Jessie is clearly following in her father's footsteps which leads to escape from the world, not only from the world of family, but also from the pain and loss attached to failed relationships. Daddy's sign GONE FISHING is not just a retreat to nature, it is an escape from life itself.

For Jessie, death in its complete sense of absence is an entering into the world of the father. Death is "quiet" so "nobody can get me" (18). This world of quiet is definitely the world of the silent father. Death offers her the perfect escape, one that will work. Death also becomes an act of grand defiance: "This is how I say what I thought about it all and I say no" (75). Her negation is the same as her father's. Here, of course, is the powerful illusion that somehow the choice of death will be the beautiful return to paradise, a world where the uncertainty of life is gone, a quiet world next to the father.

Jessie harkens back to a childhood paradise where she was somebody who never heard of "sick or lonely," where she was a child who "got fed and reached up and got held" (76). Like all children of the absent father, she longs for childhood paradise. She feels she has lost her sense of self: "Who I never was or who I tried to be and never got there. Somebody I waited for and never came" (96). Jessie sees what other lost children see—the failure to attain genuine selfhood. Like Nora, Julie, Willy and Pavlo, she does not know who she is and is seeking paradise by following the absent father into the reaches of death. As with Willy, suicide is a far better alternative than waiting around for nothing to happen.

Like a meticulous director of a play, Jessie orchestrates her death, the discovery of her body, and her funeral with accurate precision, and she does it following the path of the father. Mother notices that Jessie, just like Daddy, is gone even when she is present. Thelma realizes that "I can't stop you because you're already gone" (78). Thelma, however, cannot leave Jessie to go watch *Gunsmoke*. In fact, she has agreed to turn off the television. She must hear the gunshot. After Jessie abruptly announces that she has no more to say, Jessie is silent like her father was on his deathbed, and Thelma is now forced to hear the resounding "No" of the gunshot.

Missing no details, Jessie has also orchestrated her funeral to mimic her father's. She will have "the preacher who did Daddy's" (80) funeral, and mother will wear the dress she "wore to Daddy's" (80) funeral. In the end, Mother says "Forgive me, I thought you were mine" (89). Jessie, however, has taken the father's path and returned to the father. Although her path might seem heroic, it is not. The romantic death is just another illusion. Somewhat surprised by the accusation, Marsha Norman said to an interviewer, "Someone even accused me of writing about death as though it were the New City . . . you know, this great place where you get everything you want" (Harriott 157). Such an illusion, however, is not far from Jessie's notion of the beautiful death.

On the note of the beautiful death, *'night, Mother* invites comparison with Ibsen's *Hedda Gabler*. Kane notes "the technique of the concluding shot is by no means unique: Ibsen used it in *Hedda Gabler* . . . But Jessie is not interested in dying beautifully" (267). Kane may be too hasty in assuming that Jessie does not want a beautiful death, as further analysis will bear out. More to the point is Burkman's brief comparison: "Like Hedda and Miss Julie, Jessie is her father's daughter . . . and she has identified with his kind of withdrawal. Like Hedda and Miss Julie, Jessie finds some measure of redemption in a suicide that is partly an escape from a world in which she lacks the strength to act with freedom" (255).

An understanding of *'night, Mother* as a drama of the absent father can be enhanced by comparing Jessie Cates to Hedda Gabler. Both heroines appear to be only daughters. No mention is ever made of Hedda having any siblings. Jessie has one brother, but no sisters. Both are attached to fathers who are aloof and distant. Hedda is described as being seen riding with her father who is a general and a man respected in the community, yet he is distanced from other people by his social rank. During Hedda's conversations with Eilert, her father is at a distance with his back to them. Like Hedda, Jessie is also described as following her father around. He is a loner who speaks little and often disappears to be by himself.

Both women are identified by the name of the father even though they are married. Although Hedda is now Mrs. Tesman, the play is titled *Hedda Gabler*. When Eilert Lovborg meets Hedda, he calls her "Hedda Gabler" four times and notes "Hedda Gabler married? And to George Tesman!" (736). When he decides to blackmail her about revealing the identity of her father's pistol, Judge Brack says "No, Hedda Gabler—as long as you keep quiet" (775). Even though Jessie has been married, the cast list identifies her as Jessie Cates, so that she maintains her father's name. Both women connect happiness with the world of the father. Hedda does not talk about her father, but Aunt Julie notes about Hedda "She must have had a glorious life in the General's day" (696). But the General's day is gone, and Hedda finds herself trapped in a world that does not hold to the aristocratic values of her father. Jessie's fondest memories go back to a childhood world where her father gave her a pipecleaner boyfriend.

Outside the world of the father both women are lost. Their worlds are restricted and confined. Hedda finds herself trapped: "It's this tight little world I've stumbled into . . . that makes life so miserable" (730). Hedda cannot tolerate the "eternal aunts" (727) and their domestic routines of caring for and pampering people. Jessie is also confined. She has little attachment to her brother and sister-in-law and cannot see spending the rest of her life caring for her mother. Neither Hedda nor Jesse has any trusted friends they can confide in. Both cannot find fulfillment in marriage. Hedda does not love her husband and can barely tolerate him. Jessie loved her husband, but he left her.

As for motherhood, Hedda does not even want to hear about it. She tells Brack, "I have no talent for such things" (730). She also symbolically commits infanticide when she destroys the manuscript that Eilert and Thea worked on, a manuscript that is equated to a child. She cries out, "Now I'm burning your child, Thea!" (762). Jessie is a failure as a mother, and her son has become a criminal. Jessie sees her own hand in her son's behavior: "He knows not to trust anybody and he got it straight from me. And he knows not to try to get work, and guess where he got that. He walks around like there's loose boards in the floor, and you know who laid that floor, I did" (61). Neither woman has any prospects or goals in life. Jessie was not able to hold a job and certainly does not see herself as pursuing a career. Hedda cannot use the only means to obtain success open to her and inspire her husband to achieve a successful career in politics. Her attempts to influence Eilert, the would-be genius, into becoming a Dionysian hero are dismal failures. Both heroines feel almost cursed by failure. Hedda says, "What is it this . . . this curse that everything I touch turns vile" (773). Speaking about her husband, Jessie notes, "He just didn't know how things fall around me like they do" (61).

Both feel that life is a long ride that they are trapped on. Jessie compares her life to a bus ride and says "Even if I ride fifty more years and get off then, it's still the same place when I step down to it" (33). Describing her married life with Tesman, Hedda says, "The trip will go on and on" (727). Jessie wants to "get off" (33) the bus. Hedda is afraid to "jump off" of the train because someone might see her legs. Here, leaving the train has sexual implications and definite social constraints. But Hedda, like Jessie, does "get off" of the train on her own terms.

Both women feel powerless because the people around them know too much about them. Hedda feels that Judge Brack has her in his power because he can expose her to scandal. Speaking about her family Jesse says "They know things about you . . . whether you wanted them to know or not. They were there when it happened and it don't belong to them it belongs to you, only they got it" (23). Hedda, the daughter of an aristocrat, fears scandal. Jessie, the daughter of a reclusive, introverted man, does not want her brother to know about her life.

Both women feel trapped. Hedda says her only talent is "Boring myself to death" (730), and Jessie says "I'm just not having a very good time" (28). That both women might be suicidal is no surprise, but both women look at suicide as a romantic gesture of power; both are enamored of their ability to choose to die; and both see death as a return to the father. Both Hedda and Jessie know their way around guns. Hedda has inherited her father's pistols and shoots them for her entertainment. She has pointed the pistols at Lovborg and at Brack. She has even given Lovborg her father's pistol and told him to die "beautifully" (762). For Hedda, suicide is an act of courage, not despair, an act of beauty. Speaking of Lovborg's supposed suicide, she says that he "had the courage to do . . . what had to be done" (770). She considers his suicide "a free and courageous action" (772). Behind Hedda's own suicide is her father's aristocratic code and her own seduction by the beauty of choosing death. In death, Hedda not only follows her father's path but returns to the world of her father. Appropriately dressed in black, she shoots herself in the temple with her father's pistol and underneath her father's portrait.

Jessie, like Hedda, sees suicide as an act of choice. Lucid and rational, she is not in despair and has planned her suicide to the last detail. Speaking about her life, she tells her mother "It's all I really have that belongs to me and I'm going to say what happens to it. And I'm going to stop it. So. Let's have a good time" (36). Like a romantic individualist, Jessie wants to have the ultimate choice over her destiny regardless of the consequences. Jessie, like her father, can escape the world on her own terms and in her own way so that for her death will be a beautiful quiet. Jessie's suicide is very similar to Hedda's. Like Hedda, Jessie, dressed in black, shoots herself (most probably in the head) using her father's gun. Jessie also kills herself underneath the relics of her father in the attic above. For both women, the drama of their suicide cannot be comprehended by those around them. Brack exclaims "But good God! People don't do such things" (778) while Thelma assuredly states, "People don't really kill themselves, Jessie" (17). But despite cultural differences, both lost daughters do kill themselves, and they do it in the grand and orchestrated manner of a romantic heroine.

'night, Mother is not only similar to *Hedda Gabler*, but it also resembles *The Glass Menagerie*, another play of the absent father. Marsha Norman, in fact, cites her attendance at a performance of *The Glass Menagerie* as an influential event in her life (Harriott 148, Savran 180). In comparing both plays, Grieff notes the similarities between Laura and Jessie. He finds that both women have been deserted by the men in their lives; both have meddlesome mothers who match them with a man they can love but are not able to hold; and both are attracted to an absent father (224–5). Laura, no less than Tom, is a victim of an absent father. Like Jessie, Laura is shy, withdrawn, and at least in her mind, disabled. Like Jessie, Laura cannot hold a job or pursue a career, and the one man she loves is technically unfaithful to her and leaves her. Like Jessie, Laura has a garrulous mother who flirtatiously secures the attentions of a gentleman

caller who takes interest in Laura, and uses positive thinking to open her up to the experiences of life. Jim tries to build up Laura's confidence just as Cecil tries to convince Jessie she can do anything she has a mind to.

Both Laura and Jessie, however, are attached to the Father. Amanda has to pry Laura away from the Victrola and the worn-out records left by the father as a painful reminder of him, and Thelma has to speak for Jessie, who can only sit like her father. Jessie's father does give her pipecleaner animals as a menagerie of her own (Grieff 226), but Jessie does not use them as a substitute for life the way Laura does. Jessie's escape leads toward death rather than a withdrawal from reality. In the case of both lost daughters, they seek escape from the messy relationships and harsh uncertainties of life by following the path of an absent father who wants to escape entirely from family life.

'night, Mother, *Hedda Gabler*, and *The Glass Menagerie*, all focus on a daughter's unhealthy attachment to an absent father. Unlike the sons of the absent father, the daughters cannot drift through space and time but can only withdraw within the narrow confines of their houses. Jessie stays in her mother's house; Hedda remains stationary in the house her husband bought her; and Laura can hardly survive outside of her mother's apartment. Unable to venture out into unknown territories in search of the father, they withdraw into the interior world of the father and his mementoes. All their trajectories follow the universal pattern of the father/daughter narrative. A prisoner of the father, each is approached by a male suitor; however, no suitor is able to free her. All remain captives of the father, an absent father who maintains a deep psychological hold on them.

CHAPTER 7

TRAPPED IN THE FATHER'S DYING WORLD:
Beth Henley's *Crimes of the Heart*
Anton Chekhov's *The Three Sisters*

Another play that focuses on the daughter's relationship to an absent father is Beth Henley's *Crimes of the Heart*. *Crimes of the Heart* is not a play about the daughter's withdrawal into the world of the father, but it is a play in which an absent father figure dominates the lives of three women. Both *'night, Mother* and *Crimes of the Heart* started at the Actors' Theatre in Louisville, played Off-Broadway, won a Pulitzer Prize, and had successful Broadway runs. Both plays made instant successes out of women playwrights and sparked heated debates among feminist critics. Like *'night, Mother*, *Crimes of the Heart* is about relationships among women who have led troubled lives and are seeking desperate solutions to their problems. According to Morrow, the protagonists in both plays have "been influenced by mothers who were literally or figuratively abandoned by their husbands" (23). However, these protagonists are all influenced by men who are absent from the action of the play. More specifically, both feature an absent father or father figure.

Other than the feminist debate, criticism of *Crimes of the Heart* has focused on the issue of truths versus gimmicks. For some reason, critics tend to denigrate a comedy for creating a series of joke lines and for setting up contrived events. Walter Kerr sees *Crimes of the Heart* as "overloaded with quirky behavior" ("Offbeat" D3). He feels that "the characters tend to lose weight and substance as they reach farther and farther for one more brass ring" (31). Howard Kissel notes that "the story though funny, never seems true" (140). Michael Feingold feels that Henley gossips about her characters "never at any point coming close to the truth in their lives" (106). Frank Rich, however, takes an opposite view. He feels that Henley "refuses to tell jokes at all" and that her "characters always stick to the unvarnished truth and the truth is funnier than any invented wisecracks" ("Unvarnished Laughs" C21). Clive Barnes notes that the play can capture "the basic truth behind the improbabilities" ("'Crimes'" 137). Nancy Hargrove finds Henley's portrayal of the human condition "realistic" and "painfully honest" (89).

Comedy by its very nature treats behavior that is outrageous; yet critics want to validate a "serious comedy" by focusing primarily on its verisimilitude. *Crimes of the Heart* is indeed an entertaining play written to evoke laughter; yet behind the play is a psychological pattern that links the drama to the absent father.

First, much of the plot is structured around a series of absent fathers. The father of the MaGrath sisters left their mother, and his absence leads the MaGraths to move from Vicksburg to Hazlehurst so they can live with their maternal grandfather, Old Granddaddy. Old Granddaddy, a surrogate father to the sisters, is now in the hospital dying. Much of the play's action is surrounded around the absent patriarch. Also, Doc, Meg's old boyfriend whom she abandoned, is back in Hazlehurst because "his father died a couple of months ago," and Doc is "seeing to his property" (24). In other words, a dead father has brought him back to town where he will meet Meg again. Barnette Lloyd, the young lawyer who keeps Babe out of jail, is seeking revenge for the destruction of his father. He is willing to take a case against Zackery Botrelle because Zackery ruined Barnette's father: "He took away his job, his home, his health, and his respectability" (62). Barnette is interjected into the plot to revenge the wounding of an absent father. Even Charlie Hill can become a prospective husband for Lenny because he has renounced the state of fatherhood and doesn't want to raise "little snot-nosed pigs" (116). *Crimes of the Heart* is inscribed within the world of the absent father.

The most obvious absent father is Jimmy MaGrath. Like the Wingfield father, he seems to be noted for his ambiguous smile. Meg despises his "white teeth" (31), and when she sees a picture of him "clowning on the beach" (71), she says, "Turn the page . . . we can't do worse than this" (71). Babe holds him and his absence responsible for the death of her mother and the old yellow cat that the mother hung beside herself. "I bet if Daddy hadn't left, they'd still be alive" (31). The MaGrath father, who has disappeared completely from their lives, is not only held responsible for the mother's death, which has emotionally scarred the sisters, but he is also responsible for leaving them stranded in the house of Old Granddaddy, who has a disastrous effect in shaping their lives.

Critics seem to agree on the role that Old Granddaddy plays in the lives of the MaGrath sisters. E. D. Huntley notes, "The absent Old Granddaddy is in some ways the guiltiest character in the play because his 'crimes' have precipitated the self-destructive sins of the MaGrath sisters" (410). Adler contends that he has "controlled and limited their lives more decisively than the shadow of their mother's suicide" (44). And Jonnie Guerra points out how "the sister's victimization by Old Granddaddy's misguided plans" demonstrates "the destructive power of a male-dominated society" (125).

Old Granddaddy, the only father figure that the sisters identify with, is a key structural device in the play. His off-stage dying sets a deathwatch atmosphere against which the actions of the drama are played. Lenny has already moved her cot into the kitchen to "be close and hear him at night if he needed something" (19). Early in the play, the audience knows that "Old Granddaddy's gotten worse in the hospital" (12). Even though Meg has been brought home by Babe's legal problems, she and Lenny must inevitably face Old Granddaddy, who has "blood vessels popping in his brain" (20). As the sisters are beset with a series of crises, Act Two ends on the jolting announcement that Old Granddaddy has had a stroke. Act Three begins with an announcement that he is in a coma and that his death is imminent. As an absent father who controls the progress of the play, Old Granddaddy and his dying absorb a considerable portion of the drama.

Reflecting his dying, the world itself is filled with disease and decay. From Lenny's hair "falling out" (18) and Meg's "slicing pains" (20) to Mrs. Porter's tumor in her bladder, illness is pervasive. Meg reads Old Granddaddy's book on diseases of the skin and looks at "rotting away noses and eyeballs drooping off down the sides of people's faces" (66) while Babe keeps a scrapbook about the unpleasant things in her life, like her mother's death. Also, Old Granddaddy, who is turning "white and milky" (69) and has "almost evaporated" (69), is not alone among the wounded men. Shot by Babe, Zackery is in the hospital with a bullet wound in his stomach. Doc, lured by Meg to stay in a hurricane, has a crushed leg and has abandoned a promising medical career. The battered Willy Jay is uprooted and sent North. Lloyd Barnette, though not physically injured, has to give up his personal vendetta. Not to mention the fact that Mama's cat gets hung and Lenny's horse Billy Boy is struck by lightning. The world of death, disease, and loss is a wasteland world that revolves around the dying of Old Granddaddy, the absent father figure.

Although the sisters have not doubled Old Granddaddy, they have tried to live out his dreams for them. He has filled them with illusions that have led them into self-destructive lifestyles. Old Granddaddy designated Babe "the prettiest and most perfect of the three" (21). He was proud to see her married to Zackery Botrelle, "the richest and most powerful man in Hazlehurst" (22). Old Granddaddy felt that Zackery was "the right man for her whether she knew it or not" (22). It was Old Granddaddy's, not Babe's dream, that she would "skyrocket right to the heights of Hazlehurst society" (22). When asked whether she was happy on her wedding day, she can only reply that she "was drunk with champagne" (71). Babe is not suited to be among the social set. Furthermore, Old Granddaddy's dream husband turns out to be a callous and abusive man, so Babe seeks love and understanding in the arms of a fifteen-year-old black boy and shoots her husband when he strikes the boy. Following the path Old Granddaddy has pointed out for her has left Babe alienated, perplexed, and suicidal.

Old Granddaddy has also led Meg astray. He has pumped Meg up with ideas of becoming a Hollywood celebrity. He told her that with her singing talent all she needed was "exposure," and she could make her "own breaks" (23). In the American mythos, the Hollywood dream factory again provides an illusory escape for lost children. Like Tom, Austin, and Pavlo, Meg follows the path of the movies. Old Granddaddy wants her to put her foot "in one of those blocks of cement they have in Hollywood" (23). Ironically, Meg is metaphorically stuck in cement, trapped in the dream she and Old Granddaddy share. Resentfully, she tells Lenny, "I think I've heard that [Hollywood speech] and I'll probably hear it again when I visit him in the hospital" (23). Meg has also been driven to the brink of madness trying to live the role Old Granddaddy has cast her in. Unable to attain success, she winds up working for a dog food company. When Old Granddaddy sends her money to come home for Christmas, she can't because she undergoes a nervous breakdown. She psychologically loses her singing voice partially to get even with Old Granddaddy for whom she has been singing and winds up in the L.A. County Hospital's psychiatric ward.

Interestingly, Meg's trauma is connected with Christmas. Psychologists have discovered that Christmas time brings on depression and emotional crises in troubled people. But Christmas as a "holiday gone wrong" seems to be a focal theme in some of the dramas of the absent father. Nora's tragedy begins on Christmas. Jessie decides she is going to kill herself on Christmas. She even notes that "Jesus was a suicide" (18). Interestingly, Jesus does die at the bidding of the Absent Father and dies to return to the Father. The Christian ethos always points toward a return to the Father. Christmas brings forth the hope of a savior, but Meg, who cannot find a savior, goes crazy at Christmas. Chick even labels her "cheap Christmas trash" (6). At a Christmas bazaar, Babe does find Barnette, a savior figure who keeps her out of jail. However, despite his rescue, Babe attempts suicide. Thus, the Christmas theme of salvation sent from the Father reverses itself into one of despair and hopelessness.

Since Meg's Christmas rewards never come, she is forced to engage in storytelling. Like Willy, Biff, and Pavlo, she creates grandiose fabrications. She lies to Old Granddaddy, telling him she has made a record album and has a role in a movie called *Singing in a Shoe Factory*, a title which contrasts the glamour of being in Hollywood with the mundane job she has at a dog food company. Like Biff, Meg is forced to create a false identity in order to please a father figure. Meg confesses, "I hate myself when I lie for that old man. I do. I feel so weak. Then I have to do at least three or four things that I know he'd despise just to get even with the miserable, old bossy man!" (69). Whether she tries to fulfill Old Granddaddy's vision of what she should be or whether she acts to spite him, Meg is still controlled by Old Granddaddy.

Like Babe and Meg, Lenny too is acting out Old Granddaddy's image of what she should be. Old Granddaddy has made Lenny feel self-conscious about her "shrunken ovary" (34). Meg accuses Lenny of living out her life "as Old Granddaddy's nursemaid" (79). The one man she has had a relationship with she stopped seeing "because of Old Granddaddy" (79). Old Granddaddy told Lenny that the man would not marry her because she could not have children. Meg tries to convince Lenny she can have a romantic attachment and that "Old Granddaddy's the only one who seems to think otherwise" (80). Lenny feels that Old Granddaddy has always wanted to see them happy. "He went out of his way to make a home for us, to treat us like we were his own children. All he ever wanted was the best for us" (69–70). Thus, the sisters are trapped in an ambivalent relationship with a father figure. Old Granddaddy, the surrogate father, has determined what is best for the sisters, and they feel guilty not following his wishes.

However, Old Granddaddy's attempts to manufacture happy lives for his surrogate daughters have left them miserable and debilitated. The way Old Granddaddy has influenced them can be seen in the way he treated the young girls on the day of their mother's funeral. Old Granddaddy bought them "banana splits for breakfast" (72) and "shoved them down" (72) the girls until they got sick. His attempts to fill them with the rich desserts of life have left them physically and mentally ill. Meg says, "He keeps trying to make us happy and we end up getting stomach aches and turning green and throwing up in the flower arrangements" (73). Babe shoots her husband, then swills down three glasses of her favorite lemonade until she is bloated. Meg tries to harden herself against the tragedies of life by looking at pictures of crippled children, then buying "a double scoop ice cream cone" (67). When Lenny is filled full of Old Granddaddy's advice, she says "I'm gonna vomit" (81).

Although they follow the advice of Old Granddaddy, their feelings toward this absent father figure are ambivalent. Lenny has made a birthday wish that "Old Granddaddy would be put out of his pain" (95) and feels guilty when he goes into a coma. Rebelling against Old Granddaddy, Meg proclaims, "I sang right up into the trees! But not for Old Granddaddy. None of it was to please him" (99). Then, she announces in defiance, "He's just gonna have to take me like I am and if that sends him into a coma, that's just too damn bad" (99). Ironically, he has just been sent into a coma, and Meg's line provokes hysterical laughter.

Critics have commented on the difficulty of accepting this line. Leo Sauvage finds it in poor taste. He notes that nervous laughter may occur when someone falls down, but points out, "I've never heard of a similar physiological outbreak occurring when a family member is told a sick relative is in the hospital near dying" (20). Walter Kerr also comments on the difficulty of playing such a scene, but notes that the director of the Broadway production has "orchestrated the two-way personal collapse perfectly" in order to set up a perfect "alternating of grief and manic glee" ("Offbeat" D31). Brendan Gill notes that the sisters' outburst into laughter "strikes us as the most natural thing in the world to do" (183). The difficulty of playing such a scene which skirts a fine line between comedy and horror is connected to the sisters' ambivalent feeling toward an absent father figure.

This ambivalence brings up another problematic point in the play—its resolution. According to Morrow, "Lenny's birthday cake foreshadows her being surrounded by enduring and increasing circles of love" (37). Yet one is inclined to agree with Guerra's less sanguine conclusion. According to Guerra, Lenny's statement that the laughter of the sisters was just for a moment can only "remind the audience of the uncertain fates of these women and raise doubts that either their new closeness or their new selves can be sustained" (126). The resolution is uncertain because the ending is clearly linked to the sisters' reactions to Old Granddaddy. First, the mysterious, unrevealed birthday wish is closely connected to Lenny's first birthday wish that Old Granddaddy will be put out of his misery and to Babe's conclusion that birthday wishes sometimes "don't even count when you do have a cake" (96). Second, the final scene of the three sisters laughing replicates the previous laughter scene over Old Granddaddy's coma. Their laughter comes more out of hysteria than joy. Third, the scene in which the sisters begin to stuff themselves with an enormous birthday cake for breakfast reenacts Old Granddaddy's stuffing them full of banana splits for breakfast. Even though they have made some discoveries about themselves, their moment of laughter and their gorging of themselves with birthday cake can only offer them what Old Granddaddy has been offering them all along: solace and a life full of empty desserts. Perhaps those trapped in the world of the absent father can do no more than find ways to get through the bad days.

Despite its noticeable and much commented upon affinity to American Southern Gothic, *Crimes of the Heart*, like *'night, Mother*, is linked to an earlier dramatic tradition—the Chekhovian tradition. Adler feels that the "three MaGrath sisters bear little resemblance to Anton Chekhov's" (47); however, Jean Gagen and Joanne Karpinski have both uncovered remarkable similarities in *Crimes of the Heart* and Chekhov's *The Three Sisters*. Both critics find likenesses in the lives of the sisters. "Lenny, like Olga, has aged prematurely in a self-defeating effort to carry out a nurturing role and never expects to have a man" (Karpinski 230). Just as Lenny takes care of Old Granddaddy, Olga takes in Anfisa, the old family nurse (Gagen 119). Babe, like Masha, feels stuck in an unhappy marriage and finds a more sympathetic partner outside this bond. And like Meg, "Irina gets sidetracked in a meaningless job despite lofty career expectations and has doubts about making a commitment to a man that truly loves her" (Karpinski 230). Both plays are also full of the details of daily life (Gagen 120) and display "infiltrations of the comic into depictions of frustration, disenchantment, and failure" (Gagen 121), creating a "tragicomic tone" (Karpinski 234).

A more significant comparison lies in the structure of the two plays. Gagen notes that in both plays "most of the significant action, whether external or internal, takes place offstage and is reported" (120). This focus on offstage action sets up the drama of absent characters, the most noticeable being the absent father. Gagen notes that both plays have "invisible characters who never appear on stage, yet play significant roles in the action" (120). She points out the two absent fathers: the "father of the Prozorov sisters, who was responsible for bringing them to the provincial town which they despise" and "Old Granddaddy, who has been an obvious force in the lives of the MaGrath sisters" (120). Karpinski also notes how "both sets of sisters have inherited a suffocating value system, reinforced by emotional ties to a dominating male figure not present on stage" (230).

Both dramas open on the death or dying of an absent father figure. The first line of *The Three Sisters* is "It's exactly a year ago since father died" (73). In fact, Olga reenacts the death of the father. As the clock strikes twelve, she relives her father's death and says, "The clock struck twelve then too" (73). Early in the first act of *Crimes of the Heart*, Old Granddaddy's worsening condition is announced. Thus, the dying fathers are very present. Both plays combine death and dying of the father with the distorted celebration of a birthday. The anniversary of the Prozorov father's death and its reenactment in Olga's opening monologue takes place on Irina's name day, just like Lenny's birthday coincides with Old Granddaddy's dying. Both birthdays are filled with unusual celebrations. Chick gives Lenny a box of left-over Christmas candy, which Meg destroys. Irina's brother-in-law gives her a pedantic book which he had already given her as an Easter present. And the old doctor who was in love with Irina's mother (a spurious father figure) inappropriately gives her an anniversary present. In the world of the absent father, a celebration of renewal is tinged with incongruities, thus casting doubt on the efficacy of the celebration.

Both sets of sisters have been given unrealistic expectations by their absent fathers. Just as Old Granddaddy gave the MaGrath sisters unsuitable goals, the Prozorov father has overeducated his children. Andrew, the brother of the Prozorov sisters says "Our father . . . inflicted education on us" and "thanks to Father my sisters and I know French, German, and English, and Irina knows Italian too" (84). But Masha bemoans that in a small town this knowledge is a "useless luxury" like "having a sixth finger" (84). The father has raised them to expect a cultured life and then left them in a small town where they cannot reach their potential (Karpinski 232). Tied to a life of drudgery, Olga, like Lenny, feels "her youth and energy draining" and "would marry the first man who would come along provided he was decent and honest" (119). Masha, like Babe, married at eighteen. Like Babe, she married a man who would fit the expectations of her absent father. She thought her husband would be "the wisest of men," and he turned out to be a disappointment. Masha, a general's daughter, also remembers the officers that graced her father's parties. She believes that the "most civilized and cultured people are the military" (93). She engages in an affair with Vershinin, an officer who served in the same brigade as her father and knew him personally (another father substitute), and she is disappointed when he is sent away to Poland. Irina is also disappointed in her prospects for the future and in a prospective marriage partner. When most of the town is on fire, and her brother has mortgaged off the paternal estate, she can only say, "I can't remember the Italian word for 'window' or 'ceiling' either" (119). The education that her father gave her is receding into the past, just like his world. She realizes that she "is losing touch with everything fine and genuine in life" (119). Just as in *Ghosts* and *Miss Julie*, the world of her absent father is burning down around her, and the patriarchal estate is being jeopardized.

Both plays end with a final tableau of the three sisters together consoling one another and looking forward to better times. Gagen believes the MaGrath sisters have more "hope in the end" and Karpinski finds the ending of *Crimes of the Heart* to be in "a brighter key" (283) than the finale of *The Three Sisters*. Yet both plays are held bound by the attachment to the absent father. The MaGrath sisters are condemned to repeat Old Granddaddy's eating ritual and the Prozorov sisters listen to the "rousing tune" (139) of a military band which can be compared to the "band playing when they took father to the cemetery" (73). Significantly, his funeral was held on a day of "heavy rain and sleet" and just like Willy's funeral "not many people came" (73). Both plays end on a nostalgic longing for a childhood world and vague, uncertain hopes for the future.

The lost daughters in *'night, Mother*, *Hedda Gabler*, *Crimes of the Heart*, and *The Three Sisters* are all haunted by an absent father. The mysterious fathers have no first names. Daddy Cates, General Gabler, Old Granddaddy, and the Prozorov father are shady patriarchal figures connected with death and dying. They have all trapped their daughters in a world of illusion. As the daughters double or live out the dreams of the father, they find themselves facing death or a childhood world of dreams and fragile hopes. Whether the father represents a dying aristocratic order as he does in *Hedda Gabler* and *The Three Sisters*, the shallow values of materialistic success as in *Crimes of the Heart*, or the private world of withdrawal and renunciation of family as in *'night, Mother*, the trajectory of the daughter is propelled by his absence and what he represents.

CHAPTER 8

THE SEARCH FOR GOD, THE FATHER:
John Pielmeier's *Agnes of God*
Peter Shaffer's *Equus*

Like *'night, Mother* and *Crimes of the Heart*, John Pielmeier's *Agnes of God* focuses on the absence of a father; however, *Agnes of God* has never gained acceptance into the critical canon and thus has attracted very little critical attention. Reviewers accused the play of stooping "to cheap theatrics" (Hughes 382) and of being too "concerned with being theatrical" (Barnes "'God' Is Powered" 322). One critic concluded, *"Agnes of God* amounts to little more than old-fashioned melodrama" (Beaufort 325). Despite the negative reactions of reviewers and the neglect of academic critics, *Agnes of God* deserves just as careful an analysis as *'night, Mother* and *Crimes of the Heart*, for it recreates the dynamics of the absent father through several layers of the text, and unlike the other two plays, confronts the metaphysical dimension of the profound absence of the father.

Just like the MaGrath sisters Agnes is abandoned by a father and raised for a time by a "crazy" mother. Agnes, a lost child, is not only isolated from other children but also is physically and sexually abused by her deranged mother, who predicted that Agnes would have an illegitimate child. When her mother dies, Agnes seeks refuge in a convent and becomes a nun; however, Agnes fulfills a maternal prophecy and has a child. Like her own father, the father of Agnes' child is unidentified and absent. When Agnes is accused of strangling her illegitimate child, Dr. Martha Livingstone tries to determine if Agnes is sane, leaving the psychiatrist faced with the mystery of the virgin birth, the miraculous hand of God.

Agnes of God is structured around what Claude Levi-Strauss would call binary opposites (234) and is bound together by a series of external texts (especially those of Christian theology), which would fit the description of what Roland Barthes defines as cultural codes (205). Also, the play moves back and forth between the two extremes of the tragic and ironic modes as described by Northrop Frye. By examining the sets of binary opposites, explicating the plurality of texts, and tracing the patterns inherent in the mythos of tragedy and irony, the reader can discover an emerging pattern, a deep structure which shows an imbalance in the world order precipitated by the dominance of the Terrible Mother and the absence of the Spiritual Father, thus leaving the world order vulnerable to an illusory chain of meaningless substitutions. Living in a wasteland where the spiritual essence and the vital forces of procreation have been drained of significance, a hero/victim, in touch with the divine presence, seeks to transcend the world of illusions and to reincarnate the presence of the Spiritual Father. However, the world is controlled by the high priest of the God of Reason, who dissects the hero/victim, severing this hero from the Spiritual Father and creating a mechanistic world of bondage. Thus, the quest for the father leads to destruction.

But the drama is more than a metaphysical mystery play. It reaches deep into the mythic consciousness and brings to life the terror and pain of the primeval archetype known as the Earth Mother. In *The Great Code*, Frye describes the Earth Mother as *natura naturans*. As the "womb of all forms of life" as well as the "tomb of all forms of life," she "embodies the cycle of nature (birth, death, rebirth)—the eternal cycle of the seasons, night and day, sleeping and waking" (68). However, when she is in the cycle of death and the earth is barren, she takes on the form of the Terrible Mother. According to Erich Neuman, "Blood sacrifice and dismemberment belong to the fertility ritual of the Great Mother. Both fecundate the womb of the earth, as can be seen from the number of rites in which pieces of the victim—whether man or animal—are solemnly spread over the fields" (189). Jung points out that the negative side of the mother archetype "may connote anything secret, hidden, dark, the abyss, the world of the dead, anything that devours, seduces, and poisons, that is terrible and inescapable like fate" (*Four Archetypes* 17).

In *Agnes of God*, as in *The Pelican*, *Miss Julie*, and *The Basic Training of Pavlo Hummel*, the overwhelming presence of the Terrible Mother permeates the structure of the text. Early in the play, Mother Miriam Ruth, the mother superior in Agnes' convent, urges Dr. Livingstone not to call her "Mother" because "the word brings up the most unpleasant connotations in this day and age" (5). As far as the text is concerned the word "mother" radiates negative connotations.

Like Mother Miriam, Dr. Livingstone also has conflicting feelings about motherhood. In order to spite her mother, Dr. Livingstone becomes engaged to a Frenchman; however, when she becomes pregnant, she refuses to accept her role as mother: "I was pregnant and I didn't see myself as a . . . as well, my mother" (39). Since she is now childless, one can probably assume that her child was aborted, which is tantamount to murder in the code of Catholic theology. Dr. Livingstone has also stopped menstruating, cutting off the possibility of motherhood.

Mother Miriam is called mother even though as a nun she is required to take the vow of chastity. In her case the sign *Mother* is empty of significance. However, the play pulls a twist. Mother Miriam is no ordinary nun since her vocation is a belated one. Being a widow with two angry daughters who have disowned her, she admits her "failure as wife and mother" (48).

Even worse is Agnes' mother, a severely disturbed alcoholic who ridicules Agnes' naked body and molests the young girl by burning her genitals with a cigarette. In the voices buried in Agnes' psyche, her mother comes forth as the omnipresent force of the Terrible Mother, mocking Agnes, prophesying that

Agnes will have an illegitimate child, and labeling Agnes as "a mistake" (59). Like the harpies and witches of old, Agnes' mother looms over the world of the drama as a thoroughly malignant power.

Even the innocent, loving Agnes doesn't want to be a mother. After the birth of her daughter, Agnes "tied the cord around her [daughter's] neck, wrapped her in the bloody sheets and stuffed her in the trash can" (108). The umbilical cord, the sign of maternal nurturing, is turned into a noose, a deadly instrument of strangulation.

The traits of the Terrible Mother not only inflict the major characters but also pollute the entire world order. Menstruating nuns have only the unfulfilled "possibility of motherhood" (52). Yet, as surrogate mothers, these nuns wreak destruction. The mother superior who is supposed to watch over Marie (Dr. Livingstone's sister) refuses to call a doctor, allowing Marie to die of appendicitis. Dr. Livingstone's first grade teacher explains the death of the doctor's innocent friend as the wrath of God coming down to punish a little girl for neglecting her morning prayers. In *Agnes of God*, the word "mother" indeed has "unpleasant connotations." The world of the play is haunted by the forces of a sinister maternity, torturing, abandoning, maiming, killing the innocent

However, the world is out of balance not only because the Earth Mother shows only her dark side, but also because the spirit of the father is absent. In *Agnes of God*, the text is rife with absent fathers. Dr. Livingstone never mentions her father (absent from the discourse). As for Maurice, the father of Dr. Livingstone's child, Dr. Livingstone hasn't "thought of him in years" (39) (absent from memory). Mother Miriam never discusses the father of her daughters except to acknowledge his death (absent from the living). Agnes' father could have been "any one of a dozen men" (64) (absent as an identity). Agnes even sees fatherhood in terms of absence. She says, "Bad babies cry a lot and make their fathers go away" (24).

This absence of the father plays a part in the central enigma of the text: "Who is the father of Agnes' child?" Mother Miriam wants to believe that God allowed the ovum in Agnes' womb to divide on its own, thus obliterating the very concept of paternity (absent from existence). However, the mystery surrounding the father of Agnes' child moves into a higher sphere. Is the father of her child a man, or is he God? On this point the text is ambiguous.

When Agnes describes the "man" who came into her room, she states, "He sees me" (103). Later in confusion, she says, "I hate him" (105). When finally pushed to identify the "man," she says, "God did it to me . . . I hate Him" (105). The script always uses the upper-case letter to indicate the deity and the lower-case letter to indicate mortals. To complicate this matter, Agnes describes the vision of a beautiful being with the "moon shining down on Him" (109). "He opened His wings" (109) and lay on top of her. Is the father of Agnes' child a man, or is He God? This strange ambiguity is built into the text. Since

Agnes is not writing these statements, she could have no way of indicating whether she is using "him" or "Him". Capitalization is a function of written discourse. In fact, no actress could indicate whether she is saying "him" or "Him." An unidentified and absent voice buried in the discourse has manipulated the linguistic code to create ambiguity.

In the final analysis, the text does not resolve the ambiguity. After Agnes relives her alleged rape and the murder of her daughter, she sings a song about Charlie, who went to town to get his girl some candy. Dr. Livingstone wonders if this story is a seduction song or "simply a remembered lullaby" (111)—a lullaby one could attribute to an absent father.

Is the father of Agnes' child a man, or is he God the Father? Both seem to be absent. The text of the play has overdetermined the code of female relationships. *Agnes of God* is about mothers, daughters (Mother Miriam's two angry daughters, Agnes' daughter), and sisters (Dr. Livingstone's dead sister, Agnes' mother, who is Mother Miriam's sister). In such a text even the Divinity is a mother. Mother Miriam says about saints, "occasionally one might appear among us attached to God. But we cut the cord very quickly" (72). In other words, divine grace flows through God the Mother's umbilical cord.

Yet the play is heavily coded in the text of Catholic theology which envisions deity in terms of fathers and sons. This patriarchal God seems absent from the text; however, he has not disappeared altogether, for he is hidden in the counter text of the Catholic Mass, sung in Latin, a dead language understood by the privileged initiates. Agnes, who embodies the voice of God, sings sections from the Catholic Mass, a drama symbolizing a father's sacrifice of his only son in order to redeem the world. The "Gloria" states, "Agnus Dei, Filius Patris, Qui tollis peccata mundi" (12). ("Lamb of God, Son of the Father who takes away the sins of the world") and the "Credo" professes belief: "Et in unum Dominum Jesum Christum, Filium Dei unigenitum. Et ex Patre natum ante omnia saecula . . . Genitum, non factum, consubstantialem Patri per quem omnia facta sunt" (38). ("In one Lord, Jesus, the only begotten Son of the Father, born of the Father, before all ages. Begotten, not made, of one being with the Father by whom all things were made"). In the text of Catholic theology, God the Father and God the Son are one. There is no Mother in the Deity. According to orthodox Catholic theology, the Virgin Mary or Blessed Mother is given a privileged status among humankind as the mother of the human Christ, but she is not divine. The Father "begot" the Son, an act of male creation. Also, the only way to reach the Father is through the Son. The Judeo-Christian God is a patriarch who stands outside of that cycle of birth and death that is ingrained in the Earth Mother. Frye notes:

> The maleness of God seems to be connected with the Bible's resistance
> to the notion of a containing cycle of fate and inevitability as the

highest category that our minds can. All such cycles are suggested by nature—which is why it is so easy to think of nature as Mother Nature. (*Great Code* 107)

In *Agnes of God* the absence of the father (men) becomes connected with the central enigma of the play, the identity of the father of Agnes' child (God or man), thus linking the absence of the father to the absence of God, the Father who remains hidden in the counter text of the Catholic Mass.

With the absence of the Spiritual Father, the ascendancy of the Terrible Mother, and the descent of the dying god (the final stages of the tragic cycle), humans are alienated from God and thrust into a wasteland composed of a prison-house of endless substitutions. These substitutions are reflected in the two mother figures battling for control of Agnes. In *Agnes of God*, Dr. Livingstone sees her struggle with God in terms of her struggle with her mother, taunting her mother with claims that "God was a moronic fairy tale" (39). When her mother dies, she becomes obsessed with smoking: "Smoking is an obsession with me. I started smoking when my mother died. She's an obsession too. I'll stop smoking when I become obsessed with something else" (23). She does stop when she becomes obsessed with Agnes, a substitute for her sister Marie, whose death in a convent led Dr. Livingstone to abandon religion. She is caught in the bondage of substitutions. Her conflict with God is projected onto her mother (a parent), then to the smoking of cigarettes (objects). In like manner, her conflict with God is transformed to her unresolved anger over her sister's death, then to her obsession with Agnes' problems. Also, Mother Miriam, who stopped hearing the voice of God when she was six years old, seeks it in an unsuccessful family life for which she substitutes an empty religious vocation. She too is struggling to hear the voice of God through Agnes. Moving away from direct spiritual contact with God, the Father, both women are caught in a chain of substitutions.

Into the world of substitutions enters a hero/victim, Agnes, a lost daughter who can claim only God as her father. She has the illusion that she can break the cycle of substitutions and replace it with a cycle of transcendence in order that she might reach a union with the divine presence of the father. She attempts to achieve perfect unity with the father. Following the text of Christian theology, she transcends the material world and reincarnates the presence of the Spiritual Father through union with God, the Son. In the text of Christian theology, the Father and the Son are one, and the Father can only be reached through the Son. In moving away from the endless cycle of the Terrible Mother, Agnes reinstates the presence of the Spiritual Father.

Agnes moves toward transcendence by transforming her alcoholic, abusive mother into a good mother—a saint who knows the future and prophesies Agnes' entry into the convent: "She did love me and she was a good woman, a saint"

(45). When the Terrible Mother ("Mummy") is pulling Agnes down, Agnes looks up to the Lady who throws down "a big hook" (24) to pull Agnes up. The Lady, with a capital L, is Our Lady, the Blessed Mother, who appears in the heavens. According to the doctrine of the Assumption (text of Catholic theology), the Mother of God was assumed into Heaven, subverting the cycle of death. It is "the Lady" who allows Agnes to sing. Agnes has not only converted her mother into a good mother, but she has divided mother into "Mummy" and "the Lady," thus elevating her mother to the position of the Blessed Mother.

But Agnes goes one step further, for she sees the Lady with "holes in her hands and her side" (24). The Lady becomes the crucified Christ, the Son of God. Agnes goes even higher up the scale of transcendence, for she elevates her human suffering into the visible suffering of Christ through the stigmata. Agnes is truly united with Christ, for she physically suffers his crucifixion. She transforms the senseless suffering of a battered and deserted child into the redemptive suffering of the Son of God, hence, "Agnus Dei qui tollis peccata mundi" ("Lamb of God who takes away the sins of the world"). Agnes (which means lamb) becomes the Lamb of God. This symbol raises the sacrificial victim beyond the status of the pharmakos to the status of the Redeemer God. According to the *New Catholic Encyclopedia*:

> The symbolism of the paschal lamb, the sacrifice of Christ, is not presented in the manner of a substitution where the victim bears the sins of others and expiates them by undergoing their punishment . . . it is not said that the Lamb bears, but that He takes away sin. ("Lamb of God")

In other words, Christ is no mere mimetic substitute. His sacrifice actually expiates sins. Thus, the sign (suffering) is filled with plenitude (the redemptive suffering of Christ, the Lamb of God). Agnes has transformed the suffering of schizophrenia (the demonic) into the exaltation of the Lamb of God (the apocalyptic) (Frye *Anatomy* 141–42). Also, by reinstating God, the Son, she reinstates God, the Father, for they are one (text of Christian theology). Thus, Agnes doubles the Father through doubling the Son.

However, in the modern, scientific world, such a transcendent union is rendered illusory by rational analysts like Dr. Livingstone. Transcendence is seen as a defense mechanism used by a psychotic. Reaching for the Divine Father in a world that no longer believes in miracles is a dangerous quest. Agnes' special union with the father is seen as the illusion of a psychotic who murdered her child. After confronting the repressed memory of her crime, Agnes loses her ability to sing and dies in an insane asylum. In a rational world, union with the Sacred Father becomes a dangerous illusion leading to destruction. Like other lost children, Agnes lives in a wasteland of psychosis and sexual abuse. She seeks to escape her situation by trying to reach a Transcendental Father, but her quest leads her to insanity and death.

Agnes of God can stand on its own as a drama that centers on the search for an absent father; however, few critics can analyze *Agnes of God* without mentioning its similarity to Peter Shaffer's earlier play *Equus*, a play which has attracted considerable critical attention. From its opening performance on Broadway, *Agnes of God* has paled in comparison to *Equus*. Frank Rich noted that Pielmeier "replays *Equus* . . . but this time the rhetoric is usually as pedantic as the sentiments and there is no horse in sight" ("Stage: '*Agnes of God*'" 321). Clive Barnes found that both plays "are essentially explorations into the unusual individual . . . the one touched by God," but that *Equus* is "a better crafted play" ("'God' is Powered" 322–23). Richard Corliss simply calls *Agnes of God* "an off-center *Equus*" (323). Critics are right to note the similarities between the two plays, for there are many. David Richards points out just a few of them: "a bizarre crime with mystical overtones, perpetuated by a seeming innocent; an atheistic doctor in search of hard and fast answers; an inquest that unfolds partially in flashbacks, and finally a last-minute seance of hypnosis where the deed that has tantalized us all evening is reenacted" (D1). William Hutchings notes further similarities such as the two-act structure, the self-confessing opening monologue, the bare set, and the role reversal between analyst and patient (140–42). One might go even further to say that both authors employed a similar process in writing their plays. Both plays were inspired by a real-life event of which the author had very little details. Someone told Shaffer about a boy who blinded horses, and Pielmeier saw a newspaper headline about a nun who murdered a baby. Neither author bothered to investigate the bizarre incident, but later reflected on it as an inspiration for an ontological drama. Pielmeier himself admits the likenesses between the two plays, but notes that they differ in theme: "There are a lot of similarities, but I think they're surface similarities. . . . Both plays are about psychiatrists dealing with violent young people. Yet *Agnes* is about belief, and *Equus*, although I cannot speak for Shaffer, seems to be about passion. . . . They're very different things" (Thomas 6:6). However, the comparison between the two plays is more than a surface comparison; it goes down into the deep structure of the two plays where passion and belief are not that different and where *Equus* repeats the same quest for an absent Spiritual Father that was found in *Agnes of God*.

In *Equus* the configuration of the Terrible Mother is not as clearly formulated as in *Agnes of God*; yet it is firmly embedded in the code of sterility (a key element in the play's text) and is displayed through the guise of the siren who lures the hero away from his God. In order to depict the barrenness and sterility of the world order, *Equus* shows married women as frigid, cold, and unwilling to engage in sex. Dora Strang, Alan's mother, deprives her husband of sexual contact and "doesn't give him anything" (466). Dysart's marriage is one of "antiseptic proficiency" (437), for he hasn't kissed his wife in six years. Jill's mother is a man-hater who is rude to Jill's dates. These women have removed themselves from the cycle of fertility, leaving the world barren and sterile.

However, in *Equus*, the Terrible Mother is not only displayed in the coldness of the witch but also in the seductive terror of the siren who ensnares victims into her world of illusion. Jill constantly talks to Alan about sex. She sees horses' eyes as "sexy," talks about kissing horses as a "substitute" for sex, and finds men's eyes sexier than their "bottoms" (461). She lures Alan into a pornographic movie house where he witnesses female nudity for the first time. This pornographic theatre is the house of illusions, the primitive world of the anima, the devouring female spirit who enslaves men to the bonds of compulsion (von Franz 191). Ultimately, Jill seduces Alan in the barn, the very temple of his God, Equus. Stripped naked, the couple openly attempt to commit fornication in the "Holy of Holies" (469). Like the Grail Knight, Alan succumbs to the wiles of the temptress, losing his purity and defiling the House of God.

Jill is the negative anima, the femme fatale, a version of the Terrible Mother turned temptress. To be entrapped by her is to live in the dangerous world of illusion. In "The Process of Individuation," M. L. von Franz notes the "negative mother anima" leads men toward depression and impotence. She becomes the "death demon" or "femme fatale" which "symbolizes destructive illusion" (187). Alan tries to achieve union with Jill, but he is haunted by the face of Equus, his God. Equus demands fidelity: "Kiss anyone and I will see" (474). Alan is pulled away from his union with God into the clutches of a deceptive siren who haunts Frye's world of demonic irony (*Anatomy* 238). Thus, the Terrible Mother in all her guises wreaks havoc.

Like *Agnes of God*, *Equus* also focuses on the absent father. In *Equus*, the absence of the father as a hidden version of the male deity is played out in the diminishing of the father's function through sterility or impotence. For example, Dysart has the "lowest sperm count you can find" (455). Frank, a voyeur, substitutes pornography for sexual union with a wife who sees sex as part of a religious experience. Although Frank is Alan's father, Alan demystifies the concept of fatherhood. Looking at men in general, he says "They're not just dads—they're people with pricks. And Dad—he's not just Dad. He's a man with a prick too" (466). The privileged position of fatherhood is reduced to ordinary "maleness." Even Alan has lost the potential to become a father, for he is impotent. When he tries to have sex, Equus warns him, "You will fail: Forever and ever you will fail. You will see ME—and you will FAIL!" (474). Like *Agnes of God*, *Equus* displays fatherhood as absent or diminished. Dysart can't be a father; Frank has lost the status of "Dad," and is now a voyeur who has stopped procreating; Alan is impotent, unable to perform the procreating act.

Yet also, like *Agnes of God*, *Equus* has a counter text. Through the voice of sacred scriptures (the text of Christian theology), God, the father is heard in the voice of Equus. In order to bring forth Equus, Alan goes through a series of "begats." Tracing male lineage is a crucial issue in the text of Christian theology. Christ, the Messiah, must be descended from the House of David. Through a ritual chant of the "begats" (the father's power to procreate), Alan conjures up Equus: "And Spankus begat Spankus, the Great, who lived three score years . . . and Neckwus begat Fleckwus, the King of Spit." And finally, he says, "Behold—I give you Equus, my only begotten Son" (428–9). This voice is unmistakably the voice of God, the Father, and corresponds directly to the text of the Catholic Mass heard in *Agnes of God*. God, the Father is heard in the voice of Equus, but Equus only speaks through Alan and Dysart. The spiritual Father is hidden under layers of texts. Thus, God is hidden (absent yet present). In discussing tragedy, Lucien Goldmann states: "That God should be always absent and always present is the real centre of the tragic vision" (37). This corresponds with Frye's view of tragedy as the point on the mythic cycle when the god is dying, fading away into complete absence (*Anatomy* 21–2). In both *Equus* and *Agnes of God*, the Father God is absent and must be brought into presence.

Just like in *Agnes of God*, the whole world in *Equus* is moving farther away from a sense of oneness with the divine presence and is vanishing into a hall of mirrors. Jill kisses horses as a substitute for sex. Sexual encounters are substituted for religious ecstasy. Mother Miriam complains, "The closest thing we come to a miracle today is in bed, and we give up everything for it. Including those bits of light that might still by the smallest chance, be clinging to our souls, reaching back to God" (71). Frank Strang exemplifies the extreme case of the cycle of substitutions. For sexual union he substitutes pornography, which becomes the religion of absence. First, Frank Strang reduces religion to "bad sex" (415). Then, his son Alan sees "bad sex" as bogus religion. Alan describes the porno house: "All around they were looking. All the men—staring up like they were in church. They were a sort of congregation" (463). For union with God, men have substituted sexual union; for sexual union, they have substituted the watching of sexual union. For the watching of sexual union, they have substituted the watching of simulated sexual union since in pornographic movies the sex act may only seem to take place, or if it does take place, the feelings are acted out and not spontaneous. For the watching of simulated sexual union, they have substituted the watching of a moving picture of simulated sexual union—Substitutio ad nauseum. A depletion of the sign.

More than any other character, Dysart is aware that he is trapped in a chain of substitutions. Dysart longs to reach the passion of pagan worship. His wife reduces the sacred acrobats to "absurred" (435) freaks and equates the heroes of the Iliad with "ruffians" (436). He cries out, "Oh the primitive world . . .

what instinctual truths were lost with it" (455). Alienated and alone, Dysart knows he has lost contact with these primitive truths and is hopelessly trying to regain them. For communicating with the gods, Dysart substitutes the vicarious experience of reading books on "the cultural shelf" (455). Instead of reaching up to the gods, he brings home "Kodachrome snaps of Mount Olympus" (455). The power of the gods rests in the Hellenic pantheon. Mount Olympus is a metonymic substitution for the Hellenic gods, and a photograph is an iconic representation of a metonymic substitution. Also, Dysart touches "a reproduction statue of Dionysus" (455). The power and essence of the god is replaced by the physical presence of the god, which is replaced by the statue of the god, which is replaced by a reproduction of the statue. Again the power of the sign has been depleted. Union with God becomes the touching of a reproduction of a statue (metonymic substitution). Cut off from the presence of the Divine, the world is saturated with reproduced objects. All that is left of "the glory that was Greece and the grandeur that was Rome" are "four bottles of Chianti to make into lamps and two china condiment donkeys labeled Sally and Peppy" (436). The world is flooded with meaningless idols paying homage to "the Hosts of Philco" and "the Hosts of Remington" (447). Man is obsessed with a boundless series of fetishes. The power of the sign has been depleted. Man has moved from the signified (communion with God) to the diminished signifier (a world of material reproductions).

Like Agnes, Alan also escapes the world of substitution by moving into the world of transcendence. When his father replaces the picture of "Our Lord on his way to Calvary" (423) with the picture of a horse, Alan does not substitute the horse for God; he turns the horse into God. He takes the fairy tale story of Prince, whom no one could ride but his young master, and combines it with his mother's story about American natives, who, upon viewing the Christian cavalry, "thought that the horse and rider were one . . . a god!" (412); then he reinterprets the nature of the horse in the *Book of Job*. The horse in the *Book of Job* signifies the power of God. But for Alan, the power of the horse (the signifier) is the power of God (the signified). The signifier and the signified are one. Alan elevates fairy tale, legend, and scriptures to turn a horse into a god. But this action is not substitution. The union of horse and rider is the union of God and man.

But Equus is no pagan idol; he is unmistakably the Judeo-Christian God, "born in the straw" (442) (stable of Bethlehem) and wearing the "sandals" (444) of Christ. As Christ suffered for mankind, Equus "takes the punishment" for Alan's sake. The Ark of the Covenant symbolizing the contract between God and man becomes the "Ark of the Manbit" (445), which Alan holds in his mouth. The lump of sugar becomes Equus' "Last Supper" (446). Alan beckons Equus, "Take my sins. Eat them for my sake" (446). Equus is Jesus, the Son of God, the Redeemer who takes away the sins of the world. Just as Christ launched his attack against the House of Mammon, Alan launches Equus against their mutual "foes": "The Hosts of Philco" and "The Hosts of Remington" (447), the rulers of the shallow and materialistic world of substitutions. Equus is Alan's redeemer, the "Godslave" (446). This use of oxymoron is described by Joseph Campbell as "a device to point past those spheres of opposites by which all logical thought is limited . . . We term such speech anagogical (from the Greek verb . . . 'to lead upward') because it points beyond itself, beyond speech" (88-9). The term Godslave is not only a form of anagogical speech, but it is also a concept central to the texts of Christian theology. Frye notes:

> Jesus' claim that he was a real king, though of a spiritual kingdom "not of this world," while at the same time behaving like a servant . . . is intended . . . to resolve the master-slave dialectic on which the whole of human history turns. History symbolically ends at the point at which master and slave become the same person and represent the same thing (*Great Code* 91).

Through the anagogical concept of Godslave, Alan uses Jesus, who is hidden behind Equus, to transcend the cycle of history, which Frye links with the master/slave dialectic, and thus, Alan goes beyond the Marxism of his biological father. Finally, Alan achieves unity with God. Since Alan was taught to see sex as a "spiritual" matter leading to a "higher love," he elevates the sexual union into a spiritual union—"the two shall be one" (text of Christian theology)—and finally moves this union to a higher plane, the union of God and man: "Equus, I love you! Now! Bear me away! Make us One Person" (448). Georg Lukacs explains this concept of union by comparing the mystic to the tragic hero: "The former leads across the deeply personal world of his ecstasies; the latter loses selfhood at that moment of his highest exaltation" (82). Like Agnes, who suffers the stigmata, Alan, with the Manbit in his mouth, elevates human suffering to the position of tragedy, reincarnates the Spiritual Father, and achieves union with the divine presence, transcending the world of substitutions. But he, like Agnes, will encounter a greater threat than the world of substitution. Both come face to face with the scourge of modern times, the ultimate threat to spiritual union—the terror of dissection. Sparagmos.

In both plays the hero/victims try to reset the imbalance in the world order; however, they both come under the spells of rational analysts who embrace the philosophy of the intellectual father and who proceed to dissect the divine presence. After explaining how the Earth Mother has been reduced to mere matter (objects and substitutes), Jung states, "what was the spirit is now identified with the intellect and thus ceases to be the Father of All. It has degenerated to the limited ego-thoughts of man; the immense emotional energy expressed in the image 'Our Father' vanishes into the sand of an intellectual desert" ("Approaching" 85).

The texts of both plays are heavily encoded with the images of dissection. Psychoanalysts are surgeons of the mind, cutting up innocent victims. In *Equus*, the stage is set up like a "dissecting theatre" (399). Dysart, whose name sounds like dissect, dreams of dissecting children. He "slices them elegantly down to the navel" (477), always "cutting and snipping" at their minds, able only to pull them apart, not to give them "passion" (476). In the end, he says, "I stand in the dark with a pick in my hand, striking heads" (476). As the high priest of the "God of Health" (440), he reduces children's sublime exaltations to the banality of the normal: "The Ordinary made beautiful . . . the Average made lethal" (440) and cuts "from them the parts of their individuality repugnant to this God, parts sacred to rarer and more wonderful Gods" (440). Although he realizes that there is "nothing worse one can do to anybody than take away their worship" (453), he separates Alan from the God Equus.

Images of dissection also appear in *Agnes of God*. Dr. Livingstone is a "surgeon" who will "cut open" Agnes' mind and "take her apart" (97). Dr. Livingstone also has dreams of cutting people up, of being a midwife ready "to cut the baby out" (95). She is always ready to "cut the cord" of anyone "attached to God" (72). Agnes accuses her: "I know what you want. You want to take God away" (46).

Both Dysart and Dr. Livingstone are rational analysts. Dysart, who can't even conceive of Equus without being "subversive" (402), realizes that the fundamental questions "have no place in a consulting room" (450). He can only speak in what Frye calls descriptive discourse—a discourse which holds that "the criterion of reality is the source of sense experiences in the order of nature, where God is not found and 'gods' are no longer believed in" (*Great Code* 15). Although Dysart wants to believe in a world that is "only comprehensible through a thousand local Gods" (438), he cannot reach beyond the limits of his discourse. Neither can Dr. Livingstone. Pointing to her head, she says, "I realized that my religion is this. The mind. Everything I do not understand in this world is contained in these few cubic inches . . . God is not out there . . . he's in here" (16).

Both analysts view human beings as dissected entities. Dr. Livingstone sees Agnes as "the sum of her psychological parts" (91). Dora rejects the psychoanalytical concept that the individual is a series of parenting voices. She warns Dysart, "Every soul is itself. If you added up everything we ever did to him, from his first day on earth to this, you wouldn't find why he did this terrible thing" (451). Yet both rational analysts are trapped by the limits of descriptive discourse. Dysart cannot understand the fundamental; Dr. Livingstone cannot accept the miraculous. Mother Miriam explains these limitations: "Miracle is an event without an explanation. That's why people like you fail to believe, because you demand an explanation, and when you don't get one, you create one" (88).

And so the rational analysts reduce the language of the sacred to the language of pathology; the apocalyptic to the demonic. Those "special" or "touched" by God are "neurotic" and "sick." Union with God becomes "hysteria." According to Frank Strang, another rational analyst, the Passion of Christ is seen as "an innocent man tortured to death" (415). The Savior is reduced to a pharmakos; the sacred becomes the sadistic. Mother Miriam describes the world of the rational analysts: "No freaks here. We're all solid sensible men and women . . . Our minds dissected, our bodies cut open . . . No God up there, no heaven, no hell. Well we're better off. Less disease" (71). Goldmann explains:

> The God of the rationalist . . . is no longer man's guardian; he has become a general and universal rule which guarantees man's right to free himself . . . But at the same time, he leaves man alone in the face of a silent and static world of things and individuals (37–8).

What is left of the dissected world is indeed Jung's "intellectual desert."

Ultimately, the rational analysts have the final victory. Their victims are put under hypnosis or given placebos, what Dysart calls "tricks," demystified magic. Under these spells Agnes is forced to reenact the murder of her child; Alan, the blinding of his God. The voice of the Terrible Mother is summoned up. Agnes hears the voice of "Mummy" beckoning her to kill her child, "God's mistake" (107). Alan hears the voice of his Mother ("God sees you" (427) in the taunts of Equus ("God seest. God seest" (474).

What is left is not a world of tragedy, but a world of irony as defined by Frye, a world of "prisons, madhouses . . . the nightmare of social tyranny" (*Anatomy* 238–39). Agnes goes to the asylum, stops singing, stops eating, stops living. The instrument of God is silenced, a victim of a false society—a society which Raymond Williams explains thus: "Society is not merely a false system, which the liberator can challenge. It is actively destructive and evil claiming its victims because they are alive" (104). The ironic world prevails.

Alan lives, but his fate is worse than death because he must conform to the Normal. Frye describes this conformist world as demonic. He states, "the demonic human world is a society held together by a kind of molecular tension of egos, loyalty to group or leader which diminishes the individual" (*Anatomy* 147). Alan will enter the assembly line where his "private parts will become as plastic as the products of the factory to which he will be sent" (476). He will enter Frye's City of Destruction, "the labyrinthine modern metropolis, where the main modern stress is on loneliness and lack of communication" (*Anatomy* 155). His "Field of Ha Ha" will be exchanged for "Normal Places . . . multi-laned highways driven through the guts of cities." He will "feel nothing at his fork but Approved Flesh . . . without much passion" (476).

But what is most terrible of all is that Alan's God will be diminished. The mighty horse Equus will be reduced to a "nice mini-scooter." "He will trot on his metal pony through the concrete evenings" (476). Finally, he will trade in his scooter for a car run on horsepower. The power of the sign is again diminished. The Living God is reduced to a machine.

In both plays, the search for union with the father leaves the protagonists open to a process of demystification that returns them helpless to the rational wasteland. Given the world order in which they live, their quest to reach the spiritual father and to go beyond the physical confines of their everyday environment is ultimately a destructive one.

CHAPTER 9

BATTLING WITH GOD, THE FATHER:
Peter Shaffer's *Amadeus*

Equus is not the only play by Shaffer that treats the absent father; *Amadeus* also focuses on the search for the father. In both plays, lost sons are searching to reach God, the Father. Each play has a rational son who cannot understand or achieve the creative ecstasy of a more passionate son. *Amadeus* was a successful play both in London (1979) and in New York (1980), where it garnered five Tony Awards. Peter Shaffer won a Tony for best play and got an Academy Award for the screenplay of the movie version of *Amadeus* (1984). Despite acclaim, many critics attacked Shaffer's approach to *Amadeus*. Stanley Kauffmann accused Shaffer of creating a large-scale production and reducing it "with gimmicks" (79). Janet Karston Larson affirmed Kauffmann's assessment, noting that "gimmicks and slapstick keep a play going that has nowhere to go" (580). Robert Brustein also considered *Amadeus* to be "overinflated costume drama masquerading as a tragedy" ("Triumph" 23). On the opposite side, London critic Michael Billington enjoyed the spectacle but criticized Shaffer for trying to "elevate the play into a majestic homily on the death of a god" (11).

Shaffer is one of the few playwrights who is taking on the grand theme of the search for God, which puts him in the tradition of Eugene O'Neill among the moderns. O'Neill was interested in "The death of the old God and the failure of science and materialism to give any satisfactory new one for the surviving religious instinct to find a meaning for life in" (Krutch xvii). Like O'Neill, Shaffer states that he faces a struggle "between the secular side of me, the fact that I have never actually been able to buy anything of the official religion—and the inescapable fact that to me a life without the sense of the divine is perfectly meaningless" (qtd. in Connell 7).

Shaffer's plays focus squarely on a search for God, who seems to be unreachable or unfathomable. He is haunted by an image of a dying God. His plays like *Royal Hunt of the Sun*, *Equus*, and *Amadeus* arise from apocalyptic images "seeking their confirmation in public show . . . the Sun God dead in his square, the Horse God dead in his stable, the God in music dying in his slum" (Shaffer *Observer* 37). Michael Hinden places Shaffer's work in the older modernist tradition, noting "For many of the postmodernists the passing of God, philosophy, and religious institutions is no more a matter of concern as it is a foregone conclusion" (50). Shaffer, however, is "obsessed with man's longing for divinity" (50).

From its opening scene, *Amadeus* is a drama played out before an absent God. Although Mozart's music explodes throughout the drama, *Amadeus* "fills the theatre with the mocking heavenly silence that is the overwhelming terror of life" (Rich "Theater: '*Amadeus*'" 65). Even the audience is left in a quandary because the play's actions "are not validated by the presence of an anthropomorphized God who could confirm the audience's judgement" (Arens 167). *Amadeus* falls into a pattern found in Shaffer's later dramas. T. E. Kalem notes that in Shaffer's later plays "Two men are pitted against each other under the baleful and indifferent eye of a God who is present but never made manifest" ("Blood Feud" 67). Shaffer's dramas definitely explore the absence of God, but this God in *Amadeus* is connected to the Father, who is also absent.

Along with the attack on what they felt was Shaffer's shallow depiction of a trumped-up existential conflict, critics objected vehemently to Shaffer's depiction of Mozart (Barber 15; Fenton 43; Nightingale 735). Although Shaffer admits that he is writing drama, not history, he holds that his depiction of Mozart as puerile, undisciplined, foul-mouthed, and arrogant has a basis in fact. Another area of contention concerns the influence of Mozart's father, Leopold, over his son Wolfgang. Admitting that Leopold did manipulate and exploit his son, Jeffrey Berman believes that "there is no evidence that Mozart fell apart upon hearing of Leopold's death . . . or that the composer remained permanently haunted by the image of his father" (562). C. J. Gianakaris, however, finds that Shaffer is "accurate in creating the image of a nagging and guilt-projecting father" ("Fair Play" 131).

The question of historical accuracy is a matter of deciphering sources and verifying their reliability, but the question of the absent father in *Amadeus* and his effect on Mozart is clear. Rich feels that "Mozart's father . . . is dragged into the text (but never on stage) in a last-minute effort to produce a gratuitous Freudian analysis of his son's life and opera librettos" ("Theatre: 'Amadeus'" 64). But the absent father is not just a gratuitous motif. Gianakaris notes: "Though Shaffer did not write a part for Leopold in *Amadeus*, the elder Mozart nonetheless exists as a strong presence, affecting the hero's attitudes and actions at every turn" ("Fair Play" 131).

In general, Shaffer's plays dwell on father and son conflicts. According to Berman, in Shaffer's drama "the father is the origin of both creativity and psychopathology. There is not a single loving father-son relationship in any of his plays" (575). Dennis A. Klien confirms this assessment, stating, "Fathers and sons have been alienated in Shaffer's works since his 1957 radio play 'The Prodigal Father'" (35).

Amadeus is clearly a drama of fathers and sons. In the play, Salieri, a lost son, rejects the mediocre world of his earthly father in order to bargain with an ideal Heavenly Father. Under the illusion that he can achieve immortal fame in a paradise world, Salieri seeks to become an extension of God, the Father, to become his instrument. However, like other lost sons, he finds himself condemned to a wasteland where he can only duplicate the mediocrity of the earthly father he sought to reject. Like Salieri, Mozart is also haunted by an absent father who has rendered him an eternal child. Rebelling against the father and the father figures of the court leaves Mozart in a wasteland of poverty where his genius goes unrecognized. The lives of both Salieri and Mozart are intertwined around the figure of the absent father as Salieri attempts to become both Mozart's avenging father and an evil minister of God, the Father. In the end, Mozart regresses to the infantile world, a world dominated by the father, and Salieri sinks into senility. Both are destroyed in their attempts to appease or rebel against the absent father.

Amadeus opens with the aged Salieri, an author/narrator, summoning up The Ghosts of the Future, his audience whom he will detain from 3:00 a.m. to 6:00 a.m. As he is about to die, he gives his version of Mozart's death. Preparing to kill himself, he tells how he killed Mozart. In pretence, he has begged Mozart's forgiveness just like Mozart implored the forgiveness of his own father, Leopold. Salieri's conjuring up of the audience compares to his "raising of gods" (7) in the invocations of his operas; thus the audience members become godlike, ideal fathers, and Salieri implores them, "Be my confessors" (5). Now they become father confessors, representatives of the divine father. The play opens with the dying Salieri promising to reenact the death of Mozart, thereby trying to connect himself to Mozart through parallel death narratives. Also, by using the audience as representatives of the divine Father, Salieri plays out his drama before an Absent Father God. William Sullivan rightly affirms about *Amadeus*: "Over all, there hovers the figure of God, the Father, variously conceived by both protagonists" (49).

Salieri next begins to tell about his rise to fame. First, Salieri rejects the lifestyle of his absent father, "a Lombardy merchant" whose notion of God was "a superior Hapsburg emperor" who would "protect commerce and keep them forever preserved in mediocrity" (7). Inspired as a young boy to music, "God's art" (8), Salieri desires "to join all the composers who celebrated His glory through the long Italian past" (8). Salieri wants to escape his own father and follow the glorious patriarchs of the past who served God through music, a group of ideal fathers. Salieri then decides to bargain with God, "an old candle-smoked God, staring at the world with dealer's eyes" (8). In dealing with his "God of Bargains" (8), Salieri wants fame in exchange for a life of virtue, good works, and service to God through music. When his projected God tells Salieri "Go forth, Antonio, and serve me and all mankind and you will be blessed" (8), Salieri then promises to be "God's servant for life" (8). Soon his prayers are answered as a kindly father figure pays for his music education in Vienna and he is taken into favor by Emperor Franz Joseph II, another surrogate father.

Unbeknownst to him, in trying to escape the mediocre world of his merchant father, Salieri follows it perfectly. His father bargains with God in the form of a merchant-protecting emperor so that he can prosper in the world. Likewise, Salieri bargains with God for fame, another form of prosperity. Both Salieri and his father seek the protection of a Hapsburg emperor, an earthly representative of God, the Father, in the form of a divine right monarch. Salieri becomes not "God's servant" (8) but one of the "learned servants" (10) of the Emperor who will "celebrate men's average lives" (10), not "honor" (8) God "with music." In the end, he lives among courtiers and sacramentalizes "their mediocrity" (11). Thus, in this world, he, like his merchant father, is "forever preserved in mediocrity" (7). Unconsciously, Salieri followed the path of the absent father he tried to reject.

According to Berman in "kneeling before the 'God of Bargains,' Salieri acts out the son's ambivalent relationship with the father." This relationship is one where neither "father nor son" is "able to give love freely and unconditionally." It is a Faustian relationship in which a "frustrated child can win love only through artistic achievement" (563).

For a time, all is well between the God of Bargains and Salieri until Salieri hears Mozart's music and feels intense pain. Salieri beckons his "sharp old God" (18) because he has "heard a voice of God" issued from the "voice of an obscene child" (19). Salieri, the good son, cries out to God "Let your voice enter me! Let me conduct You." Salieri wants to be the chosen son who inherits the Father's gift, but it is Mozart who transcribes "music completely finished in his head" (45). Salieri sees himself trapped in his fate: "I feel my emptiness like Adam felt his nakedness" (46). Salieri has eaten of the tree of knowledge and can see how the "giggling child" Mozart can put down "casual notes" that turn Salieri's notes to "lifeless scratches" (46). Having been banished from the paradise of his smug self-satisfaction, Salieri is left with a terrible longing that he can never fulfill. The lost son wants his Father God to make good on His bargain. Even though Salieri has done God's will, "pursued virtue," "labored long hours" to help his fellow men, and "worked the talent" God "allowed him" (47), God has blessed "spiteful, sniggering, conceited, infantile Mozart—who never worked one minute to help another man" (47). Following the path of his own merchant father, Salieri wants God to make good on his bargain and to trade talent for pious service. But the Father God he pursues is not a simple merchant. He is a God who seeks out prodigal sons and fallen sheep. Like Cain, another rejected son, Salieri will now try to destroy God's favorite and rebel against God.

According to Berman, "Salieri's rejection of his biological parents' 'mediocrity' and his short-lived bargain with God imply a pattern of early disappointments and broken promises. Salieri's image of God changes quickly from that of 'good' to 'bad' father suggesting unstable parenting" (567). Salieri's pursuit of the Absent Father and His favor leads him down a path of self-destruction. However, before analyzing Salieri's battle with God, the Father, it is necessary to show the wasteland world that Salieri inhabits and the father figures he manipulates and appeases.

Salieri has organized his life well and programmed his career opportunities diligently; yet he lives in a wasteland devoid of the divine presence. He is a respected court composer with plenty of students; however, his life is without passion. He has chosen a wife to suit his career needs, one with a "lack of fire" (10). Even though he lusts after his pupil Katherina Cavilieri, he remains faithful to his wife because of his vow to God. Later, when he turns against God, he takes Katherina for his mistress. But the jaded Salieri, "slick as a cat" merely displays his showpiece mistress who has become "fat and feathered" (82). Living an empty and sterile life, he consoles himself by consuming sweets. He says, "All my life I have never been able to conquer a lust for the sweetmeats of northern Italy, where I was born" (7). He connects his appetite for sugar-coated but unnourishing candies to the childhood world of his father and mockingly says he eats sweets out of "patriotic feelings" (7), a statement that may be truer than he wants to admit. According to Sullivan, Salieri's oral fixation, which goes beyond his sweet tooth, is related to his identification with "his God, and therefore with his father(s), accepting the inherent aggressivity of capitalism" (477), an economic system based on consumption. Even Salieri's religion is dominated by the psychology of an exchange economy.

However, Salieri, the small-town boy, is led deeper and deeper into the world of shallow glitz as he grows famous on "golden opinions" (54). He says "My own tastes were for plain things . . . but I denied it. The successful lived with gold and so would I" (55). Salieri becomes absorbed in the world of the court, a world of "salons and soirees." He worships "the season round at the altar of sophistication" (55) and absorbs himself in the shallow world of materialism and pretense. As Werner Huber and Hubert Zapf note, "The essential quality of the court is its unreality; it is depicted as an artificial, hypocritical, mediocre world of appearances with 'fetes and fireworks' on the surface and intrigues and power struggles beneath it" (30). The court as a symbol of treacherous illusions has been a standard of English drama since the Renaissance, and Salieri is another of a long line of court intriguers. However, the golden opinions of the world cannot buy him self-satisfaction.

Ironically, Salieri gets exactly what he bargained for: God makes him the "most famous musician in Europe" (93). But fame is hollow and fleeting to him: "I was to be bricked up in fame! Embalmed in fame! Buried in fame—but for work I knew to be absolutely worthless" (93). God, the Absent Father, has kept his bargain. But the bargain is as ambiguous as the prophecies of the Delphic oracles or the pronouncements of the witches in Macbeth. Londre notes that God granted "Salieri exactly what he had asked: not musical brilliance but fame" (117). But even Salieri's fame is ephemeral. He complains "I must survive to see myself become extinct" (93). His world of fame and fortune is a wasteland. In the end, he bemoans "Mozart's music sounded louder . . . and mine faded completely" (93).

In his position and in his music Salieri mimics his father figures. He imitates the Emperor in telling Mozart to be less enthusiastic in his praise (72); follows clearly in the tradition of his mentor-father, Chevalier Gluck and seeks the position of Giuseppe Bruno, the first Royal Kappelmeister who seemed "apparently immortal" (10) but died granting Salieri his "dearest wish" (72) as Salieri inherits the position of the aged father figure. Salieri is able to manipulate and duplicate the world of fathers, but his reward ironically is not satisfaction but despair for he is rendered "'distinguished' by people incapable of distinguishing" (93).

Salieri's nemesis is Mozart, Amadeus Mozart, God's beloved. Yet Mozart is more than a foil for Salieri. Hinden believes that "Mozart is Salieri's rival, not his double" (57). But in many ways both men are doomed by the search to appease and reject the absent father. According to Berman, "Both men display deep disappointment toward their fathers. Salieri's rage toward God parallels Mozart's aggression toward Leopold" (568). Both men also connect the father to a godlike projection. Londre finds "Both Mozart and Salieri's attitudes toward God were apparently shaped by their relationships with their fathers. As the son of a merchant, Salieri tried to make a deal with God. Mozart served as an instrument first of his father and ultimately with God" (124). Mozart, like Salieri, is bound to the absent father. Sullivan notes "Leopold Mozart, although he never appears in propia persona in the play, exercises from the distance of Salzburg, and from even farther off after his physical death, an almost complete control over Mozart's emotional and psychological being" (50).

Leopold is depicted as a "bad-tempered Salzburg musician" (13) who made Mozart "play the keyboard blindfolded with one finger" (13). He has dominated Mozart, yet Leopold has spoiled Mozart too. When Mozart's music is not ingenious, Salieri labels him "Leopold's swanky son—nothing more" (20). Moreover, the father still controls Mozart who waits for Leopold's consent to marry. Constanze tells Mozart that he would not marry without his father's consent: "You're too scared of him" (17). Repeating the words of the absent father, Constanze pronounces the father's curse: "If you marry that dreadful girl, you'll end up lying on straw with beggars for children" (17). He marries without his father's consent and carries out the father's prophecy. Ailing and impoverished, he later tells Constanze, "Papa was right. We end exactly as he said. Beggars" (78). Thus, Mozart fulfills the father's prophecy.

Like Salieri, Mozart, too, lives in a wasteland. He is told that his music has "too many notes" (28); his operas are all given minimal performances; he cannot get enough pupils to support himself. When he loses the position as tutor to Princess Elizabeth, the voice of the father speaks to him. "My father always writes I should be more obedient. Know My Place" (53). Yet Mozart cannot accept his place among the mediocrities of the court. Even when he is given a position, he does not get enough money to support himself. Eventually, Mozart, the darling of Europe, finds himself dying in a slum.

Mozart ends up regressing more and more into a childhood world from which he cannot extricate himself. His wife Constanze says about Leopold "He kept you a baby all your life" (78). In the end, Mozart and Constanze are reduced to playing nonsense games in which Mozart's endearments move from "pussy-wussy" to "Pappy" to "Pappa-Pappa" (80), echoing Papageno's lines in *The Magic Flute*. Mozart's signs of affection become the child's call to his absent father. Even as father of a child, Mozart is "a baby himself" (81).

Unlike Salieri, who could manipulate the substitute fathers, Mozart can only alienate them. Like his father, Mozart is "a little stubborn" (30). He cannot control his mouth, calling Salieri a "musical idiot" (32) and labeling the Emperor "Kaiser Keepit" (33) for his stinginess. He knows that he should control his mouth. He remarks "I shouldn't have said that, should I . . . Forgive me. It was just a joke" (33). Rebelling against his father, he is not able to hold to his father's advice: "My father's right. He always tells me I should padlock my mouth" (30). He attacks the Italian court musicians as "Foppy wops," which he converts to "Foppy Poppy" (33), seeing them as negative father figures.

Sullivan notes that the closest figure to Mozart's father is Van Swieten who tries to help and advise Mozart, getting him fugues to arrange and supplying him with donations from brother Masons. When Van Swieten chides Mozart for writing vulgar farces, Mozart hears the voice of his father. Van Swieten says, "When I reproved him, he said I reminded him of his father" (56). In the end, Mozart alienates Van Swieten by revealing the secrets of the Masons in *The Magic Flute*. Sullivan notes about Van Swieten that "the parallels with Leopold . . . the provider, the restrainer, and the wounded progenitor, are clear" (51). In the end "Leopold/Van Swieten is [Mozart's] 'candle-smoked' God" (52). Mozart, like Salieri, is trapped in the world of the absent father. Salieri is driven mad because he cannot form "adequate relationships with authority figures (whether his middle class 'God of Bargains' or the Emperor Joseph II, whom he so obligingly serves) . . . Mozart suffers a similar fate rebelling against the very authorities upon whom he most depends" (Morace 41).

The power of the absent father over both men is seen most distinctly in Salieri's self-destructive attempt to destroy Mozart. Salieri seeks revenge on the Father God by trying to eliminate God's creature. Obsessed with rage against the father, he wants to murder the father by killing the son. The Transcendent Father is absent, but his creature provides an adequate substitute. Salieri easily finds Mozart's weakness in his relationship with his father Leopold. When Mozart's father would not grant consent for his marriage, Salieri, the father surrogate says, "My advice to you is to marry and be happy" (30). When Mozart believes that Salieri has gotten him a court post, he begs Salieri's forgiveness just as he would beg his father's forgiveness. He tells Salieri "Oh forgive me! You're a good man!" (71).

Mozart, the rebel son, accuses his father: "He's a bitter man, of course. After he finished showing me off around Europe, he never went anywhere himself. He just stayed in Salzburg . . . kissing the ring of the fart bishop" (68).

Mozart confesses "He's jealous . . . He'll never forgive me for being cleverer than he is . . . Leopold Mozart is just a jealous dried up old turd" (68). When Mozart describes his father to Salieri, he could just as well be speaking of Salieri, for it is Salieri who is a "bitter man," a man who plays up to the Emperor the way Leopold does to the bishop. It is Salieri who is "jealous" and who will "never forgive [Mozart] for being cleverer than he is." Salieri and Leopold are one. When Leopold dies, Mozart proclaims "There's no one else. No one who understands the wickedness around me. I can't see it" (69). Salieri, of course, is the one who has been watching Mozart, and Salieri is the one who sees the wickedness. Tormented by guilt at his betrayal of the father, Mozart yells in pain "Oh God" (69), then Salieri says "Lean on me" (69) and "opens his arms in a wide gesture of paternal benevolence" (69). Mozart does not accept the embrace, but calls out "Papa" (69). Salieri links Mozart's father to the Ghost Father in *Don Giovanni*. This absent father appears on the backdrop "a giant black figure in cloak and tricorn hat" who "extends its arms menacingly and engulfingly toward its begetter" (69).

Salieri sees Mozart haunted by the grey figure of the angry father, but he also beholds the other side of the father in the High Priest in *The Magic Flute*: "I saw his father! No more an accusing figure but forgiving . . . the highest priest of the Order . . . his hand extended to the world in love" (83). But Salieri tries to get beyond the forgiving father, and masked as the figure in grey, haunts Mozart. Mozart is writing a Requiem for the father, but in the father he sees God, the Father. He tells Salieri, who is masked as the Death Father, "God can't want it unfinished . . . Here's the Kyrie . . . Take that to Him . . . He'll see it's not unworthy" (87). Mozart even repudiates his former work and says "I've written nothing finally good!" (87). The scene is overdetermined with the presence of the absent father. Salieri, who is battling with the absent Father God, is dressed like the Ghost Father in *Don Giovanni*, who is a representation of Mozart's father Leopold. Mozart sees Salieri as the avenging father figure representing God, the Father, who is a projection of Mozart's father. Because of his need for forgiveness, Mozart gives the Father God the Kyrie, a plea for mercy and absolution. Speaking for God, the Father, Salieri tells Mozart "God does not love you Amadeus . . . He can only use. You are no use to him any more" (88).

Both Salieri and Mozart are united under the power of the absent father. Moreover, Salieri eats Mozart's music in a mock communion and says "We are both poisoned, Amadeus. I with you: you with me" (88). Mozart, however, regresses to a child and sees Salieri as his father: "Take me Papa. Take me. Put down your arms and I'll hop into them. Just as we used to do . . . Hold me close to you Papa. Let's sing our kissing song together" (89). Mozart, like many a lost son, wants to escape into a childhood paradise. He returns to the father as a child. Salieri destroys Mozart but cannot destroy Mozart's music. In one last desperate attempt, he tries to gain immortality by making people believe he is Mozart's murderer. But the people only see him as "a deluded old man" (96). Just as Mozart grows infantile, Salieri becomes senile. Mozart escapes to a childhood world that is forever in the lost past while Salieri creates an illusory future that can never be.

In the beginning of the play Salieri has summoned up the audience just as if he were invoking the gods. In the end, he reverses the situation and treats the audience as mediocrities. He diminishes the world around him and partakes of the greatest illusion of all. Instead of being a servant of God, he becomes like God with the power to absolve the sins of mediocrities, not only in the present, but for all time. He proclaims "Mediocrities everywhere . . . now and to come . . . I absolve you all. Amen!" In the pastoral gesture "He extends his arms upward and outward to embrace the assembled audience in a wide gesture of benediction" (97). The deluded Salieri, as he did with Mozart, extends the embrace of the father in an attempt to become the Father.

Amadeus is a play about the search for an absent father and the need to be his chosen son. Both Mozart and Salieri begin life in a protected world of the father. Mozart is a pampered and spoiled young man. In the world of harsh realities, Mozart cannot understand why the paternal paradise has vanished: "Once the world was so full, so happy . . . Everyone smiled at me once . . . the king of Schonbrunn; the princess at Versailles—they lit my way . . . my father bowing . . . with such joy! 'Chevalier Mozart, my miraculous son!'" Mozart asks, "Why has it all gone? . . . Why? . . . Was I so bad? So wicked? . . . Answer for Him and tell me" (88). Mozart questions God and asks Him what sins he has committed to deserve the loss of paradise. His only hope is to regress into an infantile state and join the father.

Salieri also starts out in the protected world of the court, enjoys success, and achieves fame, but he knows he is not the chosen son and cannot achieve immortality. Like Mozart, he questions God, for he believes he has done everything he can do to appease God, the Father. Like Mozart, he too finds himself disillusioned and escapes to the father through an illusion. He becomes not only "the Patron Saint of Mediocrities" (95) but assumes God's power to forgive and absolve the human race, once and for all time. In a last gesture he folds "his arms high across his own breast," a gesture of "self-sanctification" (97). In the end, both men are destroyed by their obsession with an absent and elusive father.

CHAPTER 10

THE FATHER AND THE CLASS STRUGGLE:
John Osborne's *Look Back in Anger*

Issues of race, class, and gender have been foregrounded in many recent British and Commonwealth plays so that it is no surprise that the figure of the absent father in these dramas has ideological overtones. For instance, in John Osborne's *Look Back in Anger*, Athol Fugard's *Master Harold . . . and the boys*, and Caryl Churchill's *Top Girls*, the absent father lurks behind the shadow of the patriarchy. Jimmy Porter in *Look Back in Anger* finds himself trapped by a class structure that leaves him doomed to reenact the losing battle of his revolutionary father. Hally in *Master Harold . . . and the boys* wants to usher in a new world order but is hopelessly caught in the racist social structure of his father. Marlene in *Top Girls* tries to escape the imprisoned life that her father imposed on her mother only to become an oppressor like her absent father. In all three plays, the figure of the absent father looms behind the ideology of oppression.

Upon its opening, *Look Back in Anger* confused many critics, who like Derek Monsey saw Jimmy as a "nasty type of pretentious bore" (44). However, many scholars today would agree with Ruby Cohn, who declares: "By now, it is traditional to date the new English theatre from May 8, 1956, the premiere of *Look Back in Anger*" (4). According to Michelene Wandor, *Look Back in Anger* is a compelling and powerful play which helped "initiate a new way of showing contemporary life in theatre" (*Look Back* 8). No doubt the play was a daring new work which has now become landmark in the history of modern British theatre.

Noting some of the innovations in *Look Back in Anger*, John Osborne declared, "It was almost a rule when I first started working in theatre at all that you never discussed anyone on the stage who never appeared . . . In *Look Back in Anger* there are about 27 people referred to and only five of them actually appear" (qtd. in Hinchliffe). Absent characters are indeed central to *Look Back in Anger* in order to project the world of the play through Jimmy Porter's view. His past, as well as his present, dominates the lives of the other characters. The play has been called a "monologue with interruptions or monologue with echo" (Haymond 17). Gordon Rogoff finds that "what seemed to be a five character play was really a monologue" (30–1). Out of all the absent characters in Jimmy's life, none is more significant than the absent father. Critics were quick to notice the influence of the father's death on Jimmy Porter, even though they were puzzled about its significance.

Monsey finds that Jimmy "is looking back so angrily, apparently, because he watched his father die" (44). Robert Tee notes that Jimmy "was a post-war failure. Partly, according to the author, because he saw his father die" (46).

Eric Keown grudgingly admits, "All that can be claimed in the man's favor is an unhappy childhood" (56). Finally, Milton Shulman, who sees no clear motivation behind Jimmy's anger, queries sarcastically, "What has turned him into this pugnacious bore other than the fact that he saw his father die?" (41).

Looking closely at the play, "the fact that he saw his father die" is central to understanding Jimmy Porter and to the interpretation of *Look Back in Anger*, for Jimmy has renounced the world to follow the path of the absent father. His mourning has been projected onto the world order against which he rages.

When Osborne was eleven, he witnessed the dying and death of his father, a sickly man in and out of sanitoriums for tuberculosis. Osborne "spent many hours reading to him before his death" (Goldstone 23) and said later, "I had great affection and feeling for him. I thought he was a man of tremendous probity and integrity" (Wager 76). Knowing the death and loss of a father at an early age, Osborne was able to infuse some of the pain of a father's absence into his character Jimmy Porter.

As Jimmy, in an extensive monologue, relives the moment of his father's death, he illustrates how the concept of a deathwatch has become focal to his world view. He says, "Anybody who has not watched somebody die is suffering from a pretty bad case of virginity" (58). Death and sex are inextricably linked in Jimmy's mind. As a ten year old boy, Jimmy watched his father's dying for a year because during the Spanish Civil War "certain god–fearing gentlemen there had made such a mess of him, he didn't have long to live" (57). Although Jimmy's family knew his father was dying, they were embarrassed by the whole business. Jimmy remarks, "As for my mother, all she could think about was the fact that she had allied herself to a man who seemed to be on the wrong side of all things" (57). Jimmy's mother only wanted to be "associated with minorities, provided they were the smart, fashionable ones" (57). His family sent Jimmy's father money and "hoped he would get on with it quietly, without too much vulgar fuss" (58). Jimmy affirms, "But I was the only one who cared" (58).

Jimmy was the only one who stayed with the father through his dying: "All that feverish failure of a man had to listen to him was a small frightened boy" (58). The father poured out "all that was left of his life to one, lonely bewildered boy. . . . All he could feel was the despair and the bitterness, the sweet sickly smell of a dying man" (58). As a boy, Jimmy learned what it was like to be "angry and helpless" and he "can never forget it" (58). He tells his wife "I knew more about . . . love . . . betrayal . . . and death when I was ten years old than you will probably know all your life" (58). Like Orestes and Hamlet, Jimmy is outraged that his father has not been properly mourned and has been betrayed by his mother. Like them, Jimmy extends his mourning and projects it onto the world at large.

Jimmy's monologue about the death of his father also points out Jimmy's obsession to follow in the path of the father and, in some way, to avenge his father's death. First, Jimmy identifies the men who wounded his father as "god-fearing gentlemen," connecting them with hypocritical religion and shallow nobility, two social structures which Jimmy finds inimical. Jimmy has spent his life waging war on the "god-fearing" and the genteel. He rails continuously against religious hypocrisy and attacks the British class system. Like his father who was a "failure" on "the wrong side of all things" (58), Jimmy is also a failure, unsuccessful as a journalist, an advertising agent, and a vacuum cleaner salesman. Although he has had some university education, he works at a sweet stall. Apparently, according to Helena, there is no use in this world for Jimmy, who seems to belong in the French Revolution.

Jimmy has also absorbed from his father's deathbed his sense of "despair and bitterness" so that the England he knows is a foul wasteland to which he is condemned. In this world, he can only feel as he felt at his father's bedside, "angry and helpless." He also holds his mother accountable for betrayal of the father and for supporting only "smart, fashionable" minorities. Jimmy's life becomes centered either on an attack against the mother or on a need to replace the mother. He projects the image of his own "bad" mother onto Alison's mother and onto Alison, his wife, while he searches for the "good" mother to replace the mother who betrays. Of course, this quest plays havoc with his relationships. However, Jimmy survives the agony of the search for the absent father either by creating an illusory world of the fathers in a mysterious past or by escaping to a childhood paradise of games and toy animals.

Jimmy, like other lost sons, lives in a wasteland world of lost hopes where "nobody thinks, nobody cares," and there are "no beliefs, no convictions and no enthusiasm" (17). He finds it "pretty dreary living in the American age" (17), an age dominated by shallow materialism and shoddy Hollywood fantasies. His life is enclosed in a world of nauseous repetition. Every Sunday is the same: "Always the same ritual. Reading the papers, drinking tea, ironing" (15). The book reviews he reads are the same even if the books are different. Jimmy is able to replace one woman with another. After Alison leaves him, and he takes Helena as his mistress, the stage directions note that Alison's things on the dressing table "have been replaced by Helena's" (75). Both Jimmy and Cliff, who shares the apartment with Jimmy and Jimmy's women, are still reading the two boring Sunday papers. Like Alison before her, Helena wears Jimmy's shirt and stands ironing as the two men perform vaudeville skits and roughhouse. Helena does Cliff's clothes just as Alison did. The woman is different; the tension in the scene is less than the one with Alison, but the routine is the same.

Jimmy is also surrounded by religious hypocrisy. The "god-fearing" enemy who has killed his father is reincarnated into the Bishop of Bromley who "wants all Christians to do all they can to assist in the manufacture of the H-Bomb" (13) or in the American evangelical enthusiasts who nearly trample a woman to death in their Christian zeal. As for the "gentlemen" who killed his father, they reappear in the form of Nigel, his wife's brother: "He and his pals have been plundering and fooling everybody for generations" (20). He feels that the aristocracy will "kick you in the groin while you're handing your hat to the maid" (21). His wife Alison is "pusillanimous" (21) and "a monument to non-attachment" (21). His marriage is "a narrow strip of plain hell" (60). All heroism was played out in "the thirties and forties" (84), the generation of his father. He tells Cliff, "There aren't any brave causes left. If the big bang does come, and we all get killed, it . . . will be about as pointless and inglorious as stepping in front of a bus" (85). Thus, the despair he learned at his father's side is evident in Jimmy's vision of a futile death for the whole human race.

Lost in a world of mourning, Jimmy can only see the world as absurd. For Jimmy, people have become absorbed in the trivial. Scholars are concerned that Shakespeare was a transvestite and are arguing over Milton's braces. Jimmy is also disturbed that the people are resigned and noncommittal, especially his wife. Jimmy cries out "Oh Heavens, how I long for a little ordinary enthusiasm" (15). Jimmy, however, knows that he is out of place in the world and that he is a "lost cause" (95). According to Helena, "he doesn't know where he is or where he is going. He'll never do anything." Like his father, Jimmy will follow the path of heroic failure. Alan Carter notes how Jimmy's attitude toward his father's death has shaped his view of the world: "Jimmy cannot bear the thought that he may end his days in the same way as his father. This is his plea, 'Is there not something wrong with a society that permits such a death and goes about its everyday life?'" (54–5). In other words, Jimmy is reenacting the death of his father and railing against society because of its indifference to his father's death.

In this wasteland world, Jimmy finds himself compelled to repeat the deathwatch of the father. His witnessing the death of his friend's mother replicates his witnessing his father's death. Jimmy must go to the deathbed of Hugh's mother because, like his father, "she hasn't got anyone else" (62). The one-year vigil with his father has been reduced to a day, but Jimmy still feels the pain. "For eleven hours, I have been watching someone I love very much going through the sordid process of dying" (73). Hugh's mother, like Jimmy's father, happens to be on the wrong side, "a woman who said all the wrong things in the wrong places" (73). But like his father, Jimmy feels she should "be taken seriously" (73). Because his wife would not come with him, he casts her in the role of his betraying mother. He bemoans, "I'll be alone again. Because that bitch won't even send her a bunch of flowers" (73).

In Jimmy's deathbed vigil of the father, Arnold Hinchliffe sees Jimmy's sense of helplessness: "It is a helpless Jimmy, one who fails to measure up, if through no fault of his own, to the requirement of the moment. He does not want to fail again with the death of Hugh's mom" (17). Jimmy's feeling of helplessness makes him see only the the hopelessness and futility of his life and clouds all his relationships. Herbert Goldstone finds that Jimmy is proud that he is responsible for his father, but the suffering placed "a tremendous burden on him" (42). He felt "however much he tried that he couldn't help [his father] enough," and "perhaps he has continued to feel that way" (42).

Like the fathers of Osvald, Hedda, Jim, Pavlo, and the Prozorov sisters, Jimmy's father is connected to a heroic military world that is receding into the age of the romantic past. Thus, Jimmy searches for a father substitute in a military figure like his father. According to Robert Egan, Jimmy is "guiltily yearning for the heroic militancy of his father, fatally wounded in Spain" (418). He finds a model of this warrior in his boyhood friend, Hugh. Jimmy and Alison lived with Hugh in his flat above a warehouse. Hugh and Jimmy held Alison as "a hostage from those sections of society they had declared war on" (43). Together Hugh and Jimmy gatecrashed the parties of Alison's upperclass friends, the world of "gentlemen," the same enemy that Jimmy's father fought. Hugh, who "takes the prize for ruthlessness" (43), liked to "invade enemy territory" (44) and "carry out raids on the enemy" (44). Hugh and Jimmy "went on plundering" Alison's friends. Alison notes, "Hugh fairly revelled in the role of barbarian invader. Sometimes I thought he might even dress the part—you know furs, spiked helmet, sword" (44). Hugh and Jimmy were quite adept at "guerilla warfare" against the gentry. Hugh, however, disappoints Jimmy. He gives up on England which has been overrun by "Dame Alison's mob" (46), and according to Alison, goes off to "find the New Millennium on his own" (46). Jimmy's father was defeated; Hugh gives up. Again, Jimmy feels abandoned and helpless.

Jimmy also identifies with another father figure. Ironically, it is Alison's father, a Colonel in India, another warrior figure. Jimmy seems to understand "Daddy": "The old Edwardian brigade do make their brief little world look tempting . . . bright ideas, bright uniforms, the long days in the sun . . . what a romantic picture" (17). Jimmy describes the military man as a plant "left over from the Edwardian Wilderness that can't understand why the sun is not shining any more" (66). Interestingly, Colonel Redfern concurs with Jimmy's assessment. He wants to remember England as it was in 1914. Although he is not an absent father, he represents absence, first, by his removal from the England that was changing while he was away in India, and second, by his nostalgia for living in the past. For him India was the same paradise Jimmy describes, "Cool evenings upon the hills, everything purple and gold" (68). Even though his heroic vision of grand regiments is the reverse of the slaughter fields that Jimmy's father was wounded on, both men have lost the battle. Colonel Redfern says, "I think the last day the sun shone was when that dirty little train steamed out of that crowded, suffocating Indian station and the battalion was playing for all its worth, I knew in my heart it was all over then" (68).

Both Alison's father and Jimmy's father were military men on a grand crusade who came back to England with a sense of despair. What they fought for either vanished or never did materialize. Jimmy ironically sympathizes with

Alison's father in the passing of the Edwardian paradise: "Still I even regret it, phoney or not. If you have no world of your own, it's rather pleasant to regret the passing of someone else's" (17). Jimmy, of course, is searching for an illusory world buried in the past. John Russell Taylor points out about the Edwardians, "Their security in an apparently insecure world is eminently to be envied by someone, like Jimmy, who finds no certainty anywhere outside himself or within" (47). Hugh, who seeks a new social order, and Colonel Redfern, who yearns for the old social order, both offer Jimmy illusory worlds, one in a future that can never be and the other in a past that perhaps, in fact, never was. In the absence of a heroic father, neither the glorious barbarian nor the aristocratic warrior can transform the English wasteland into a new paradise.

Jimmy, however, is not deterred from taking on the persona of a warrior. But, like his father, he is no soldier hero. Alison notes that in fighting for her, "Jimmy went into battle with his axe swinging round his head, frail and so full of fire" (45). He was a knight "except that his armor really didn't shine very much" (45). In the end, he ironically sees himself as a "victorious general" who is "sick of the whole campaign, tired out, hungry and dry" (81). Trying to go beyond the image of his defeated father, he declares himself victorious, but his victory is undercut by his despair. Like his father, he is too sick to carry on the battle. As a conquering knight, he is frail, and his armor does not shine, and as a victorious general, he is exhausted and war-weary. The world of the father substitutes he identifies with, along with the chimerical military personas he adopts, leave Jimmy more defeated than ever.

Brian Murphy sums up Jimmy's plight in his quest for the absent father: "Finding an absence of real values of any sort in his world, Jimmy turns wistfuly to the lost world of the Edwardians and then angrily on those who, like Nigel, betrayed all those old values. So then he turns to love, to private relationships and asks of them some of the passion and possibility of that lost culture" (373). Jimmy tries to fight his father's battle in the private sphere. In a world where great causes have vanished "social frustration is taken out on personal relationships" (Innes 98). Michelene Wandor comments on Jimmy: "His sense of class hatred is sublimated into sexual hatred and venomous attacks on women in general" (*Carry on Understudies* 142). As in *Miss Julie*, *Look Back in Anger* interlinks the class conflict with the battle of the sexes.

Jimmy's battle against women, however, is played out in the battle against the Terrible Mother, a destructive imago that reigns supreme in the absence of the father. Because Jimmy's mother betrayed the father, Goldstone believes, "Jimmy felt a strong conflict of loyalties so far as his mother and his family were concerned" (42). Jimmy's mother was embarrassed by the father and his ability to wind up on the losing end of issues. She is also somewhat of a social snob in her allegiances to liberal causes and will only support "smart, fashionable" minorities. Furthermore, there seems to be a class difference between mother and father. Cliff tells Alison, "Some of his mother's relatives are pretty posh, but he hates them as much as he hates yours" (30). Jimmy blames his mother for her class pretensions and for her lack of support of the father.

Jimmy's anger towards his own mother, however, becomes transferred to Mummy, Alison's mother, who is seen as the central force of evil. Mummy is a castrating force who will "kick you in the groin" (21). She wouldn't hesitate to "cheat, lie, bully and blackmail" (52). In a grotesque image of motherhood, Jimmy sees her bellowing "like a rhinoceros in labor" (52). Like some terrible earth mother, she is "over-fed" and "flabby," yet "armor plated" (52). He eventually pictures her as dead, the mother goddess of corruption. "She will pass away leaving a trail of worms gasping for laxatives behind her" (53). Mummy is symbolized by a storage tank in the middle of the apartment. Helena puts a slip cover over the tank labeled "Mummy" but "Mummy is still present, built into the apartment as she is built into English life" (McCarthy 151). Wander notes that motherhood is problematic in Jimmy's life: "Both Jimmy's and Alison's mothers are 'bad'—Jimmy's because she didn't care about him, Alison's because she is such an upper-class cow" (*Look Back* 12).

Jimmy's horror of the Terrible Mother is carried over in Strindbergian fashion to his paranoid delusion about a conspiracy of women. He once lived in a flat below two women and was run out by "the eternal racket of the female" (25). The din of the Terrible Mother is reinforced by her ability to dismember or dissect. He describes his wife as a "refined sort of butcher" (24). Her "hands would have your guts out in no time" (24). Jimmy feels that Alison has the "passion of a python" (38). "She devours me whole every time, as if I were some over-large rabbit. That's me, the bulge around her navel . . . buried alive down there" (38). Egan notes, "In a grotesque progression of images combining his sexual fears of Alison with the Oedipal need of her, he figures himself in her belly, a rabbit in the entrails of a python. Mother and child become predator and victim" (420). In other words, he transforms his wife into a devouring mother.

Alison also notes that Jimmy wants her to be "a cross between a mother and a Greek courtesan" (91). This demand sets up an ambivalent relationship towards her. Like his mother, Alison is seen as betraying Jimmy by remaining in contact with her upper-class parents and by walking out on him when he needed her. This ambivalence started out at the very beginning of their marriage. According to Roy Huss, "Jimmy's anger over Alison's virginity was based on his uneasy feeling that she resembled more the sexually taboo mother figure than the acceptable courtesan figure" (22).

Ambivalent and terrifying motherhood haunts Jimmy's world. Other than the betrayal of his mother and his battle with the ogre-like Mummy, Jimmy's image of his wife's mother, there is his old girlfriend Madeline who "was nearly old enough to be his mother" (71). Even Helena possesses a "matriarchal authority" that makes men "anxious not only to please but impress" (39). Jimmy creates a song entitled "My mother's in the Madhouse—that's why I'm in love with you" (79), connecting the woman he loves to the image of the "crazy" mother. The landlady "old mother Drury" (71) might be an "evil high priestess" (76). Jimmy reads in the papers that in the Midlands where he lives there are "evil and grotesque practices" and "midnight invocations to the Coptic Goddess of fertility" where a debutante drinks blood "during an evil orgy" (76). This ceremony links the upper-class women in Jimmy's life to the debutantes who worship the Great Mother goddess through blood sacrifices. As he lets his friend Cliff leave him, he resigns himself to becoming a victim of the devouring mother: "No there's nothing left for it, me boy, but to let yourself be butchered by women" (85).

Jimmy's strongest attack on motherhood is launched against his wife in the form of a curse which is ironically fulfilled. Again, as in *Ghosts*, a realistic drama takes on a mythic superstructure as Jimmy's curse imposes a final attack on the Terrible Mother. He tells Alison "If you could have a child and it would die . . . if only I could watch you face that" (37). She not only has a child that dies but she also loses the ability to have any more children. Jimmy takes her back and together they escape into a childhood world of games. Only after he has destroyed all possibility of motherhood does he accept his wife.

Unable to bear the horrors of life in a world bereft of the father, Jimmy escapes to the paradise world of childhood. Jimmy and Alison become children in a nursery playing "bears and squirrels." According to Alison, in this game, they form "a sort of unholy priesthole of being animals to one another . . . full of dumb uncomplicated affection . . . playful careless creatures in their own cozy zoo for two: a silly symphony for people who couldn't bear the pain of being human beings any longer" (47). As Alison comes crawling back in pain to Jimmy, he escapes through this game into a youth he never had. He says "We'll live on honey and nuts . . . And we'll sing songs about ourselves—about warm trees and snug caves and lying in the sun" (96). As in *Miss Julie*, the sun becomes the image of paternal light, a way out of rainy Sundays.

According to Christopher Innes, the ending shows Alison "trapping Jimmy in a sterile, regressive fantasy" (99). Jimmy, the boy who became "a veteran" (58) in life at his father's deathbed ends up escaping into a childhood world that never existed for him. Goldstone notes that in seeing the helpless Alison return to him "Jimmy could feel again as he did earlier with his father, that he is responsible for what happened and therefore has another intolerable burden to assume" (51). Jimmy Porter has sought to reincarnate the absent father and to vindicate him; both tasks are futile. In the end, he can only be an innocent child in a sunny garden world.

Several critics have noted the similarities between *Look Back in Anger* and *Hamlet*. For Mary McCarthy, Jimmy is Hamlet; Alison, the scorned Ophelia, "an ally of the corrupt court"; and Alison's mother, Polonius, "looking behind the arras" (154). Both Jimmy and Hamlet "have declared war on a rotten society" (155), cannot accept "their normal place in the world," and "suffer from horrible self-doubt that alternates with wild flashes of conviction" (155). McCarthy's comparison is apt, but G. Wilson Knight points out a more crucial connection as he notes about Jimmy:

> As a boy he had nursed his dying father, whose death weighs on his mind as the death of Hamlet's father on his. Like Hamlet's, his thoughts are dominated by death. The extent to which death is almost driving him mad is evident when in the manner of Hamlet's words to Claudius, he deliberately torments his wife with an imagined description of her mother's body undergoing dissolution. (50)

Both plays are about sons in mourning for an absent father. Hamlet's enemy can easily be identified as Claudius, the evil father, and in the end, Hamlet kills him. In Jimmy's case the figure of the evil father is more pervasive. It is masked behind a patriarchal system that cannot be destroyed. Thus, for Jimmy, revenge is transformed into indiscriminate rage.

Although *Look Back in Anger* is a realistic drama, its mythic framework conveys the agony of a lost son who is haunted by the image of a dying father and doomed to follow the path of a failed father. The play also shows how the son seeks dubious father substitutes that offer him illusory paradises, none of which he is capable of accepting. In the end, his search for the absent father leaves him, like other lost children, trapped in a regressive fantasy.

CHAPTER 11

THE FATHER AND RACIAL STRIFE:
Athol Fugard's *Master Harold . . . and the boys*

Like Look Back in Anger, *Master Harold . . . and the boys* also looks at the absent father in a light of social oppression, using the family conflict to investigate larger social issues. *Master Harold . . . and the boys* is one of those rare serious plays that receive almost universal praise. In its American production, it has been called "a triumph of playmaking" (Barnes 307), "an incomparable theatre experience" (Wilson 308), and a "stunning play" (Watt 309). Frank Rich of the New York Times raved: "There may be two or three living playwrights in the world who can write as well as Athol Fugard, but I'm not sure that any of them has written a recent play that can match 'Master Harold and the Boys'" (305).

Like Osborne did in *Look Back in Anger*, Fugard calls directly on autobiographical material in *Master Harold . . . and the boys*. The play was germinated by a painful incident out of Fugard's past. As a young boy Fugard spat into the face of Sam Semela, a black employee of his mother and a close friend of Fugard. Fugard writes about the incident in his *Notebooks*: "Don't suppose I will ever deal with the shame that overwhelmed me after I had done that" (3-61). He openly confesses, "*Master Harold* deals with one specific moment I am trying to exorcise out of my soul" (Von Staden 42). This incident is not all that Fugard wells up out of his past. Indeed, *Master Harold* is the "most totally and immediately autobiographical of his plays" (Gussow 47). Like Hally in the play, Harold Athol Lannigan Fugard had the nickname, Hally. (Like Roger Samuel Shepard, Fugard discarded his father's first name.) Fugard knew the black men, Sam Samela and Willie Molopo. Fugard's mother operated a cafe called the St. George's Park Tea Room, as well as the Jubilee Hotel. Because Athol's father, like Hally's, was a cripple and an alcoholic, both the scene in which Sam helps Hally fly a kite and the incident where he carries home the inebriated father are memories from out of Fugard's past (Gussow 47,52,55).

Master Harold . . . and the boys is a play about fathers. Concerning the play Fugard confesses, "I was dealing with the last unlaid ghost in my life, who was my father. Our relationship was as complex as Master Harold expresses it in the play. I had resentment at his infirmity and other weaknesses but as Master Harold says 'I love him so'" (Vandenbroucke 190). Fugard's relationship with Sam Samela was no less complex. Fugard praises Sam: "He radiated all the qualities a boy could look to and recognize as those of a man . . . I thought I could model myself on that" (qtd. in Gussow 55). Sam and Athol Fugard did things that a father and son should do. But his relationship with Sam as surrogate father was an awkward one. Fugard explains, "But there was ambivalence in my relationship with him: a love-hate thing. I couldn't come to terms with the difference" (Vandenbroucke 185). Fugard dedicated the first draft of the play, "For Sam." Only on later drafts did he add "and H.D.F.," the initials of his father, Harold D. Fugard. Interestingly, the name is hidden behind the initials, and the claim of fatherhood is absent.

Despite the fact that the play has more autobiographical moments than previous works, Fugard still maintains the elements common to most of his works. Russell Vandenbroucke notes:

> He [Fugard] focuses upon an intense relationship and the impediment to it, happy memories quickly give way to the recovery of the past through its vivid recreation; characters again play with language they love; games are initiated and rules assumed; important offstage characters precipitate onstage action; hopes and dreams are entertained then shattered; and a character's consciousness and self-awareness are deeply transformed. (186)

Not only the focus on the recovery of the past and the destruction of illusions, but also, more importantly, the pivotal use of off-stage characters, specifically Hally's father, place *Master Harold . . . and the boys* squarely within the dramaturgy of the absent father.

Hally's father is absent at several levels. Not only is he not present on stage, but also he is away from home in a hospital. His physical illness has distanced him physically as well as psychologically from his son. At another level, he is an alcoholic who has escaped his role as a responsible father and abandoned his son, if not physically, at least spiritually. The drama is focused around the unnamed father's possible return and his son's attempt to prevent such a return. Early in the play Hally is concerned about Sam's remark that Hally's father may be coming home. Hally's first reaction is denial. "No, it can't be. They said he needed at least another three weeks of treatment" (12). After a while Hally becomes more frantic "No, Sam, they can't be discharging him" (13). Then he blurts out "If anything, it sounds like a turn for the worse . . . which I sincerely hope it isn't" (13). Hally's remark is a form of wish-fulfillment which he guiltily tries to cover up. He finally satisfies his fantasy that his father's homecoming will be long delayed by convincing himself, "She's at his bedside in the hospital helping him pull through a bad turn. You definitely heard wrong" (14).

Then Hally soon forgets about his father and starts enjoying himself when the phone rings and his mother informs him that his father, indeed, does want to come home. Hally desperately tries to prevent his father's return. He urges his mother to say no to the father: "Be firm with him. You're the boss" (33). The father represents failure to Hally, and his return will lead to Hally's failure.

Hally will fail his exams if he has to "spend half the night massaging his [father's] gamy leg" (30). Hally will also be faced with the pain and helplessness of the father the same way Jimmy Porter was. Both sons must deal with the father's shame, a shame that like Orestes' shame, diminishes the son and prevents him from acquiring his identity within the father's line. Finally, Hally himself takes on a fatherly role with regard to own his father. He tells his mother: "If he is going to behave like a child, treat him like one" (33). Just like Jimmy, Hally has had to take care of his helpless father. Because of this reversal in the father/son relationship, Hally is forced to become the father of his father.

Hally continues to prevent the return of his real father because that return will only reinforce his despair over the absence of a true father. After the threat of his father's return Hally groans "Life is just a bloody mess, that's all and people are fools" (34). Hally's life is haunted by the presence of an absent father who assures him that life is ruled by "the principle of perpetual disappointment" (35). Even though Hally wants his father at a distance, he mourns the absence of a father, and his mourning, like Jimmy's, is projected onto social order that surrounds him.

After venting his frustration and despair, Hally is raised to new hopes of a better social order only to have another phone call dash his hopes. He bemoans, "Just when you're enjoying yourself someone or something will come along and wreck everything" (47). When Hally sees the return of the father as inevitable, he loses all hope in the harmony of the world and turns his frustration and rage on Sam, his surrogate father. Thus, just as in *Miss Julie* the entire plot of *Master Harold . . . and the boys* is structured around the absent father and his threatened return.

To Hally, the father represents not only a world of filth and excrement with "stinking chamber pots full of phlegm and piss" (48) but also a world of deception and thievery where everyone has "to keep an eye on the till" (48) because Hally's father will steal money to buy alcohol. The father who should be guiding Hally is really a child, an alcoholic who cannot care for himself and who cannot be trusted.

Deprived of a father, Hally lives in a wasteland. In the St. George's Park Tea Room where he awaits messages about the father, there are no heroes who can slay dragons, only the refuse of a less-than-fashionable diner, harboring "a few stale cakes under glass," "a not very impressive assortment of sweets," "sad ferns in pots," "an old style jukebox," and a price list scribbled on a chalkboard in an "untrained hand" (3). Also, no customers ever come into the tea room. Entering this tea room from out of the storm, Hally is offered the same bland diet of soup and meat pie. The rainy weather and the absence of sunlight, a motif also found in *Ghosts* and *Look Back in Anger*, again symbolizes mourning for the lost father. Hally is also sick of constantly getting caught in disputes between his parents and frustrated with the physical and moral decay of his father. Hally's life at school is no better. He is frustrated with his math teacher, and finds his homework assignments inane. Obviously a bright young man, he has repeatedly failed examinations.

Even the days of his early youth in a rundown hotel, ironically named the Jubilee Boarding House, "are not remembered as the happiest ones of an unhappy childhood" (25). The boardinghouse brings back memories of complaining guests, disreputable prostitutes, "unappetizing cooking smells" (25), and the stench of the servant's lavatory. The loss of appetite and the disgust of excrement seem always to overwhelm Hally. Hally's disgust with his living conditions goes beyond his immediate surroundings. Like Jimmy Porter, Hally sees the despair in his own life reflected in the desperate conditions of the social order. Unlike Jimmy, he wishes for a better world, but in the absence of a father, he often falls into despair. Commenting on police brutality, he tells Sam, "It's a bloody awful world when you come to think of it" (15). As a lost son, Hally finds himself in a world that is in a state of decay and confusion, a wasteland of perpetual mourning.

Living in a diminished world that is haunted by the presence of an absent father, Hally seeks father substitutes. He rebels against "old fart-face Prentice" (14), his math teacher, by drawing caricatures of him. He wants to write an essay that will irk old Doc Bromley, his English teacher, who like Hally's father "doesn't like natives" (43). Proud of his essay on black ballroom dancing, he gloats, "This will teach the old bugger a lesson" (43). Rebelling against these father figures only allows him to dodge his rebellion against his father. Even the police who beat blacks fill him with disgust. In Hally's case the hatred of suppression is derived from his hatred of the absent father. According to Leon Lewis:

> Hally's crippled father—never seen on stage—embodies the whole system. His debilitating disease is the racism that has ruined his country's dreams. His "gamy" leg is a symbol of infirmity, but it is not as serious as the psychotic hatred that has reduced the man to drunken ranting. (1061)

Lewis sees a crucial connection between the alcoholic father and the decadent patriarchy in South Africa, a patriarchy that veils its own weaknesses by maintaining a system of oppression. Lewis may be somewhat overemphatic about the exact cause of the father's alcoholism, but he does hit on the link between Hally's hatred of the father and his attempt either to displace his anger onto father surrogates or to replace his father with an ideal father.

Like other lost sons, Hally conjures up the romantic vision of a heroic father. Hally is still waiting for the great reformer to arrive, a world redeemer. His inflated vision of the ideal father is projected upon a world savior, a mysterious figure who will alter the life not only of his lost child but also of the whole world. Discussing this savior figure, Sam notes that "maybe he hasn't even been born yet," and Hally resigns himself, "so we just go on waiting" (16). While waiting for the redeeming father, Sam and Hally search through history to find a mighty patriarch, "a man of magnitude" (18) (unlike Hally's father, who is a diminished man). Hally reaches for Charles Darwin because Darwin went back to the origins of things. Origins, of course, are the domain of the father. Hally is also enamored of Leo Tolstoy, the paternal reformer, with his "long beard," his "visionary eyes," and his "face of a social prophet" (21). Hally admires a man who can shovel manure with peasants (a far cry from his father, who wallows in his own excrement). Praising Tolstoy, he tells Sam, "Here's a man, Sam!" (21). Hally, however, rejects Jesus but concurs with Sam on Alexander Fleming who discovered penicillin. It seems easier for Hally to identify with a father-hero who can cure physical ailments rather than one who calls for complete moral reform, for Hally can only allow his disgust of his own father to reach his father's physical decrepitude and not his moral decay.

The most complete father substitute for Hally, however, is not a great father from history, but Sam himself. It is Sam whose discussions help Hally to succeed in school and Sam who shelters and comforts Hally. In the Jubilee Hotel, Sam's room was a haven. Like Nora and Julie, Hally escaped the world of the father by going down to the servant's quarters. He tells Sam, "If it wasn't for your room I would have been the first certified ten-year-old in medical history" (25). When Hally was humiliated by his father's public drunkenness, Sam took the despondent, young Hally kite-flying. As he often did with his father, Hally felt ashamed about the kite-flying and hoped there weren't "any other kids around to laugh at" them (29). He expected, "Like everything else in my life, here comes another fiasco" (29). But Sam's makeshift kite flew, and for a moment, "the miracle happened!" (30).

Like other lost sons, Hally is looking for miracles. Hally remembers the incident, "I was so proud of us" (30). Hally also remarks about the strangeness of the event: "Little white boy in short trousers and a black man old enough to be his father flying a kite" (31). Hally wants to retreat back to his childhood haven and into the paradise world of the ideal father: "Our days in the old Jubilee. Sad in a way they're over. I almost wish we were still in that little room" (32). Hally wants to regress to the world of his surrogate father in order to escape the oppression of growing up in the world of his real father. Even though Sam and Hally are still together, Hally notes "It's just that life felt the right size in there . . . Wasn't so hard to work up a bit of courage. It's got so bloody complicated since then" (32).

However, as with most lost sons, the return to childhood is an illusion that will not work; but Sam offers Hally another illusion, the dream of utopia, envisioned through ballroom dancing. Sam convinces Hally that dancing is more than a "simple-minded" activity (39). Dancing in the finals of ballroom competition is "like being in a dream about a world in which accidents don't happen" (45). Sam creates a paradise world in the ballroom similar to Williams' Paradise Dance Hall. In ballroom competition, dancers can dance without bumping into one another, and everyone can "get it right, the way we want life to be" (46). For a moment, Hally buys the beautiful illusion of a world without collisions, a world guided by sanctified fathers, like Mahatma Gandhi and the Pope. Hally even sees the United Nations as "a dancing school for politicians" (47). Hally, like other lost children, projects his own father-hunger onto the world and tries to envision a childhood paradise that can be absorbed into the sociopolitical system. Sam's world without collisions leads Hally into the dangerous illusion of foreseeing a world devoid of all conflict. In the middle of the vision comes a call from the father that will destroy Hally's illusion.

Hally cannot escape the world of his absent father. In his search for an ideal father, he finds himself doomed to double the real father he both loves and hates. Early in the play, Hally treats Willy like a child and shouts at him: "Act your bloody age! . . . cut out the nonsense now and get on with your work" (13). He thinks of himself as a benevolent patriarch: "Tolstoy may have educated his peasants, but I've educated you" (23), he tells Sam. When he feels the pressure of his father's return, he becomes more belligerent. He tells Sam, "And remember my Mom's orders . . . you're to help Willie with the windows" (35). When the two waiters disturb him he "grabs a ruler and gives Willie a vicious whack on bum" (38) and accuses the two black men of "acting like bloody children" (38).

The phallic stick, the source of patriarchal power and its brutalizing force has been introduced earlier. Hally's math teacher gives Hally a whack on the bum, "six of the best and his are bloody good" (14). In a sadistic father/son ritual, blacks in South Africa are stripped and given "strokes with a light cane" (15) on their naked backsides and Willie gives his girlfriend Hilda a "hiding" (7). The violence of the patriarchy which pits white against black, man against woman, is pervasive and the cruel resonance of the word "ruler" as a punitive device fits well with Hally's strutting "around like a despot, ruler in hand giving vent to his anger and frustration" (38). He calls the two black men a "pair of hooligans" (38) and insists he has been "far too lenient with them" (39). Anxious about the return of his absent father, Hally becomes more and more like the "bad" father he wants to disavow. He is becoming more and more like the patriarchal oppressor that he abhors.

As the play reaches a climax and Hally realizes that his father is really coming home, his illusions crumble and the substitute fathers fall as Hally completely transforms himself into his own father. Hally demolishes the illusion of a world without collisions by interjecting the image of cripples. Earlier in the play, the image of the cripple has been introduced in the context with dancing. Sam jokingly says Willie will have difficulty dancing because he has "leg trouble" (10), and his dance partner has "gone a bit lame" (12). For Hally, cripples like his father will "turn that dance floor into shambles" (51). Hally turns the paradise world of the dance floor into a nightmare world: "Nobody knows the steps, there's no music, the cripples are out there tripping up everybody" (52). The prize is a chamber pot "filled to the brim with piss" (57). Like Jimmy Porter, Hally has watched the physical decay of his father. Although the father is not critically ill, his alcoholism and progressive illness become a form of prolonged dying. The image of the dying father only fills Hally with despair, not only for himself but also for the whole world. This despair, however, helps him reify the patriarchal ideology that renders the power structure, no matter how shaky, as unalterable.

When Sam tries to stop Hally from degrading his own father, Sam invokes the sacred bond between father and son: "It's a terrible sin for a son to mock his father" (52). But Sam, like Pastor Manders in *Ghosts*, is talking about fatherhood in the abstract, an ideal father who is absent in the case of Hally. At this point, Hally turns on Sam, stating, "You're only a servant here and don't forget it" (52). Hally then invokes the employer/employee hierarchy, another power structure supposedly based on a benevolent paternalism which only disguises ruthless exploitation. Hally points out to Sam, "As far as my father is concerned, all you need to remember is that he is your boss" (53). The patriarchy often rules through capitalist oppression. But in the case of Hally's father, the patriarch is also an absent breadwinner, and Sam reminds Hally that Hally's mother runs the business. Finally, Hally invokes the patriarchal privilege of master/slave which defines a racist society. Here and here alone can the absent father be empowered. Hally puts Sam in his place with regard to Hally's father: "He's a white man and that's good enough for you" (53). In a racist society even a white father who absents himself from all the responsible roles of fatherhood can reduce a black man to the position of submissive son or "boy." Sam's notion of the absent ideal father is now transformed by Hally into the absent ideological father of racist oppression.

Entrapped within the patriarchal system, Hally attacks Sam, his good father, and follows in the footsteps of his real father, the bad father. Hally now insists that Sam call him "Master Harold" and taunts Sam, "Somebody who will be glad I've finally given it to you will be Dad" (55). Now, Hally joins forces with his Dad and tells Sam a racist joke he and his Dad share about a "nigger's arse" not being "fair." Feeling degraded, Sam bares his behind to Hally and tells him to tell his Dad "I showed you my arse and he's quite right it's not fair" (56). In retaliation, Hally spits in Sam's face, but Sam reminds him "the face you should be spitting in is your father's . . . but you used mine because you think you're safe behind your fair skin" (57). At this point, Hally has used Sam to vent his rage against his absent father. Rich notes that Hally "in absence of his real father takes out all his anger on his surrogate father" ("Life as a Dance" 305), and Kalem notes: "For the father he cannot strike Hally substitutes the father who cannot retaliate" ("Dance Marathon" 306).

Sam describes to Hally a scene in which Sam, along with the young child Hally, went to a barroom to carry Hally's father home and clean him up after he messed in his pants. It was this repressed incident that filled the young Hally with shame and led Sam to make a kite for Hally. Sam knew a boy could not become a man bearing the mark of shame. Sam says "The one person who should have been teaching you what that means was the cause of your shame . . . that's why I made the kite. I wanted you to look up, be proud of something of yourself" (58). Sam, however, left Hally alone on a bench as Hally flew the kite. Hally's father was absent when he needed him, and Sam was absent for Hally on the bench when Hally was scared because the bench was a "Whites Only Bench." Ron Koertge states, "Thus under pressure the father/son relationship is perverted to master/slave. And in this light we come to see how Sam is not, and under apartheid, could never be Hally's real father figure" (226). The illusion that Sam could be an ideal father is broken. Sheila Roberts points out that Hally "dreads the responsibility of his bedridden, alcoholic father but . . . can no longer accept Sam, a black man, as his father. All he can do is try to reduce Sam to the degrading position of his own father, and thus decrease his own inner conflicts" (33).

Sam offers Hally the choice of coming off the "Whites Only" bench and being man enough to reconcile himself with Sam so that they could fly kites again. Sam is willing to make amends and not leave Hally as a loser. In this scene, one recalls Hally's remarks to Willy, whom Sam and Hally allowed to win at checkers. Hally explains that not letting someone come out a perpetual loser "is more than fair," it is an "act of self-sacrifice" (12). Sam has moved beyond dark and fair, just and unjust and has become a true father. But Hally is too entrenched in the climate of his real father as he reminds Sam, "You can't fly kites on rainy days" (59).

The play ends with Willy and Sam dancing to a Sarah Vaughan song. The lyrics read: "Johnny won your marbles / tell you what we'll do; / Dad will get you new ones right away" (60). The song notes the presence of a nurturing father that remains absent for Hally. In *Master Harold . . . and the boys*, the search for the father draws the lost son into a political morass where the path of the absent father leads to a shadowy patriarchy built on the foundations of exploitation and racism. Jimmy Porter could only get beyond the class structure of the patriarchy by escaping into a childlike romance, his own private Eden. Hally's future is uncertain. Speaking about the "Whites Only" bench, Sam tells Hally, "You know what that bench means now and you can leave it any time you choose. All you've got to do is stand up and walk away from it" (60). But Hally, like his father, may be too "crippled" to stand up.

The ending of the play is ambiguous. When Fugard was asked whether the play showed a hopeful ending for Hally, he replied: "A play is not a novel. A novel must not leave that question unanswered. A play must answer that question in production" (Von Staden 46). The play, however, does not create the world of a romantic dance as Sam describes it, a "love story with a happy ending" (5). It is a complex work about absence and mourning. Fugard advises the audience, "*Master Harold* reflects a measure of grief at the way things happen in certain circumstances . . . What the audience must do is grieve, but forgive" (Gussow 93). The grief that comes out in *Master Harold . . . and the boys* is clearly over the absent father for "the innate power of this archetypal father-son conflict is one reason for *Master Harold*'s impact" (Vandenbroucke 191).

CHAPTER 12

THE FATHER AND THE INVISIBLE PATRIARCHY:
Caryl Churchill's *Top Girls*

The archetypal conflict with the father not only appears in *Master Harold . . . and the boys* but also emerges in Caryl Churchill's *Top Girls*. *Top Girls* opened at the Royal Court Theatre in London on August 28, 1982, and was transplanted to the Public Theatre in New York in December of 1982, with the original British cast. The play was favorably received, won an Obie, and was produced worldwide. Caryl Churchill is one of the few women dramatists in Britain to be distinguished as "a major playwright" (Innes 471). She is the only woman represented out of the fourteen playwrights appearing in Methuen's *Landmarks of Contemporary Drama* (1986), and the play that is featured is *Top Girls*.

Caryl Churchill's dramas are deeply concerned with feminist issues and modes of performance. Churchill's plays espouse "the social concerns of contemporary feminists: gender stereotyping, the division of labor according to sex, the proprietary family, the oppression of sexual variety through compulsory heterosexuality, class struggle, ageism, and ethnocentricity" (Marohl 377). Her methods of play construction are in line with feminist theories of performance. She attempts to "raise the audience's consciousness . . . through the actual events of performance: woman playing man, man playing woman, one person playing two or more persons, the deconstruction of history and geography (and the related unities of time, place, and action) in order to dramatize the cyclical progress of political and social events in history" (Marohl 377). In other words, Churchill tries to shatter realistic conventions in order to create an alienation effect that calls attention to social issues instead of using them solely as a context for emotional identification.

Many of these techniques of defamiliarization are employed in *Top Girls*, a play which interjects the historical plight of women into an individual drama of two sisters from opposite end of the social spectrum. *Top Girls* opens on a dinner party in honor of Marlene's promotion to manager of the 'Top Girls' Employment Agency. In attendance are five women of renown from out of the past: Isabella Bird (1831–1904), Victorian world traveller from Edinburgh; Lady Nijo (b. 1258), the Japanese Emperor's courtesan who later became a Buddhist nun travelling on foot throughout thirteenth-century Japan; the legendary Pope Joan (c. 854), a woman impostor who became the head of the Vatican; Dull Gret (c. 1562), a woman out of a Brueghel painting who led a charge through hell; and Patient Griselda (c. 1400), the submissive wife who appears in Chaucer's *Canterbury Tales*. These women from history, fiction, and art sit down for an elegant meal with Marlene and proceed to describe their exploits and tribulations. What starts out as a celebration ends up in shambles with Nijo crying and laughing, Joan vomiting, and Marlene getting drunk.

In Act Two, the scene shifts to the 'Top Girls' Employment Agency, where highly paid women gossip, berate their clients, and conduct a series of interviews. Angie, Marlene's niece (who is really the daughter she abandoned), comes to visit Marlene. Howard Kidd's wife comes in to plead the case of her husband who was passed over in promotion for Marlene, a woman. Marlene ousts Mrs. Kidd, is unaffected by Howard's sudden heart attack, and declares that Angie will never amount to anything.

The last act is a flashback to a year earlier when Marlene visits her sister Joyce. The two women argue about Marlene's choice to leave her child and work her way up the corporate ladder and Joyce's choice to raise Marlene's child and stay home trapped in a working class environment with limited options. *Top Girls* casts seven actresses in sixteen roles, mixes fantasy and reality, shifts time schemes, and alternates seemingly random scenes. Churchill notes about the play, "What I was intending to do was to make it first as though it was celebrating the achievement of women—by showing the main character, Marlene, being successful in a very competitive capitalist way—and ask what kind of achievement is that?" (Betsko and Koenig 82).

Critical interpretation of the play varies. Colin Chambers and Mike Prior feel that "the successful but empty Marlene emerges as a crude Thatcherite while Joyce is the one who has kept faith in her working-class politics" (196). For Amelia Howe Kritzer, the play's resolution is not so clear and simple: "Instead it ends with an unresolved argument that denies vindication to both sides and testifies to an urgent need for alternatives to the existing opposition between caring and competition" (142). Michelene Wandor has a similar response: "It is not a play which celebrates bourgeois success and it's not a play which campaigns for working class loyalty. It is quite apolitical in attributing values to either class" (125). When asked why there were no feminist role models in the play, Churchill responded, "I quite deliberately left a hole in the play rather than giving people a model of what they could be like. I meant the thing that is absent to be present in the play" (Stone 80).

The prototype for the modern feminist is not the only absence seeking presence in the play. Also, absent from the play, but powerfully present, is the father and the patriarchal system he represents. His most notable absence is seen first in the absence of male characters on stage. Joseph Marohl finds that "the absence of male characters on stage diminishes the importance" of those cultural codes which "define gender differences" (381). However, it is clear that the absence of the father and his patriarchal representatives is just another way that the patriarchy can assure its ideological repression of women by turning them into doubles of the patriarchal oppressors. Patriarchy, like all ideologies, oppresses less by force than by conditioning. This ideology leaves the daughter always longing for the lost father, looking always for Daddy's approval. The real father is not as important to the process of conditioning as is the absent father behind the patriarchal system. In *'night, Mother*, women absorb themselves in their struggles over absent men whereas in *Top Girls*, women simply turn into patriarchal oppressors and live out the script of the absent father in a new guise.

In examining the dinner party of impressive "top girls" from history, one can see that Marlene's toast to the "extraordinary achievements" (13) of these women only glosses over the painful realization that all of them have been trapped in a wasteland inhabited by death and disappointment. In the wasteland, the lost children are always obsessed with the mourning of the father. Thus, they cannot detach themselves from the patriarchal father. Isabella feels guilty about her world travels and comes home to wear herself out "with good causes" (18), like her father did. Nijo, by following her father's dictums, has spent half her life in sin and the other in repentance. She says, "I'm not a cheerful person, Marlene. I just laugh a lot" (8). In her attempt to become a man and to duplicate her rational father, Joan has lost touch with her ideals and has become alienated from her woman's body. Gret has lived her life in misery and squalor and can only strike back at mythological demons, mere phantoms of the Evil Father. Griselda has given up her life with her children for a shallow pretense concerning wifely duties. The whole idea of notable women sharing a common bond of achievement falls apart.

Kritzer holds that the women "eventually do perceive a commonality in their dead lovers, lost children, and angry response to injustice. This commonality, however, is intrinsically negative because imposed on them by oppression" (145). In other words, what they share is not their success, their escape from patriarchal oppression, but rather the very bonds of their oppression that holds them bound to the absent father. Christopher Innes is even more pointed than Kritzer when he notes that "what unites them is their submissiveness to the men in their lives—authoritarian fathers, sexist lovers, brutal husbands—and it is in the gruesome tribulations they have overcome that they find a common bond" (465). What exactly has been overcome is still a point of contention in the play. However, Innes does locate the cause of misery in the power of the fathers.

Each of the women from the past follows the path set for them by an absent father or father figure. Nijo follows her father's wishes. In a night of excessive drinking, Nijo's father gives her over to the Emperor and thus she becomes a medium of exchange between two patriarchs. Even though Nijo was frightened, she did not consider the Emperor's actions as rape. She tells Marlene "No, of course not, I belonged to him" (3). Nijo's father also scripts the path of her whole life. He tells Nijo, "Serve his Majesty, be respectful. If you lose his favor, enter Holy Orders" (3). Nijo moves from father to Emperor. When she falls out of favor with the Emperor, she follows her father's wish and becomes a Buddhist nun. Nijo imitates the wandering priests and becomes a wandering nun. When Marlene says that Nijo's father meant for Nijo to go into a convent, she says "I still did what my father wanted" (3). She not only becomes a nun, but follows the path of the patriarchal priests. All her life, Nijo continues to reenact the command of the father.

Isabella also follows the path of the father. She says "I tried to do what my father wanted" (3). Of course, like a good child, she "tried to be a clergyman's daughter" (3). She did needlework, took part in charitable events, read the metaphysical poets, and learned Latin even though she was a woman. However, she felt that she was more suited to "manual work" (4). Despite her ventures around the world, Isabella feels compelled to immerse herself in the charitable schemes of a "clergyman's daughter." She says, "My travels must do good to someone besides myself" (18). After her husband's death she goes back to sewing "a complete suit in Jaeger flannel" (12).

Joan's pursuit of the father shows a variation on the "search for the father" motif. Though she does not mention her peasant father, she is absorbed with her intellectual father, John, the Scot, a medieval philosopher, and her spiritual father, God. Joan is a child prodigy with a love for the truth which is embodied in the logos or word of the father. To pursue learning, she not only becomes a man but also a priest, a father without children, a male whose fatherhood depends on an absent father. Eventually, she goes one step higher to become Pope, the Holy Father, the Vicar or stand-in for God, the Father. Joan denies her femaleness to work her way up the hierarchical chain of absent fathers. Nijo, the monk; Isabella, the clergyman's daughter, and Joan, the priest, are absorbed not only with the patriarchal father but also with the Transcendental Father who is always out of reach.

Griselda's father is approached by Walter, the local marquis, who asks for Griselda's hand in marriage. Even though Walter did not order the marriage, Nijo insists, "And your father told you to serve the Prince" (21). Griselda replies, "My father could hardly speak"; the peasant could hardly deny the ruler. Where else but from her father could Griselda have learned her place in the patriarchy? "A wife must obey her husband. And of course I must obey the Marquis" (21), states Griselda. The hierarchies of class and gender are too strong for Griselda, who can only see herself as a submissive daughter, an obedient wife, and a loyal subject.

In the case of Nijo and Isabella, whose stories dominate the women's social event, the death of the father becomes a key point. Isabella is shocked by her father's death: "My father was the mainspring of my life and when he died I so grieved" (4). Nijo's father was saying his prayers in a sort of sleep state. When Nijo aroused him, he spoke, but died before finishing the sentence. Nijo has regrets about waking him: "If he died saying his prayers, he would have gone straight to heaven" (4). Joan, of course, sees death as a return to the spiritual father: "Death is the return of all creatures to God" (4).

The women project the death of the father onto the deaths of their lovers.

Isabella could have married Rocky Mountain Jim, but he couldn't give up whiskey. Of course, Isabella had never seen her father drunk, thus sobriety was associated with the father; so Jim, an alcoholic, was not right for her because he did not duplicate the father. One day she had a vision of Jim and on that day he died "with a bullet in his brain." Isabella transferred the love of her father to the love of her sister Hennie and from Hennie to Doctor Bishop, the physician who treated Hennie during her final days: "He and Hennie had the same sweet character. I had not" (11). Just when Isabella began "to love him with" her "whole heart . . . it was too late" (11). Doctor Bishop wasted away of anemia: "He faded away and left me. There was nothing in my life" (11). Patriarchy controls less by actual fathers than by the absent father, who is forever being transformed into a chain of substitutes or vanishing into an incorporeal being.

Nijo's life follows the same pattern. She transfers love and obedience from father to emperor. She is unfaithful to the Emperor, but her lover goes to hell. She says, "When father died I had only his majesty. So when I fell out of favor I had nothing. Religion was a kind of nothing and I dedicated what was left of me to nothing" (7). Nijo connects the death of the Emperor closely with the death of her father. "My father and the Emperor both died in the autumn. So much pain" (26). Autumn, of course, is also the season of the dying god. In order to be with the Emperor, Nijo hid in the room with his coffin. She fell asleep and had to chase the funeral procession in her bare feet. But she saw "only wisps of smoke in the sky, that's all that was left of him" (26). Thus, the father figure is always elusive, a desire that is unsatisfiable. Like Isabella's Doctor Bishop, Nijo's father substitute just "faded away." Both women are left with nothing.

Like Isabella and Nijo, Joan too is absorbed with an absent father. Joan had an argument over the nature of God with her lover, who disagreed with her over the teachings of John the Scot, her intellectual father. Joan says "We quarreled. And the next day he was ill. I was annoyed with him all the time I was nursing him . . . But then I realized he'd never understand my arguments again and that night he died. John the Scot held that the individual disintegrates and that there is no personal immortality" (11). Thus, for Joan her lover disintegrates. He becomes another version of the vanishing and absent father.

Isabella's Jim, the unredeemable drunkard, gets a bullet in his head while Dr. Bishop, the father substitute, wastes away. Nijo's lover Aniake dies and will go straight to hell while the Emperor, her father surrogate, goes up in smoke. Joan's lover, who cannot understand the philosophy of Joan's intellectual father, dies and disintegrates. Griselda's lover does not die, but he rejects her. Her father lives, but he can only weep for her when she is cast off. Nijo says, "At least your father was not dead. I had nobody" (24). The father sets the pattern of life for his daughters, but the father and his substitutes are always an unattainable, a vanishing substance, or an object of loss—in other words, an absence.

In *The Daughter's Seduction*, Jane Gallop observes: "By giving up their bodies, men gain power—the power to theorize, to represent themselves, to exchange women, to reproduce themselves, to mark their offspring with their name. All these activities ignore bodily pleasure in pursuit of representation, reproduction, production" (67). This powerful bodiless male figure holds a fascination for the historical women in *Top Girls*. These women have given themselves up to the incorporeal father who vanishes or disintegrates and have attached themselves to the symbolic father. Beth Kowaleski-Wallace and Patricia Yaeger state: "The Lacanian father is a disembodied entity, a law or function who is essentially bodiless. Yet it is precisely this bodilessness that so compels and obsesses his daughters" (xiv). The daughters in *Top Girls* are truly obsessed with the bodiless or absent father. These women, however, (with the exception of Griselda) go beyond the bounds of the common daughter narrative in which the daughter is so bound to the father that in order for her to escape the father, an "outside rival male must arrive and create a magnetic pull on the daughter, who otherwise remains within, in psychological bondage to her filial bonds" (Boose 32). Indeed, these daughters go out into the world and project themselves through time and space, yet they maintain an unyielding link to an absent father, a disembodied father who maintains power over them through subtle means. He need not bind them to a house or castle like the dominant father in narrative discourse; instead, he creates a space, an absence that is always filled by his shadow figure, a double who eventually vanishes. The corporeal presence of a father can be attacked, but an absent father can easily draw his daughters on a path of substitutions that imprisons them in a quest for an illusion, an invisible father hidden behind lovers, husbands, or the patriarchal structure of the church. The invisible father, only a step away from presence, is what ensnares his daughters and holds them bound to him.

In this bound world of the absent father, the Terrible Mother arises as motherhood is seen in terms of rejection or destruction. Isabella substitutes horses for children. Nijo's daughter by an illicit lover is taken away from her and raised by her lover's wife who has no children. Another child is taken from her at birth and Nijo never sees it again and a third child is abandoned at the death of her lover. Joan does not even recognize that she is pregnant because she isn't "used to having a woman's body" (16). During a procession, the baby comes out of her into the street. Both she and her baby are killed. One of Gret's children dies on the wheel and another is run through with a sword. Griselda would allow her husband to take her children away and kill them. Griselda accepts the condition that her child is "Walter's child to do what he like[s] with."

Motherhood fares no better in the realistic scenes. Like Nijo, Marlene gives up her daughter to a woman who has no children (her sister Joyce) so she can hold a position of status in a man's world. Joyce has a miscarriage because she has to take care of Angie, Marlene's child. Joyce resents her sacrifice, and Angie wants to kill her mother. Marlene, who has been on the pill so long she is "probably sterile" (81) has had two abortions and doesn't like "messy talk about blood" and "gynecology" (81). According to Chambers and Prior the issue of children is central to the play: "What pulls the threads together is children—the conflict for women between rearing children and independence and the problem of living a full and caring life without children in a male-dominated competitive society" (194). Churchill, however, does not see the problem of children as a central issue. The idea of Angie as Marlene's daughter instead of her niece was a late revision. Churchill notes "Of course women are pressured to make choices between working and having children in a way that men aren't, so it is relevant, but it isn't the main point" (Betsko and Koenig 82).

Much more to the point is what happens to women who become a part of the patriarchy, a world of absent fathers. In Marlene's world, the absent patriarch has an even more subtle grip on his daughters than in the world of the historical women. Thinking that she is being liberated, the daughter becomes absorbed into the patriarchal structure. Marlene blames the problems she had in her family on her father. Marlene's father was a drunk who beat Marlene's mother. Marlene is convinced that her mother went "hungry because he drank the money" (85). Marlene feels that her mother's life was wasted because she was "married to that bastard" (84).

Marlene's decision to leave home is predicated on the behavior of the father. In her drunken rambling, she babbles, "I know when I was thirteen, out of their house, out of them, never let that happen to me, never let him, make my own way out" (85). Apparently the alcoholic father was absent to his children. When Angie remembers her grandfather holding her in a towel, Marlene says about her father "I don't think he ever gave me a bath . . . He probably got soft in his old age" (73). Marlene left home to escape the world of the father. She didn't want to "marry a dairyman who'd come home pissed" and call her "fucking bitch" (79). Her hatred of the father is also projected upon the working class. "I hate the working class . . . I don't like beer guts and football vomit and sagging tits" (85).

Joyce, of course, plays the opposite role. She stays at home, marries a man who tries to dominate her and then leaves her. However, she defends her father as a man who has to vent his rage because he is "working in the fields like an animal" (85). Both women are attached to the absent father. Marlene accuses Joyce of following in her father's footsteps: "Bosses still walking on workers' faces! Still Daddy's little parrot. Haven't you learned to think for yourself" (84). In fact, the drunken rift between Joyce and Marlene seems like a replay of what happened the night their father died. Marlene tells Angie that Marlene and Joyce "got drunk together the night your grandfather died" (72). Though the scene goes undescribed, the deathwatch of the father is pivotal to the conflict between

Joyce, who still tends the father's grave and Marlene, who continues to renounce the father. As in *'night, Mother* and *Look Back in Anger*, the deathwatch of the father is central to the play's conflict.

Joyce seems hopelessly stuck in her dismal situation, but Marlene is no better off. Marlene has tried to reject the father, but she too has followed in his path. He was a drinker, a man who mistreated his family and who was insensitive to women and children. Marlene is also a drinker. At the dinner party, Marlene is continually ordering drinks. She even drinks Isabella's brandy. At Joyce's house, she initiates the drinking. Marlene has also abandoned her family. At work, Marlene "never talks about her family" (66). She has "no memory for birthdays," and "Christmas seems to slip by" (67). She tells her sister Joyce, "I don't know what you are like, do I?" (69). Marlene hasn't seen her daughter in six years and is also willing to abandon her own mother. She tells Joyce that Joyce doesn't have to visit their mother. Joyce says "How would I feel if I didn't go?" Marlene answers "A lot better" (79). Joyce merely parrots her father's liberal philosophy, but Marlene, like her father, truly neglects her family.

Moreover, in her flight from her brutish father, Marlene follows in his path. Marlene and the women at 'Top Girls' are insensitive to the plight of women. Marlene gets to be a manager because she has "got far more balls than Howard" (46). Marlene convinces her client Jeanine to give up her aspirations for travel, conceal her future marriage plans, and take a job as a secretary at a lampshade firm so she can be in charge of other girls who come in later. Marlene's coworkers also urge women to lower their expectations or their salaries. In addition, role playing is expected of corporate women. One client, Louise, survives in an ungrateful business world because she can "pass for a man at work" (52).

The callous attitude of the patriarchal father is also expected from the working women. Another client, Shona, will go far in sales because of her insensitivity: She says, "I never could consider people's feelings" (61). Angie is impressed that Marlene can tell Howard's wife to "piss off" (59). And Marlene can write off her own child along with all those who are "stupid, lazy, and frightened" (86). Marlene believes that at best Angie will be a clerk in a grocery store, but "she's not going to make it" (66). Assessing the "top girls," Kritzer points out : "Their toughness . . . has served to validate rather than challenge patriarchal power" (144). Marohl notes that they are "enforcing a patriarch-like matriarchy based on tyranny and division" (381). According to Reade W. Dornan, the women in the play have "cut themselves off from normal relationships with men, women, and children" and have made choices that "require suppression of common human impulses: the desire for intimacy, a trust in family ties, and concern for others" (1615). In other words, they have linked themselves to the absent father who stands outside the bounds of family ties.

Marlene's brutal and insensitive father may be absent, but he has not been left behind, and he has not disappeared. He is present in his daughters who have become the oppressors. It is significant that none of the women in Marlene's world with the exception of Mrs. Kidd, the wife of a male employee, is called by her surname. Like Miss Julie and Nora, none of these women bear the name of the father, yet all of them could pass for his double. For Marlene, success may be a ticket out of the poverty of her childhood. But her success is an illusion, for although she has not condemned herself to marrying the father, she has condemned herself to becoming the father in his worst aspects.

Like the women from the historical past, Marlene is also trapped by the absent father. In her attempt to flee the abusive father and his substitutes, she becomes the father/abuser. She too is willing to abandon her mother and daughter and to oppress the men and women with whom she works. Like the absent father, she stands outside of the family, a disconnected entity enmeshed in an intricate network of power plays in which success means transforming oneself into the patriarchy, not destroying it or changing it. This power of the absent father to stand both as the hated figure and the ideal model, to be reviled in one form but emulated in another, and to offer a path of escape that will only become a road to imprisonment is what makes him so dangerous to pursue.

In all three dramas—*Look Back in Anger, Master Harold . . . and the boys,* and *Top Girls*—lost children follow the path of an absent father who is connected to the patriarchal structure. In their personal quests to vindicate, escape, and/or replace the father who has died or who is in the process of dying, they become victims of the invisible structure of the patriarchy which consumes them in illusions or leaves them in despair. In these plays, the absent father stands hidden behind a social structure based on the ideological system that repudiates fatherhood at the same time as it guarantees the rule of the father.

CHAPTER 13

CONCLUSION

The modern dramas covered in this study are not only dramas that take place at the wake of a dead god, but they are also dramas about the absence of fatherhood. The transcendental father and his representatives are becoming more elusive in twentieth-century drama. Although the dramas analyzed in this study cover the span of modern drama from the 1880's to the 1980's, they show a remarkable similarity in structure, a structure which points to the death of fatherhood, a death that thrusts the universe into perpetual mourning. Trying to recreate and rehabilitate the image of the father leads only to greater mourning and finally to melancholia, the state of inertia, despair, and death.

The modern dramas focused on in this study are propelled by the absence of the father, a father who has died, gone away or completely abandoned his lost children. At a crucial moment in Nora's life, her father is dying, and when she desperately needs him to sign a loan agreement, he is dead. Her father's absence on Midsummer's Eve leaves Miss Julie vulnerable. The memorial to the dead father haunts the world of *Ghosts* like the picture of the dead father haunts Hedda's living room. The mourning of the absent father and the smell of his funeral pervade the world of *The Pelican*. In these dramas the father is absent, but his lingering or imminent presence becomes a disrupting and often destructive force.

Jessie forgives her father for abandoning her through death; yet she cannot let go of him and uses his gun the way Hedda uses her father's pistols, as a force of power, the ultimate power of self-destruction. Pavlo's unidentified father, Willy's father who abandoned the family when Willy was a boy, Tom Wingfield's father who skipped the light fantastic over distance and space—all become figures of everlasting pursuit, controlling forces, hypnotic and seductive in their absence. The deathbed scene of Jimmy's father is always pursuing Jimmy like the masked figure of the dead father looms over Amadeus Mozart. The absent father is connected with death or is forever dying like the MaGrath sisters' comatose Old Granddaddy and Hally's crippled, incontinent father.

These dead and absent fathers are paradoxical figures who are a part of the family, yet outside of it. They are often shady figures, symbols of the social order, yet transgressors against it so that the ordered universe is on shaky ground, and the pater familias becomes an ambivalent figure. Nora's father, the model citizen, has been involved in questionable business deals. Julie's aristocratic father holds a dubious title built on fraud and prostitution. Captain Alving, the pillar of the community, is a dissolute reprobate. Mr. Wingfield and Papa Loman are American pioneers who have deserted their families. The great white father in *Master Harold* is a sickly, irresponsible alcoholic and Marlene's father, the champion of the working class, is a drunkard and a wife-beater. The father is not only absent, but his position as father within the family and the social order is in question.

Even though the name of the father is a signifier that determines subjectivity, the father's name is partially or completely unspoken. Nora's father is unnamed. Julie's father becomes subsumed under his title, the Count. The father in *The Pelican* is simply known as Father. The father in *True West* is called the Old Man, just like the grandfather in *Crimes of the Heart* is called Old Granddaddy. Pavlo cannot pry the name of his unidentified father out of his crazy mother, just as no one is able to name Agnes' father or the father of her child. Hally's father goes unnamed. While the fathers of Willy, Tom, and Jimmy have the same last name as their sons, no mention is made of their first names. Even when the name of the father is used, it is displaced. Both Hedda and Jessie are marked by their father's names even after they are married. Thus, the name of the father which determines identity or subjectivity is somehow as absent as the father himself. Therefore, that which is supposed to construct identity is itself ambiguous and vague.

In the drama of the absent father, not only is the father's reputation in question and his name elusive, but motherhood, when present at all, is also ineffectual or distorted. Thus, the family structure has no balance. The mothers in *A Doll House* and *Hedda Gabler* go completely unmentioned and Willy's mother is barely spoken of. Mothers are also ineffectual and flighty, like Amanda Wingfield, who lives in a dream world or Austin's mother, who is somewhat scatterbrained. Crazy mothers also appear. Pavlo's mother is a loose woman who torments her child. Julie's mother tries to reverse all the gender roles on the family estate. Agnes' mother is a psychotic who abuses Agnes. Jimmy's mother is not insane, but in Jimmy's mind she is projected onto Alison's mother, and seen as a monstrous woman. Motherhood in Jimmy's world is similar to motherhood in *The Pelican* where the mother figure becomes another version of the Terrible Mother, vindictive and destructive. Thus, the primal forces of maternity and paternity are both disrupted, leaving the lost children unable to construct a self.

With the father absent and the mother missing, ineffectual, or perverse, the lost children are alienated and confused, unable to come to terms with their mental and physical ailments. The confused Nora is living in a fantasy world that is falling apart around her. She eventually realizes that she does not know who she is or where she belongs in society. Julie is disoriented, cut off from herself, unable to separate her ideas from the ideas of her father. Longing to be free, she feels condemned to the father's aristocratic code. Similarly, Hedda is torn between her desire for the libertine's life and her aristocratic fear of scandal. Osvald wants the joy of life, but he is hampered by his father's physical and moral disease. The sickly and malnourished children in *The Pelican* can find no purpose in life and seek to exonerate the father by burning themselves up in his house.

Tom feels imprisoned in the domestic and industrial world; yet his flight in the path of the father leaves him an aimless wanderer. Willy is a lost man who cannot figure out why the world has changed around him. Living on illusions, he does not know who he is and eventually realizes that no one even knows him anymore. Pavlo is alienated from himself, unable to communicate with those around him. Like Willy, he tries to fabricate an existence for himself and becomes the object of ridicule. Austin is unable to adjust to the world around him and longs to return to the father. Jimmy Porter, having absorbed his father's despair, has turned into a frustrated, angry man, hopelessly adrift in a society he cannot understand. The young Hally, ashamed of his father, lives in a state of perpetual disappointment. Trying to live out Old Granddaddy's dream, Babe is left desperate and suicidal. Jessie, who has inherited her father's epilepsy and learned his technique of withdrawing from the world, has made a mess of her life and has lost touch with her husband and child. Marlene, trying to escape from the father's world, has completely detached herself from all her emotions.

These lost and alienated children live in a world that is turning into a wasteland. The ornamented world in *A Doll House* is filled with false Christmas gaiety, a facade which falls apart the way the wilting Christmas tree does. In *Miss Julie*, the festivity of Midsummer's Eve has turned the world upside down. Man and woman, master and slave, have been reversed. Festive songs have turned into dirty little ditties, and human action has frozen into paralysis. Hedda's honeymoon has taken her through the dusty libraries of antiquity and into the sterile world of Falk villa, a house which she detests because it reeks of the smell of old age and death. With the exception of her father's pistols, she is trapped in the world of sentimental bourgeois objects. In *The Pelican*, the world has lost its warmth, and the food has no nourishment.

The wasteland is also a gloomy world shaded from the sun. A dreary soulless world, for instance, clouds the lives of the characters in *Ghosts*. The world of the St. Louis tenements in *The Glass Menagerie* is one of entangled clothes lines and garbage cans, a desperate world of hanging fire escapes. Willy's world is crumbling around him. The refrigerator doesn't work; the car is breaking down; the house needs repair. The large apartment buildings have blocked out the sun and left him hemmed in. Pavlo lives in a world of old ammunition barrels. Austin can no longer recognize the streets he drives, and his mother's house is turned into a junk heap of modern appliances. Salieri lives on empty sweets, and parades around with his shallow golden ornaments, symbols of the hollow success he has achieved. Hally's world is a bland tea room with stale cakes and poorly written signs. Like Osvald's and Jimmy's worlds, it is a world of rain and cloudiness, one which does not allow him the freedom to fly kites. Jessie's world is filled with routine chores, lists, and objects which have no meaning for her. She does not even like the special cocoa her mother has made for her. The world of the absent father is one of profound mourning. Life itself is either thrust into meaningless rituals or brought to a standstill amidst decay and rubble. The wasteland is a world which deprives its inhabitants of physical and spiritual sustenance.

In the wasteland, the attempt to celebrate the rituals of life only bring on the "holiday gone wrong." According to Rene Girard, ritual sacrifice deflects violence. However, the deritualized festival or "holiday gone wrong" is one that "has lost all its ritual characteristics. It has 'gone wrong' in the sense that it has reverted to its violent origins. . . . The festival ceases to function as a preventative measure and lends support to the forces of destruction" (125). In other words, rituals of celebration have lost their efficacy, leaving only the empty world of meaningless ritual and its violent consequences. The Christmas festivities in *A Doll House* turn to disaster. During Christmas holidays, Jessie starts to think about suicide. Meg goes insane at Christmas time. Midsummer's Eve turns into a night of illicit lust and ends in Miss Julie's suicide. Hedda's honeymoon turns into a series of deaths. Aunt Juliana points out the ritual of life, noting that Aunt Rina, the elderly woman, has died, but soon the family will be celebrating the christening of Hedda's child. However, both Hedda and the unborn child are destroyed. Father's funeral in *The Pelican* continues to haunt the family as the funeral is followed by the daughter's wedding. The memory of the father's funeral also clouds the name day ceremony of Irina in *The Three Sisters*. Furthermore, the celebration is marred by inappropriate gifts as Irina gets anniversary presents on her name day. The conjunction of birth and death is seen in Lenny's birthday party, celebrated on the day old Granddaddy is dying. The predictable presents she will receive on her birthday only makes Jessie more resolute to kill herself. In essence, the ceremonies of celebration turn out disastrous. Birth and death, wedding and funeral are subverted from their normal cycles. Celebrations of hope turn into despair. Carnival is transformed into confusion and death.

One way to relieve the pressure of living in the wasteland is to escape into an illusory world, a childhood past or a fantasized future. Nora lives in a childhood world of fantasy, forever her father's child. She creates fantasy saviors to rescue her. Julie dreams of a childhood paradise and creates a fantasy world in Switzerland where she and Jean can live among the orange groves of Lake Como. Hedda fantasizes beauty in a romantic death. Osvald sees the Parisian world of sunlight and innocence as an escape from the dreary climate of his fatherland. Son and Daughter in *The Pelican* harken back to their childhood holidays. Willy remembers the Edenic world of elm trees, sunshine, and family gardens. He longs to recreate the green world in a country house. Laura lives in the world of old victrola records and high school yearbooks while

Tom escapes through movie fantasies. Austin dreams of the fifties and becomes nostalgic for the outdoor West of his childhood. Pavlo returns to the heroics of his mother's Hollywood warriors. Mozart regresses to the childhood world of lullabies on his father's knee and his days of childhood adulation. Hally remembers the good times in Sam's room. Jessie reminisces over the little stick men her laconic father gave her. Under the pressures of the wasteland world, the children try to return to a romantic past as an escape.

Alone and disoriented in the wasteland, the lost children seek or have thrust before them an ideal father. Nora looks for the father in a romantic savior figure. Mrs. Alving creates an ideal father for her son, one which represents the cherished notion of fatherhood itself. Hedda and Jessie see the father and his world as an escape from the dreariness of everyday life. Willy views his father as the self-reliant pioneer of American mythology set out on a quest for gold. Tom envisions his father as the adventurer hero who has travelled to exotic lands. Austin holds up his father as the American loner, the romantic drifter who has cut himself off from civilization. Pavlo's father emerges from the Hollywood image of the soldier. Salieri, like Agnes, recreates the father in God, the Father. Hally searches for a world redeemer while Marlene sees fatherhood in the power of the patriarchy. Whether the father is romanticized as a personal or world savior, seen as a mythological figure embodying the underlying values of the society or whether he is seen as an all-powerful transcendental father, he is inflated into an image that cannot sustain the idealization that is projected onto it. Thus, all attempts to recreate the father are futile.

The absence of the father produces an overreaction, a need to create an invulnerable father set up as the object of an intensive quest. This quest becomes an attempt to follow the father, to recreate a part of his life, or to double him. In her outward charm and her shady dealings with money, Nora reenacts the father. When she assumes the signature of the father as her own, Nora becomes the father. Following his path, however, leads her to a grim realization about herself and the world of the fathers that surrounds her. Julie is a syphon for her father's ideas and like him seeks withdrawal from shame through suicide, a suicide he was unable to go through with. Hedda also tries to escape the dreary world by following the aristocratic military code of the father and committing the noble suicide with the father's pistols.

Similarly, Jessie follows the path of her withdrawn father and tries to reenact him in life as well as recreate his funeral in her own projected funeral. Like Hedda, she seeks bliss through the use of the father's gun. Osvald inherits his father's disease as well as the father's lust for servant girls. Willy is absorbed with the father's path to fame and riches. When he fails to carve out a territory that yields riches, he decides to strike it rich like the father and cash in his life for a fortune.

Tom also tries to pursue his father's path of adventure, only to find himself lost and bewildered in a world lit by lightning. Pavlo becomes a soldier in the romantic tradition of his ideal father. His heroics, however, turn into bullying, and he is blown to bits, just like the movie-hero father his mother pointed out to him. Meg, Lennie, and Babe try to act out Old Granddaddy's dream and find themselves depressed, neurotic, and suicidal. Jimmy Porter spends a lifetime trying to reenact his father's liberal rebellion only to find himself helpless and isolated, while Hally winds up identifying with the racist father he hates. Following the path of the father is always a journey toward self-destruction. In a world where the father has become a hidden unreachable object, absent at the origin, seeking him becomes a futile quest. Doubling him locks one into a chain of aimless repetition. This pattern of repetition and doubling is common to modern drama which has created a world devoid of a teleological structure, a world in which the cycle of ritual is turned into the nausea of routine.

In depicting this world of senseless routine, modern drama keeps harkening back to some transcendental power outside of embodied presence, some romantic notion of the father. Davis notes Western culture's absorption with the Paternal Romance, which projects "the romantic theme of the father . . . as a perfect transcendental origin, usually of the entire world and the institutions of culture" (*Paternal Romance* 4). Davis finds this ideal a fiction and points out: "The textual dimension of paternal authority constantly counters the ideal by exposing paternity as a local construction, an effect of narrative—that is, paternity not as an ideal but as a social and wholly constructed version of authority within a narrative; a fiction" (*Paternal Romance* 4).

Davis also shows how the construction of the Paternal Romance was conceived in antiquity, bolstered during the Enlightenment, and then started to break down in the nineteenth century, so that by the twentieth century the Paternal Romance was beginning to unravel. Davis reiterates, "In postmodernism there is no world father, no final and absolute 'other' as a ground for the world's deeply ironic sense of otherness" (*Paternal Romance* 141). According to Davis, late twentieth century thinkers are attempting to "forget the father" through "a deliberate and methodical dismantling and dispersal of fixed references" (*Paternal Romance* 141). This process leaves the father open to constant interrogation and denies him a privileged position.

Thus, the quest for the father in modern drama is not a quest for self-discovery, but rather it is an elusive search for that which is always out of reach. The privileged position of the father as the origin of discourse has given way in the modern period to an absence at the origin. The restless search for the father only confirms his absence. Yet his absence always leaves a trace of his presence, a series of signifiers that point the way to a chimerical father. This father who is never present is always represented in the drama. He is a figure who is dead, dying or absent, but never wholly gone, never completely mourned. This failure to mourn the father has cast the world order into a state of perpetual mourning, a stultifying state of inertia or circularity. The world is a wasteland, the objects that surround the characters have lost their aura and have been turned into junk or converted into cheap souvenirs, substitutes for experiences that have been long lost. Modern drama is not only reeling from the absence of some absolute teleological certainty, it is also mourning the loss of the father, pointing always to the futility of union with the father. Doubles and substitutes, so prevalent in modern drama, only create illusory fathers. Ultimately, to search for the father is to pursue one's own destruction.

Yet the absent father is still holding a central place in the study of modern drama, not so much because he is privileged but because he is still sought after. He acts as a catalyst for dramatic action, propelling the action forward and doubling it backwards. He determines the trajectory of the modern characters who search for him in vain, and he inscribes the traces of his presence across the dramatic environment. The father is a dead or dying figure, always wished for, always demanding replication, and always being mourned even though the mourning process is never complete. Davis notes the position of the absent father in postmodern literature by turning to Donald Barthelme's appraisal of the father in his novel *The Dead Father*: "Dead but still with us, still with us but dead" (3). Davis notes how this proclamation "captures the sense of the lost but residually present Father in the late twentieth century, not completely 'remembered' but not in a position to be completely forgotten" (*Paternal Romance* 147).

The vague memory of him is still firmly planted on the margins of dramatic discourse so that the father who never makes an entrance still holds center stage.

WORKS CITED

Adler, Thomas P. *Mirror on the Stage: The Pulitzer Plays as an Approach to American Drama.* West Lafayette, IN: Purdue UP, 1987.

Aeschylus. *The Libation Bearers. Oresteian Trilogy.* Trans. Philip Vellacott. London: Penguin, 1959. 103–143.

Arens, Katherine. "Mozart: A Case Study in Logocentric Repression." *Comparative Literature Studies* 9 (1986): 141–169.

Aston, Elaine and George Savona. *Theatre as Sign System: A Semiotics of Text and Performance.* New York: Routledge, 1991.

Barber, John. "Mozart Depicted as a Popinjay." *Daily Telegraph* 5 Nov. 1979: 15.

Barnes, Clive. "'Crimes' is a Prize Hit That's All Heart." *New York Post* 5 Nov. 1981. Rpt. in *New York Theatre Critics' Reviews* (1981): 137.

_____. "'God' Is Powered by a Trinity of Actresses." *New York Post* 31 Mar. 1982. Rpt. in *New York Theatre Critics' Reviews* (1982): 322.

_____. "'Master Harold' Is Masterful Look at South African Life." *New York Post* 5 May 1982. Rpt. in *New York Theatre Critics' Reviews* (1982). 306.

Barthelme, Donald. *The Dead Father.* New York: Farrar, Strauss, and Giroux, 1975.

Barthes, Roland. *The Pleasure of the Text.* Trans. Richard Miller. New York: Hill and Wang, 1975.

_____. *S/Z.* Trans. Richard Miller. New York: Hill and Wang, 1974.

Beaufort, John. "Agnes of God." *Christian Science Monitor* 19 Apr. 1982. Rpt. in *New York Theatre Critics' Reviews* (1982): 325.

Berman, Jeffrey. "The Search for the Father in *Amadeus.*" *Psychoanalytic Review* 74 (1987): 561–578.

Betsko, Kathleen and Rachel Koenig. "Caryl Churchill." Interviews with Contemporary Women Playwrights. New York: Beech Tree, 1987. 75–84.

Bigsby, C.W.E. *A Critical Introduction to Twentieth-Century American Drama.* 3 vols. Cambridge: Cambridge UP, 1984.

Billington, Michael. "Divining for a Theme." *Guardian* 5 Nov. 1979: 11.

Blau, Herbert. "Look What Thy Memory Cannot Contain." *Blooded Thought: Occasions of Theatre.* New York: Performing Arts Journal, 1982. 72–94.

Bleich, David. "Psychological Bases of Learning from Literature." *College English* 33 (1971): 32–45.

Bleikasten, Andre. "Fathers in Faulkner." Davis, *The Fictional Father.* 115–146.

Boose, Lynda. "The Father's House and the Daughter in It: The Structures of Western Culture's Daughter-Father Relationship." *Daughters and Fathers.* Ed. Lynda Boose and Betty S. Flowers. Baltimore: Johns Hopkins UP, 1988.

Browder, Sally. "'I Thought You Were Mine': Marsha Norman's *'night, Mother.*" *Mother Puzzles: Daughters and Mothers in Contemporary American Literature.* Ed. Mickey Pearlman. Westport, CT: Greenwood, 1989. 109–113.

Brustein, Robert. "Don't Read This Review!" *New Republic* 2 May 1983: 25–27.

_____. *The Theatre of Revolt.* Boston: Little Brown, 1962.

_____. "The Triumph of Mediocrity." *New Republic* 17 Jan. 1981: 23–24.

Burkman, Katherine H. "The Demeter Myth and Doubling in Marsha Norman's *'night, Mother.*" *Modern American Drama: The Female Canon.* Ed. June Schlueter. Rutherford: Fairleigh Dickinson UP, 1990. 254–263.

Campbell, Joseph. *The Masks of God: Creative Mythology.* New York: Penguin, 1968.

Carlisle, Olga and Rose Styron. "Arthur Miller: An Interview."
    The Theatre Essays of Arthur Miller. Ed. Robert A Martin. New York:
    Penguin, 1978. 264–293.

Case, Sue-Ellen. "The Personal Is Not the Political." *Art and Cinema* 1.3
    (1986): 4.

Chambers, Colin and Mike Prior. *Playwrights' Progress: Patterns of Postwar
    British Drama*. Oxford: Amber Lane, 1987.

Chekhov, Anton. *The Three Sisters*. *The Oxford Chekhov*. Vol. 3. Trans. and
    ed. Ronald Hingley. London: Oxford UP, 1964.

Churchill, Caryl. *Top Girls*. Student ed. Ed. with Commentary and Notes by
    Bill Naismith. London: Metheun, 1982.

Clurman, Harold, ed. "Introduction." *The Portable Arthur Miller*. By Arthur
    Miller. New York: Viking, 1971. xi–xxv.

Cohn, Ruby. *Retreats from Realism in Recent English Drama*. Cambridge:
    Cambridge UP, 1991.

Cole, David. *The Theatrical Event*. Middletown, CT: Wesleyan UP, 1975.

Cole, Susan. *The Absent One*. University Park: Penn State UP, 1985.

Connell, Brian. "Peter Shaffer: The Two Sides of Theatre's Agonised
    Perfectionist." *Times* 28 Apr. 1980: 7.

Cook, Jon. "Fictional Fathers." *Sweet Dreams: Sexuality, Gender and Popular
    Fiction*. Ed. Susan Radstone. London: Lawrence and Wishart, 1988.
    137–164.

Corliss, Richard. "Sisters Under the Skin." *Time* 12 Apr. 1982. Rpt. in *New
    York Theatre Critics' Reviews* (1982): 323.

Davis, Robert Con. "The Discourse of Jacques Lacan." Davis, *The Fictional
    Father* 183–189.

_____. *The Fictional Father: Lacanian Readings of the Text*. Amherst: U of
    Massachusetts P, 1981.

_____. *The Paternal Romance: Reading God the Father in Early Western Culture*. Chicago: U of Illinois P, 1993.

Derrida, Jacques. *Writing and Difference*. Trans. Alan Bass. Chicago: U of Chicago P, 1978.

Dogra, O.P. "Miller's *Death of a Salesman*: The Collapse of the Dream." *Perspectives on Arthur Miller*. Ed. Atma Ram. New Delhi: Abhinav, 1988. 53–65.

Dornan, Reade W. "*Top Girls*." *Masterplots II: Drama Series*. Vol. 4. Ed. Frank Magill. Pasadena CA: Salem, 1990. 1613–1617.

Driver, Tom. *Romantic Quest and Modern Query: History of the Modern Drama*. New York: Dell, 1971.

Durand, Regis. "'The Captive King': The Absent Father in Melville's Text." Davis, *The Fictional Father* 48–72.

Egan, Robert. "Anger and the Actor: Another Look Back." *Modern Drama* 30 (1989): 413–424.

Erlich, Avi. *Hamlet's Absent Father*. Princeton: Princeton UP, 1977.

Esslin, Martin. *Theatre of the Absurd*. 3rd. ed. New York: Penguin, 1980.

Feingold, Michael. "Dry Roll." *Village Voice* 18 Nov. 1981: 104+.

Fenton, James. "Can We Worship This Mozart?" *Sunday Times* 23 Dec. 1979: 43.

Fiedler, Leslie A. *Love and Death in the American Novel*. New York: Criterion, 1960.

Freud, Sigmund. *Moses and Monotheism*. Trans. and ed. James Strachey. London: Hogarth, 1964.

_____. *Totem and Taboo*. Trans. James Strachey. New York: Norton, 1962.

Frye, Northrop. *Anatomy of Criticism*. Princeton: Princeton UP, 1957.

_____. *The Great Code: The Bible and Literature*. New York: Harcourt, 1983.

Fugard, Athol. *Master Harold . . . and the boys*. New York: Penguin, 1984.

_____. *Notebooks: 1970–1977*. New York: Knopf, 1984.

Gagen, Jean. "'Most Resembling Unlikeness, and Most Unlikely Resemblance': Beth Henley's *Crimes of the Heart* and Chekhov's *Three Sisters*." *Studies in American Drama, 1945–Present* 4 (1989): 119–128.

Gallop, Jane. *The Daughter's Seduction: Feminism and Psychoanalysis*. Ithaca: Cornell UP, 1985.

Garber, Majorie. *Shakespeare's Ghost Writers*. New York: Methuen, 1987.

Gianakaris, C.J. "Fair Play?" *Opera News* 27 Feb. 1982: 18,36. Rpt. in Gianakaris, *Peter Shaffer Casebook*. 127–133.

_____, ed. *Peter Shaffer: A Casebook*. New York: Garland, 1991.

Gill, Brendan. "Backstage." *New Yorker* 16 Nov. 1981: 182–183.

Girard, Rene. *Violence and the Sacred*. Trans. Patrick Gregory. Baltimore: Johns Hopkins UP, 1977.

Glicksberg, Charles. *The Tragic Vision in Twentieth-Century Literature*. Carbondale: Southern Illinois UP, 1963.

Goldhill, Simon. *Language, Sexuality, Narrative: The Oresteia*. Cambridge: Cambridge UP, 1984.

Goldmann, Lucien. *The Hidden God*. Trans. Phillip Thody. New York: Humanities, 1964.

Goldstone, Herbert. *Coping with Vulnerability: The Achievement of John Osborne*. Washington, D. C.: UP of America, 1982.

Grant, Gary. "Writing as a Process of Performing the Self: Sam Shepard's Notebooks." *Modern Drama* 34 (1991): 549–565.

Green, Andre. *The Tragic Effect: The Oedipus Complex in Tragedy*. Trans. Alan Sheridan. Cambridge: Cambridge UP, 1979.

Greenfield, Barbara. "The Archetypal Masculine: Its Manifestation in Myth and Its Significance for Women." *The Father: Contemporary Jungian Perspectives.* Ed. Andrew Samuels. New York: New York UP, 1985. 187–210.

Grieff, Louis K. "Fathers, Daughters, and Spiritual Sisters: Marsha Norman's *'night, Mother* and Tennessee Williams' *The Glass Menagerie.*" *Text and Performance Quarterly* 9 (1989): 224–228.

Gross, Barry E. "Peddler and Pioneer in *Death of a Salesman.*" *Modern Drama* 7 (1965): 405–410.

Guerra, Jonnie. "Beth Henley: Female Quest and the Family Play Tradition." Hart 118–130.

Gussow, Mel. "Witness." *New Yorker* 20 Dec. 1982: 47–94.

Hadomi. Leah. "Fantasy and Reality: Dramatic Rhythm in *Death of a Salesman.*" *Modern Drama* 31 (1988): 157–174.

Hargrove, Nancy D. "The Tragicomic Vision of Beth Henley's Drama." *Southern Quarterly* 22.4 (1984): 50–70.

Harriot, Esther. *American Voices: Five Contemporary Playwrights in Essays and Interviews.* Jefferson, NC: Mac Farland, 1988.

_____. "Marsha Norman: Getting Out." *American Voices.* 129–163.

_____. "Sam Shepard: Inventing Identities." *American Voices.* 3–16.

Hart, Lynda, ed. *Making a Spectacle: Feminist Essays on Contemporary Women's Theatre.* Ann Arbor: Michigan UP, 1989.

Hayman, Ronald. *Contemporary Playwrights: John Osborne.* Rev. ed. London: Heinemann, 1972.

Henderson, Joseph. "Ancient Myth and Modern Man." Jung, *Man and His Symbols.* 95–156.

Henley, Beth. *Crimes of the Heart.* New York: Penguin, 1982.

Hinchliffe, Arnold J. *John Osborne.* Boston: Twayne, 1984.

Hinden, Michael. "When Playwrights Talk to God: Peter Shaffer and the Legacy of O'Neill." *Comparative Drama* 16 (1982): 49–63.

Huber, Werner and Zapf, Hubert. "On the Structure of Peter Shaffer's Amadeus." *Modern Drama* (1984): 299–313.

Hughes, Catherine. "Skeletons in the Closet." *America* 15 May 1982: 382.

Huntley, E.D. *"Crimes of the Heart." Masterplots II: Drama Series.* Ed. Frank Magill. Vol. 1. Pasadena, CA: Salem, 1990. 407–413.

Huss, Roy. "John Osborne's Backward Halfway Look." *Modern Drama* 6 (1963): 20–25.

Hutchings, William. *"Equus* of Convent: *Agnes of God." From Bard to Broadway.* Ed. Karelisa Hartigan. Lanham MD: UP of America, 1987. 139–146.

Ibsen, Henrik. *The Complete Major Prose Plays.* Trans. Rolf Fjelde. New York: NAL, 1978.

_____. *A Doll House. Complete Plays.* 123–196.

_____. *Ghosts. Complete Plays.* 201–276.

_____. *Hedda Gabler. Complete Plays.* 689–778.

Innes, Christopher. *Modern British Drama.* Cambridge: Cambridge UP, 1992.

Jones, John. H. "The Missing Link: The Father in *The Glass Menagerie.*" *Notes on Mississippi Writers* 20 (1988): 29–38.

Joyce, James. *Letters of James Joyce.* 3 vols. London: Faber and Faber, 1957–1966.

Jung, C. G. "Approaching the Unconscious." *Man and His Symbols.* 1–94.

_____. *Civilization in Transition.* Vol 10. Collected Works of C. G. Jung. Trans. R. F. C. Hull. Ed. Sir Herbert Read, Michael Fordham, and Gerhard Adler. New York: Pantheon, 1964.

_____. *Four Archetypes*. Trans R. F. C. Hull. Princeton: Princeton UP, 1970.

_____, ed. *Man and His Symbols*. New York: Dell, 1968.

Kalem, T.E. "Blood Feud." *Time* 29 Dec. 1980: 57.

_____. "Dance Marathon." *Time* 17 May 1982. Rpt. in *New York Theatre Critics' Reviews*. (1982). 306.

Kane, Leslie. "The Way Out, The Way In: Paths to the Self in the Plays of Marsha Norman." *Feminine Focus: The New Women Playwrights*. Ed. Enoch Brater. New York: Oxford UP, 1989. 255–274.

Karpinski, Joanne B. "The Ghosts of Chekhov's *Three Sisters* Haunt Beth Henley's *Crimes of the Heart*." *Modern American Drama: The Female Canon*. Ed. June Schlueter. Rutherford: Fairleigh Dickinson UP, 1990. 229–245.

Kaufmann, Stanley. "Shaffer's Flat Notes." *Saturday Review* Feb. 1981: 78–79.

Keown, Eric. Rev. of *Look Back in Anger*. *Punch* 8 May 1956 Rpt. in Taylor, Osborne Casebook. 55–56.

Kerr, Walter. "Offbeat—But a Beat Too Far." *New York Times* 15 Nov. 1981: D3, D31.

Kissel, Howard. "Crimes of the Heart." *Women's Wear Daily* 6 Nov. 1981. Rpt. in *New York Theatre Critics' Reviews* (1981). 140.

Kleb, William. "Theatre in San Francisco: Sam Shepard's *True West*." *Theatre* 12 (1980): 65–71. Rpt. as "Worse Than Being Homeless: *True West* and the Divided Self" in *American Dreams: The Imagination of Sam Shepard*. Ed. Bonnie Marranca. New York: Performing Arts Journal, 1981. 117–125.

Klein, Dennis A. "*Amadeus*: The Third Part of Peter Shaffer's Dramatic Trilogy." *Modern Language Studies* 13 (1983): 31–38.

Knight, G. Wilson. "The Kitchen Sink." *Encounter* Dec. 1963: 48–54.

Koertge, Ron, and others. *Instructor's Manual to Literature: Reading, Reacting, and Writing.* Eds. Laurie Kirszner and Stephen Mandell. Chicago: Holt, 1991.

Kolin, Philip C. "Notices of David Rabe's First Play, *The Chameleon* (1959)." *Resources for American Literary Study* 17 (1991): 95–107.

_____. "David Rabe's *Streamers.*" *Explicator* 45 (Fall 1986): 63–64.

Kritzer, Amelia Howe. *The Plays of Caryl Churchill: Theatre of Empowerment.* New York: St. Martin's, 1991.

Krutch, Joseph Wood. "Introduction." *Nine Plays by Eugene O'Neill.* New York: Random House, 1954. ix–xxii.

"Lamb of God." *New Catholic Encyclopedia.* 1967 ed.

Larson, Janet Karsten. "*Amadeus*: Shaffer's Hollow Men." *The Christian Century* 20 May 1981: 578–583.

Levi-Strauss, Claude. *Structural Anthropology.* Trans. Clarie Jacobson. New York: Basic Books, 1963.

Lewis, Leon. "*Master Harold . . . and the boys.*" *Masterplots II: Drama Series.* Ed. Frank Magill. Vol 3. Pasadena, CA: Salem, 1990. 1059–1064.

Londre, Felicia H. Stradding. "A Dual Poetics in *Amadeus*: Salieri as Tragic Hero and Joker." Gianakaris, *Peter Shaffer Casebook.* 115–125.

Lukacs, Georg. "The Metaphysics of Tragedy." *Tragedy: Vision and Form.* 2nd. ed. Ed. Robert Corrigan. New York: Harper, 1981. 76–93.

Marohl, Joseph. "De-realized Women: Performance and Gender in *Top Girls.*" *Modern Drama* 3 (1987): 376–388.

McCarthy, Mary. "A New Word." *Harper's Bazaar* Apr. 1958. Rpt. in Taylor, *Osborne Casebook.* 150–160.

McDonald. David. "The Trace of Absence in a Derridean Reading of *Oedipus Rex.*" *Educational Theatre Journal* 38 (1979): 147–161.

Meyer, Michael. *Ibsen.* abr. ed. New York: Penguin, 1974.

Miller, Arthur. *Death of a Salesman.* Viking Critical ed. Ed. Gerald Weales. New York: Penguin, 1977.

_____. *Timebends.* New York: Harper, 1987.

Mitchell, Juliet. *Women, the Longest Revolution.* New York: Pantheon, 1984.

Monsey, Derek. Rev. of *Look Back in Anger. Sunday Express* 8 May 1956. Rpt. in Taylor, *Osborne Casebook.* 44.

Morace, Roberta A. "*Amadeus.*" *Masterplots II: Drama Series.* Vol. 1. Ed. Frank Magill. Pasadena, CA: Salem, 1990. 37–43.

Morrow, Laura. "Orality and Identity in *'night, Mother* and *Crimes of the Heart.*" *Studies in American Drama, 1945–Present* 3 (1988): 23–39.

Mottram, Ron. *Inner Landscapes: The Theatre of Sam Shepard.* Columbia: U of Missouri P, 1984.

Murphy, Brian. "Jimmy Porter's Past: The Logic of Rage in *Look Back in Anger.*" *Modern Quarterly* 18 (1977): 361–373.

Murray, Gilbert. *Hamlet and Orestes: A Study in Traditional Types.* New York: Oxford UP, 1914.

Neumann, Erich. *The Great Mother.* Trans. Ralph Manheim. New York: Pantheon, 1955.

New York Theatre Critics' Reviews. New York: Theatre Critics' Reviews, 1940–present. irreg.

Nightingale, Benedict. "Obscene Child." *New Statesman* 9 Nov. 1979: 735.

Norman, Marsha. *'night, Mother.* New York: Hill and Wang, 1983.

Osborne, John. *Look Back in Anger.* New York: Penguin, 1982.

Otis, Brooks. *Cosmos and Tragedy: An Essay on the Meaning of Aeschylus.* Ed. E. Christian Kopff. Chapel Hill: U of North Carolina P, 1981.

Parker, Brian. "The Composition of *The Glass Menagerie*: An Argument for Complexity." *Modern Drama* 25 (1982): 409–422.

Pielmeier, John. *Agnes of God*. New York: Doubleday, 1982.

Pirani, Alix. *The Absent Father: Crisis and Creating*. London: Arkana, 1989.

Pucci, Pietro. *Oedipus and the Fabrication of the Father: Oedipus Tyrannus in Modern Criticism and Philosophy*. Baltimore: Johns Hopkins UP, 1992.

Rabe, David. *The Basic Training of Pavlo Hummel and Sticks and Bones*. New York: Viking, 1973. Introduction by Rabe. ix–xxv.

Redfield, James. *Nature and Culture in the Iliad: The Tragedy of Hector*. Chicago: U of Chicago P, 1975.

Rich, Frank. "Life as a Dance." *New York Times* 5 May 1982). Rpt. in *New York Theatre Critics' Reviews* (1982). 305.

_____. "Stage: 'Agnes of God' in a Convent." *New York Times* 31 Mar. 1982: C23.

_____. "The Theater: 'Amadeus' by Peter Shaffer." *New York Times* 18 Dec. 1980. Rpt. in *New York Theatre Critics' Reviews* (1980): 64.

_____. "Unvarnished Laughs." *New York Times* 5 Nov. 1981: C21.

Richards, David. "Agnes of Mysteries and Miracles." *Washington Post* 8 Dec. 1983: D1+.

Ricoeur, Paul. *Freud and Philosophy: An Essay on Interpretation*. Trans. Denis Savage. New Haven: Yale UP, 1970.

Ridgeway, William. *The Dramas and Dramatic Dances of Non-European Races*. Cambridge: Cambridge UP, 1915.

Roberts, Sheila. "'No Lessons Learnt': Reading the Texts of Fugard's *A Lesson from Aloes* and *Master Harold . . . and the boys*." *English in Africa* 9 (1982): 27–33.

Rogoff, Gordon. "Richard's Himself Again." *Tulane Drama Review* 34 (1966): 29–40.

Rosen, Carol. *Plays of Impasse: Contemporary Drama Set in Confining Institutions*. Princeton: Princeton UP, 1983.

Sauvage, Leo. "Reaching for Laughter." *New Leader* 30 Nov. 1981: 19–20.

Savran, David. "Marsha Norman." *In Their Own Words: Contemporary American Playwrights*. New York: Theatre Communications Group, 1988.

Scott, Charles E. "The Pathology of the Father's Rule." *Thought* 61 (1986): 118–130.

Shaffer, Peter. *Amadeus*. New York: Harper, 1980.

_____. *Equus. The Collected Plays of Peter Shaffer*. New York: Harmony, 1982.

_____. "Figure of Death." *Observer* 4 Nov. 1979: 37.

Shakespeare, William. *Hamlet*. Folger ed. Ed. Louis B. Wright and Virginia A. LaMar. New York: Washington Square, 1958

Shepard, Sam. *True West. Sam Shepard: Seven Plays*. New York: Bantam, 1981. 1–60.

Shulman, Milton. Rev. of *Look Back in Anger*. *Evening Standard* 8 May 1956. Rpt. in Taylor, *Osborne Casebook*. 41.

Sohlich, Wolfgang. "Ibsen's Brand: Drama of the Fatherless Society." *Journal of Dramatic Theory and Criticism* 3 (1989): 87–105.

Sophocles. *Oedipus Tyrannus*. Trans. and ed. Luci Berkowitz and Theodore F. Brenner. New York: Norton, 1970.

Spencer, Jenny S. "Marsha Norman's She Tragedies." Hart 147–165.

_____. "Norman's *'night, Mother*: Psycho-drama of Female Identity." *Modern Drama* 30 (1987): 364–375.

Spoto, Donald. *The Kindness of Strangers: The Life of Tennessee Williams*. New York: Ballantine, 1986.

Stanton, Kay. "Women and the American Dream of *Death of a Salesman.*" *Feminist Rereadings of Modern American Drama.* Ed. June Schlueter. Rutherford: Fairleigh Dickinson UP, 1989. 67–102.

Stone, Elizabeth. "Playwright Marsha Norman: An Optimist Writes about Suicide, Confinement and Despair." *Ms.* July 1983: 56–59.

Stone, Laurie. "Caryl Churchill: Making Room at the Top." *Village Voice* 1 Mar. 1983: 80–81.

Stoner, Richard. "*True West.*" *Masterplots II: Drama Series.* Vol. 4. Ed. Frank Magill. Pasadena, CA: Salem, 1990. 1660–1664.

Strindberg, August. *Miss Julie. The Plays of Strindberg.* Vol 1. Trans. Michael Meyer. New York: Vintage, 1972. 113–161.

_____. *The Pelican. The Chamber Plays.* Trans. Evert Spinchorn and Seabury Quin, Jr. New York: Dutton, 1962. 155–204.

Sullivan, William. "Peter Shaffer's *Amadeus*: The Making and Unmaking of the Fathers." *American Imago* 48 (1988): 45–60.

Szondi, Peter. *The Theory of Modern Drama.* Trans. and ed. Michael Hayes. Minneapolis: U of Minnesota P, 1987.

Taylor, John Russell. *Anger and After.* Baltimore, MD: Penguin, 1963.

_____, ed. *John Osborne: Look Back in Anger: A Casebook.* Nashville, TN: Aurora, 1969.

Tee, Robert. Rev. of *Look Back in Anger. Daily Mirror* 8 May 1956. Rpt. in Taylor, *Osborne Casebook.* 46.

Thomas, Trever. "The Headline That Became a Play." *Los Angeles Times* 14 Feb. 1984: sec. 6:5.

Thompson, Judith. *Tennessee Williams' Plays: Memory, Myth, and Symbol.* New York: Peter Lang, 1987.

Tischler, Nancy M. *Tennessee Williams: Rebellious Puritan.* New York: Citadel, 1961.

Valency, Maurice. *The End of the World*. New York: Schocken, 1983.

Vandenbroucke, Russell. *Truths the Hand Can Touch: The Theatre of Athol Fugard*. New York: Theatre Communications Group, 1985.

von Franz, M.L. "The Process of Individuation". Jung, *Man and His Symbols*. 157–254.

Von Staden, Heinrich. "An Interview with Athol Fugard." *Theater* 14 (1982): 41–46.

Wager, Walter, ed. *The Playwrights Speak*. New York: Delacorte, 1967.

Wandor, Michelene. *Carry On Understudies: Theatre and Sexual Politics*. London: Routledge, 1986.

_____. *Look Back in Gender: Sexuality and the Family in Post-War British Drama*. London: Methuen, 1987.

Watt, Douglas. "'Master Harold . . . and the boys.'" *Daily News* 5 May 1982. Rpt. in *New York Theatre Critics' Reviews* (1982). 309.

Wattenberg, Richard. "'The Frontier Myth' on Stage: From the Nineteenth Century to Sam Shepard's *True West*." *Western American Literature* 24 (1989): 225–241.

Wellwarth, George E. *Modern Drama and the Death of God*. Madison: U of Wisconsin P, 1986.

Werner, Craig. "Primal Screams and Nonsense Rhymes: David Rabe's Revolt." *Educational Theatre Journal* 30 (1978): 517–529.

Wilden, Anthony. *Jacques Lacan: Speech and Language in Psychoanalysis*. Baltimore: Johns Hopkins UP, 1968.

Williams, Edwina, and Lucy Freeman. *Remember Me to Tom*. New York: Putnam, 1973.

Williams, Raymond. *Modern Tragedy*. London: Chatto and Windus, 1966.

Williams, Tennessee. *The Glass Menagerie*. New York: New Directions, 1970.

Wilson, Edwin. "A Strong Play about the Agonies of Apartheid." *Wall Street Journal* 7 May 1982. Rpt. in *New York Theatre Critics' Reviews* (1982). 308.

Wilson, Peter J. *Man, the Promising Primate: The Conditions of Human Evolution.* 2nd ed. New Haven: Yale UP, 1983.

Yaeger, Patricia. "The Father's Breast." Yaeger and Kowalewski-Wallace 1–21.

Yaeger, Patricia and Beth Kowalewski-Wallace. *Refiguring the Father: New Feminist Readings of the Patriarchy.* Carbondale: U of Illinois P, 1989.

INDEX